# THE SIGNIFICANCE OF SILENCE

# The Significance of Silence

AND OTHER SERMONS BY

LESLIE D. WEATHERHEAD

**ABINGDON-COKESBURY PRESS**

*New York* · *Nashville*

# THE SIGNIFICANCE OF SILENCE

## COPYRIGHT MCMXLV
## BY WHITMORE & STONE

K

PRINTED IN THE UNITED STATES OF AMERICA

DEDICATED TO

## THE REVEREND WILLIAM L. NORTHRIDGE
### M.A., B.D., M.Th., Ph.D.

PRESIDENT OF THE METHODIST CHURCH IN IRELAND

PRINCIPAL OF EDGEHILL METHODIST THEOLOGICAL COLLEGE, BELFAST

*BUT TO ME*

BILLY

MY FRIEND

# PREFACE

I HAVE WRITTEN RATHER A LENGTHY PREFACE IN ORDER THAT THOSE who read this volume of sermons may have, if they so desire, the background of the work of which preaching is only a part and a picture of the people to whom these messages were proclaimed.

In the spring of 1941 the City Temple was set on fire by incendiary bombs dropped from German airplanes and, except for the façade, the tower, and the lower part of the walls, totally destroyed. The famous marble pulpit, gift to my predecessor, Joseph Parker, from the City of London, was an unrecognizable heap of stones. Not one of the stained-glass windows remained. The great organ vanished in a night. The vast auditorium, seating over two thousand people, was a jumble of burned beams, twisted girders, and broken rubble. A score of firemen lived on the premises from the outbreak of war, but unfortunately the first fireman on the roof fell and was injured. By the time he was carried to safety the roof was alight in three places. Pieces of burning roof fell on the wooden pews, and in a few minutes the place was a roaring inferno.

I was on the spot before the fire was wholly extinguished and, led by Captain F. W. Ashard, our gallant verger, crawled in through a back way, but a pile of red-hot rubble and still-burning material blocked our advance. With some difficulty and circumvention we got right through to the front entrance. The gates opening on Holborn Viaduct were closed. I saw a slim figure standing on the pavement looking through the great iron gates. She did not see me. For a few seconds I watched her. She would account herself a person of no importance, standing there in the rain. But it was not the rain that made her face wet. She was crying—not hysterically or convulsively—just crying quietly there in the rain over the ruins of the church she loved, the church where she had met God. I pushed one of the great gates open and brought her in. We surveyed the destruction in silence, and then we espied the marble figure of Joseph Parker, thrown from its pedestal, but still erect, with that proud, majestic, serene, strong face, scorched by the flame and chipped by the blast of bombs, but still challenging evil to do its worst. The tears of a simplehearted girl, the triumphant expression of the old warrior—they seemed to express one's innermost feelings. On the one hand, the sadness, the unutterable sadness of our loss. On the other, the unconquerable sense of triumph; a great thankfulness that no power of hate or aggression or evil can ever dominate the church, the living entity, made, not of stones, however venerable, or stained glass, however lovely, but of loyal, loving human hearts.

I have come to admire those stout hearts. My people, be it remembered, do not live near where the City Temple stood. We have long been the only English Free Church which is technically within the City boundaries, and we could not continue to exist unless people came long distances to worship with us and support our witness. My "parish" extends from Barking in the east of London to Barnes in the west, from Barnet in the north to Banstead in the south, more than twenty miles in every direction from the City Temple. Yes, and far beyond. We used to boast seat-holders in Liverpool and Southampton, in Birmingham and Harrogate, who regularly attended on Sundays.

And what a variety of people is contained in any one congregation! Our membership includes a cabinet minister, and others of rank, position and authority, and also the lowliest and poorest—people who have been unemployed, people who have been in prison. I have seen in one service folk who can put a coronet on their note-paper, a score who can put letters of distinction before or after their names, and also hundreds who do not earn more than a pound or two a week. Harley Street doctors, an undersecretary of state, professors and lawyers, students and eminent men of commerce worship with artisans, youngsters just beginning a career, nurses, clerks, typists, young business men and women, postmen, and policemen. In the days of peace, when, unable to accommodate the congregation, we relayed both services to a crowded hall below the church, we have counted fourteen nationalities at one service. The

City Temple has been called "The Cathedral of Nonconformity." The dear old walls have embraced men and women of every nation and almost every sect under heaven. Those walls have listened to men's joyous thanksgivings, their pleas for pardon, the stifled sob of the overburdened, the resolute dedications of youth, the crying of the brokenhearted, the hopeful aspirations of the young, and the faith of the aged. Those gaunt, ruined walls, scarred now by bombs, blackened with smoke, open to the wind and rain, what a story they could tell since the days when they were first dedicated to the public worship of Almighty God!

Come with me on an afternoon's visiting! I must go first to a hospital, since an urgent message calls me there. My wife is with me. She drives the little car and plans to sit in it while she waits for me. But shrapnel is falling, and she is obliged to lock it and leave it and take shelter under the stone porch of a near-by church. In the darkened hospital the windows are nearly all boarded up against the flying glass, which in an air raid can cause horrible mutilation and is the chief cause of casualty. The corridors are now illumined only by low-power blue bulbs. I find my way to a ward. One of my members is behind the screens. I sit on her bed, and she stretches out her left hand to greet me. How often we have said, "I would give my right hand if . . ." Well, that is what she has done! She is a worker at a warden's post. "Air Raid Precautions." "Civil Defense." How ordinary the words sound! But the night before, Doris was on duty at a certain street shelter at eight o'clock. It was quite dark. An air raid was in progress. The guns were booming. Shrapnel was falling. Should she stop and take cover? She decided that she *must* reach the post at the time appointed and relieve another. So on she went. Her right arm was completely blown off. The mayor of her borough came to the hospital to congratulate her. He might well do so. One lost arm may sound little in the grim fight for freedom in which millions have been made sad and thousands killed. (In the winter of 1940-41 two hundred people a night were killed by bombs in Britain alone and an equal number injured.) But those are figures one cannot take in. Here is one girl in her twenties doing her duty in the little task entrusted to her, injured for life in the doing, and smiling up into my face, her uninjured hand in mine. She is a member of the City Temple. She is a "living stone" in an indestructible church, a temple not made with hands.

On we go in the little car. We are very interested in the Littletons. (That is not their name, of course.) There are ten children, and the father, up till recently, was unemployed. The City Temple has what I called an "Adoption Scheme." The idea is that every member, singly or with another, should *adopt* an underprivileged family. This doesn't mean patronage and charity. It means taking a loving interest in a family where life is hard. It means knowing the children's names, remembering birthdays, sharing the good things of life, lending a helping hand. The Littletons are our "family." My wife goes regularly to see them. We knew their neighborhood had suffered. One morning on my way to Broadcasting House to broadcast in the early morning service, I had seen the people sweeping up the broken window glass from the pavements as people sweep snow in winter. So we made for their home, the lower part of which had earlier been condemned as unfit for habitation. Opposite the house a factory had been gutted with fire bombs. You would have regarded their home as wholly unfit for occupation. But there they were, cheerful as ever, Jim and Harry, Evelyn and Hilda, Tommy and Bob, Gladys and Mabel the twins, and the tinies, grinning as only Londoners can.

Why aren't they evacuated? you ask. They were. Their mother took a long journey, a new and frightening experience for her. She went with seven of her brood, including twin babies eight months old, to the address given. But something had gone wrong. "There's only one bed in this house," the owner told her crossly, "and I'm sleeping in that." Mrs. Littleton felt homesick and unwanted. She spent the night in a grocer's shop, the nearest A.R.P. post. Then back home she went, and she's not feeling very keen on further adventures. On the whole, the evacuation scheme from the big cities has "worked," but so big a scheme is bound to break down at some point. So Mrs. Littleton is going to "stay put."

The next visit is heart-rending indeed! In a small house lived a father and mother and two daughters. One of the girls was a nurse on night duty. The other worked in the City. When the nurse returned from her duty in the early morning, she could not find her home. It was just a heap of rubble. Underneath were her father and mother and sister. Both the parents were killed. The sister owed her life to wonderful presence of mind. When the explosion was over, she was still alive. She pushed out her hand amid the rubble around her until she felt the alarm clock which had been near her bedside. Grasping it with the only hand she could move, she wound the hands round on the broken dial until the bell rang. The men in the demolition squad heard the bell, dug down to her, and rescued her. Both her feet were broken, but she is still alive and very brave.

Our last visit that afternoon was to a little shop kept by two elderly ladies. How would you feel if the little business which was your only means of livelihood were ruined through war? They are too old to start again elsewhere. There is no one with youth and energy and capital to set them on their feet again. They are casualties in the war for freedom. We talked to them for a little while, saying the things that can be said. Then we had to leave them, face to face with disaster and possibly destitution.

Of course, one could cover pages with such stories. That is merely the record of one afternoon. Every minister who spent the winter of 1940-41 in London, when night after night the "blitz" went on from dusk till dawn, could tell the same heart-rending tale. Underneath some churches shelters were constructed in which hundreds of people were accommodated every night through the whole winter, and pastors saw and took the chance to minister to them in spiritual, cultural, and physical ways. This was not possible at the City Temple. Our people live many miles from their church, and there are only a handful of people at night in the City of London proper. But we have kept in touch with our folk in all their hardships, dangers, and sorrows, and we shall do all we can for them till the horror ends.

A word might be said about our organizations. It was once said that the City Temple was a preaching place only. If ever it was that, it isn't so now. The officers in charge of these organizations are all church members, and membership is a matter which we do not view lightly. My able and devoted assistant, Miss Winifred Barton, interviews every prospective member, and to be a member of the City Temple is reckoned a high privilege.

Membership expresses itself in various ways. Every member is encouraged to join at least one of the organizations, for membership in a church without an active part in its work and close fellowship with others is scarcely worth calling membership at all.

One of our most fruitful organizations is the Friday Fellowship, which I have fully described in my book *This is the Victory*. Every Friday evening "young" people of all ages and both sexes meet to think and pray together about some aspect of the Christian life, particularly an aspect which presents a problem of difficulty.

It was here that we grew to know one another. We met together first of all for a few moments of worship. Then we broke up into groups, each group having its own leader and "scribe." The leader kept the group relevant in its thought and speech, though not with too great a strictness. The "scribe" jotted down, and afterward reported to the whole fellowship, the findings of the group and especially any point which needed further discussion. Then we had forty of fifty minutes of free and informal conversation, lifted the theme to its practical implication, dedicated ourselves to the newly-seen challenge, and went our way. The spiritual enthusiasm was a grand tonic to me personally, and I regard the Friday Fellowship as the chief spiritual dynamo of the church. Anything said from the pulpit can here be challenged. No one gets on his "high horse." If he tries to do so, he is laughed off it. The good fellowship, the honest thinking, the passion for reality, the hatred of all that is pompous or insincere, the healthy laughter, and the presence of Christ which so often descends upon us with breath-taking, silencing nearness have to be experienced. They cannot be described.

The Samaritan League I started soon after I came. It is for men only, though soon afterward we started a women's movement doing similar work, and it flourishes. Homes have been found for the homeless, meals for the hungry (a thousand a year by the Samaritan League alone), clothes for the ill-clad, work for the workless, radios for the lonely, friendship for the friendless, medical and surgical aid for the needy. Pensions have been obtained for scores, legal advice procured, prisoners visited in jail, and five thousand visits paid to render help in evil-smelling slums where poverty, filth, and vice prevail. In all this the women are not a whit behind the men. Not only is there a flourishing Women's League of Service, but a beautiful piece of work is done on every Monday afternoon when women are given spiritual encouragement, good fellowship, and refreshment, and their individual needs dealt with. One of the sad things about the fire is the entire destruction of clothing for the poor and destitute which had been recently received and was ready for immediate dispatch.

Our Psychological Clinic is never "written up." We publish no report, no publicity articles, no balance sheet. But before war took some of them away, half a dozen Christian doctors with training in psychiatry helped me in dealing with those troubles, some with physical symptoms, all with spiritual symptoms, which distress of mind, conflict of soul, and overstrained "nerves" engender. So often in the old days a patient with "nerves" went to the minister and was told to trust God and pray, or was sent to the doctor and told to drink bromide and rest, when what was needed was a thorough search into the roots of conflict, often obscured from the patient himself, until a new and healthier orientation could be found and a new path followed to liberty and joy and peace. I restrain myself from writing in detail of this work so dear to me. When you see a patient carried into the Clinic and walking out, albeit unsteadily at first; when you meet a person in the street who says, as one did to me a month ago, "You saved me from suicide"; when you receive letters almost daily which say, "I found new health and life through your Clinic," or "Thank you so much for ever introducing me to Dr. A, B, C, or D; I am now a different person"; then you rejoice that the City Temple is doing, in this way, part of the Master's work on earth. You realize that still he moves in the city streets, bringing, though it be through others, healing in his touch.

In addition, of course, we have what every church has, its prayer circle, its children's church, its choir, its literary society, its social circle, its missionary committee, its loyal band of women who work and sew for Red Cross funds and the funds of the church. I will not write at length of these, not because they are not important, but because their story would not command the same interest.

A month after the great disaster, the City Temple suffered again, although there was little more that could be destroyed. At that time we had been graciously allowed by Dr. Sidney Berry to meet in the Memorial Hall, the headquarters of the Congregational Union. One Sunday morning in May, 1941, I set off to conduct worship with a heavy heart. All night the bombs had been dropping, the guns roaring, the shrapnel falling. I should think no one in London had had any sleep, and many hundreds had suffered. In the suburb where I live we had been fortunate this time, though my own home had been damaged by earlier raids. Yet I felt sad on this bright morning, and apprehensive of the stories of suffering my people would tell me.

Before we had gone a mile, the bright sky had disappeared and given place to rolling clouds of smoke that covered the heavens and made the streets look as though it were a November evening. How we escaped punctures I have never understood. We drove continually over broken glass and parked at last near Smithfield Market, three quarters of a mile from the Memorial Hall, but as near as the police would allow us to take the car. Then we walked. Down one side of bomb craters we went, and up the other. Skirting piles of debris, including part of the famous Old Bailey Courts of Justice, which I saw come down into the street, clambering over timber and massive lumps of masonry, threading our way between and over fire hose, we came at last to Farringdon Street, which was blazing all down one side as far as one could see. Fortunately the Memorial Hall was safe, though all approaches to it were dangerous, either from flames or from falling buildings. One could not pass up Ludgate Hill toward St. Paul's Cathedral, for the flames from both sides met in the middle of the street.

Yet the small hall in which we met to worship was crowded with people, and many stood in the corridors outside. I took for my subject "The Power of God" and read part of that glorious letter of Peter to a church suffering the agony of persecution under the monster Nero. We felt gloriously close to the infant church of the first century as we prayed and sang, with London burning all around us.

In the sermon I had to raise my voice to be heard above the hiss of the firemen's hose and the roar of the flames devouring the buildings on the opposite side of the street. One of the buildings, which the whole congregation could see through the windows, bore the advertisement "Hot Sausages Ready." I felt quite sure they were hot—too hot for the firemen to get near!

I shall never forget that service. In the middle of it a gas main exploded with a roar. The flames lit up the faces of the congregation, but only one fainted, and she had been up all night after receiving the news that her brave airman lover was "missing." I turned to Mr. Clare—our faithful church secretary, who recently died—on one side of me and to Miss Barton on the other, and we whispered in consultation as to whether we should give up the idea of an evening service. I then announced that the second service would be held as usual. And again the people crowded the hall. I spoke on the inner serenity of spirit which Christ promised to those who trusted him. We felt the Master was indeed in our midst and that no outward horror and destruction could invade our hearts.

That evening I had to go to the hospital to find out the truth about one of my best men, a member of the Church Council. In doing duty for another he had been instantly killed by an exploding bomb. I had married him a year earlier to a bride who was a widow at twenty-three. I went out to see her late that Sunday evening in her suburban home. No one, unless he had an adequate hold on God, could be anything but dejected. Yet among my own people there was and is a marvelous serenity, based on the things war cannot touch. The girl-widow I visited that night showed as fine courage as a soldier in the front line.

I have described in detail that Sunday—the worst day I have ever lived through—because it tries to paint a picture of what my people are facing and the spirit in which they are facing it. Not one of us is in despair. These are great days for religion. We are in good heart, full of hope and confidence and determination. We, the living members of the spiritual City Temple,

> Stand in the temple of our God
> As pillars—

And we refuse to be cast down. We are determined to build again on the same site and carry on our work. In the meantime, quite unsought, came the invitation of the vicar of St. Sepulchre's Anglican Church, with the full approval of the Bishop of London, to worship in that lovely shrine, only a hundred yards from our doors, on the site of which worship has been offered to Christ for over a thousand years. The vicar, the Rev. G. H. Salter, Anglican son of a Methodist father, has made a gesture which will do more for the cause of Christian unity than many discussions and conferences. His brotherly action and friendly spirit have endeared him to us all forever. We can the better bear the sight of the gaunt walls of the ruined City Temple if all that has happened leads us to demolish the walls of misunderstanding which have separated the Christian denominations. St. Sepulchre's, or more correctly, the Church of the Holy Sepulchre, more famous than our own, has itself suffered terrible damage from the enemy. The verger's house is entirely destroyed and also the historic old watchtower, from which watch was kept against the body snatchers who stole bodies from the graveyard for dissection in St. Bartholomew's Hospital opposite. Vestries were wrecked. Lovely stained-glass windows were blown in. But at St. Sepulchre's we meet twice every Sunday. The vicar conducts his services in the Church of St. Bartholomew-the-Less in the precincts of the famous hospital (Bart's) of which he is the chaplain. We have to arrange our week-night activities as best we can. At the time of writing every organization is meeting except the literary society. That did become impossible. We had 2,200 registered members but cannot now find either accommodations or lecturers.

The sermons that follow were mostly preached at St. Sepulchre's, but that church also suffered repeated damage from the flying-bomb horror in the early summer of 1944. On one occasion the window substitutes were blown out by blast within forty-eight hours of being put in. We have had to move again and again. The Fyvie Hall in Regent Street and the Portland Hall in Titchfield Street have had to be used. But now we are back at St. Sepulchre's and hope to remain there until the end of the war, though even as I write this Hitler's V-2 bombs are falling on London. One fell after this manuscript had gone to press which injured the verger's wife and five hundred others, of whom three hundred were detained in St. Bartholomew's Hospital. One hundred sixty-three were killed. More windows at St. Sepulchre's were destroyed. My secretary, Miss Winifred Haddon, deserves high praise. She retyped this manuscript in circumstances of personal danger and remained at her post through the whole of the war.

I have kept the direct method of address and printed the sermons in the main as they were preached. Although I have omitted sermons commonly called topical, in which one tries to relate the events of the day to the great truths of God, I have in my selection sought to include expository, psychological, devotional, social, and evangelistic sermons, sermons for the young and for the old, for the student and for the "plain man." I should like to think that if any people read this book who criticize the church and yet who never go to one, they might be induced to join in fellowship. The church needs everyone of good will to help it in its work. But it has something of inexpressible value to offer—namely, for individuals, communities, and nations, a new integration of life on the soundest of all bases. Some of us believe that, because the Spirit of Christ still lives in his church and acts through it, it is, in spite of division and failure, the great hope of the world. It is easy to stand outside and criticize. Why not come in and help to make the vision a glorious reality?

LESLIE D. WEATHERHEAD

*The City Temple*
*% The Church of the Holy Sepulchre*
*Holborn Viaduct, London, E.C.*
*Easter, 1945*

# CONTENTS

# THE SIGNIFICANCE OF SILENCE

I WANT TO SHOW YOU THREE WAYS IN WHICH SILENCE IS SIGNIFICANT. I shall ask you to note first the significance of silence in the hour of the soul's exaltation; second, the significance of silence in the hour of the soul's grief; and, third, the significance of silence in the hour of the soul's refusal to come to grips with reality.

I think the hour that stands out most in my memory of my last summer holiday was an hour of silence. I was staying at Jordans in Buckinghamshire, that lovely, secluded Quaker settlement, with its old-world garden, its ancient barn built from the timbers of the "Mayflower," and its sense of quietude. It always seems like Sunday afternoon at Jordans.

One September morning I got up at a quarter to seven, walked through the kitchen garden, up through the orchard where the owls were still crying, through a gate, and into a meadow. But not only into a meadow, into a great silence. It was in the meadow that I met God. The ground was so drenched with dew that it looked as if it were covered with hoar frost. The sun was peeping over the horizon, throwing long shadows upon the grass. It was an hour of bewitching loveliness. Magic was in the air and awe in my heart. I had that strange impression, which probably you have had many times, that I was being allowed to be present just as God had concluded the creation of the world, that I was seeing the world all new and fresh from his hand. There was a solemn hush which seemed to fall over the whole field and everything in it.

In a way it was a strange experience. You don't *plan* such hours of insight when you go for a summer holiday. Yet at the end of that holiday, having done perhaps all the things you planned to do, you realize the thing that stands out most is an hour of silence when the soul was caught up in rapturous worship and allowed to behold part of the beauty of God. You know that God was near, that he was speaking to you, that he brought you to that hour and to that place, in order to say things to you in the silence that otherwise you would not have stayed to hear.

I had a similar experience some years ago after preaching in Lincoln. I didn't know who was going to be my host, but after the meeting, which was very hot, very noisy, and very uncomfortable, a simplehearted farmer came up, almost shyly, and said that he was to be my host. He apologized for not having a car. If only he could have known how my heart exulted as we bowled through the narrow lanes in a gig. I felt like a child in fairyland. The gig lamps lighted the chestnut haunches of the mare, threw strange, thrilling shadows on the hedgerows and the lower branches of the trees, and frightened here and there a chattering blackbird from its roost. We drew up with a glorious clatter of hoofs on the cobbles of a farmyard. I felt it had all happened before, perhaps a hundred years ago. One has that feeling sometimes. Men shouted and ran to the unharnessing, and then supper followed in a huge kitchen with a mighty log fire. Hams hung from the ceiling. Dogs pushed their noses into your hand in friendly welcome. The kettle sang on the hearth. A great ginger cat sprawled on an oak settee in the chimney corner. We sat down to a white wood table scrubbed as clean and spotless as linen could be. Then followed pipes and talk and a prayer together, and then the never-to-be-forgotten experience. I was led to a bedroom filled with moonlight and the fragrance of lavender sheets. The bedroom window was thrown up, and when I was alone, I knelt at the open window, and the sound that thrilled me was the sound of a very distant train. Chug, chug, chug . . . then a lot of quick chugs together. It sounds foolish to say that I was thrilled by the sound of a train, however far off. But the fact is that sounds of that nature interpret the silence. They alone make one apprehend how utterly still and quiet is the night. The silent majesty of that moonlight night, lying upon the hushed fields like the supernatural glory of God, needed some gentle sound to interpret and emphasize it. Then the second interpreting sound—also far away—a village clock striking twelve. I shall never forget that night. I felt so wrapped in the presence of God that I didn't want to lose it in sleep.

I felt that I understood a little better that strange experience of Elijah. After the wind and the earthquake and fire he heard "a still small voice," or if we interpret the original more literally—and you will find the words in the margin of the Revised Version—"a sound of gentle stillness." The sound interpreted the silence. Let us note, then, in the first place how often the hour of the soul's exaltation is an hour of silence.

Some words of Pascal come to the mind in this regard. "All the evils of life," he said, "have fallen upon us because men will not sit alone quietly in a room." Such a statement sounds remote from the busy planning of our minds and the doing of our hands and the running of our feet, but the more I think about it the more I think it is true. Is not the truth of the matter that we live at such a speed and our lives are so rushed and hectic that God has very little chance with us? He cannot make himself heard above the bustle and the noise. And I know that I need it to be said to me, therefore I dare think you may need it to be said to you, that, when we are engaged on the very work of God himself, we are so hurried and rushed that, as it were, we are closed down to all other stations, open only on one wave length, that of our own concerns, and therefore insensitive and unreceptive to his voice.

If you agree that the soul's hour of exaltation is an hour of silence, try to receive the thought that therefore the time of silence is most likely to produce the soul's exaltation. I will not at this point go into all the psychology that lies behind that claim, but I am certain it is true. We notice and take advantage of this psychological truth in many ways. If rest is marked by relaxation, then to achieve a relaxed state will often bring the desired rest. One is glad to find that even the busy Paul has a word to those eager Thessalonians: "Study to be quiet." And we need that quiet not that we may think more positively, whipping our mind to activity, or do more and more, spurring our will to greater effort, but that we may, in quiescent relaxation of mind, receive and commune.

I find a clue in the behavior of others which helps me to understand my own needs in this matter. There are hours of exaltation when the silence of the soul is carelessly broken into pieces by the noisy burglary of one's peace of mind and the treasures of the silent hour on the part of someone else. If another can rob me of the harvest of the silent hour by some vulgar remark, how often do I rob myself and spoil a silence which God could use, by vulgarly and unnecessarily breaking into it with some petty and unimportant detail?

How exquisitely this kind of outrage is described by Rupert Brooke! I cannot spoil the lovely poem by quoting a small part of it. Listen to this:

> Safe in the magic of my woods
>     I lay, and watched the dying light.
> Faint in the pale high solitudes,
>     And washed with rain and veiled by night.
>
> Silver and blue and green were showing.
>     And the dark woods grew darker still;
> And birds were hushed; and peace was growing;
>     And quietness crept up the hill;
>
> And no wind was blowing
>
> And I knew
> That this was the hour of knowing,
> And the night and the woods and you
> Were one together, and I should find
> Soon in the silence the hidden key
> Of all that had hurt and puzzled me—
> Why you were you, and the night was kind,
> And the woods were part of the heart of me.
>
> And there I waited breathlessly,
> Alone; and slowly the holy three,
> The three that I loved, together grew
> One, in the hour of knowing,
> Night, and the woods, and you—
>
> And suddenly
> There was an uproar in my woods,
>
> The noise of a fool in mock distress,
> Crashing and laughing and blindly going,

Of ignorant feet and a swishing dress,
And a Voice profaning the solitudes.

The spell was broken, the key denied me.
And at length your flat, clear voice beside me
Mouthed cheerful clear flat platitudes.

You came and quacked beside me in the wood.
You said, "The view from here is very good!"
You said, "It's nice to be alone a bit!"
And, "How the days are drawing out!" you said.
You said, "The sunset's pretty, isn't it?"

By God! I wish—I wish that you were dead! [1]

How significant silence can be! Of such a silence Wordsworth
wrote, "I made no vows, but vows were made for me." And the
praying of Jesus night after night amid the silent, lonely hills that
rise from the Galilean lake would not, I feel sure, be full of wordy
petition, but of the sharing of a love-interpreted silence.

O Sabbath rest by Galilee!
   O calm of hills above,
Where Jesus knelt to share with thee
The silence of eternity,
   Interpreted by love!

"He went up into the mountain apart to pray: and when evening
was come, he was there alone."

Note, secondly, the significance of silence in the hour of the soul's
grief. What will you do if grief assails you? Will you rush into
activity! Will you try to fill your mind with other thoughts? Will
you plunge yourself into the tumult of life? Will you seek in the
whirl and rush of both duty and pleasure to dull your aching heart?

I am not minimizing the value of activity. Again and again to
get on with the next job is the best medicine you could use. But,
however severe the disease, no patient can go on drinking medicine

[1] From *The Collected Poems of Rupert Brooke*. Copyright, 1915, by Dodd,
Mead & Co. Reprinted by permission.

all the time, and, however great our grief, activity must come to an end, and then there is silence which only practice beforehand can help us to use in the hour of sorrow. Without such practice the silence may be full of bitter rebellion, bleak remorse, bitter cynicism. For the mind practiced in the use of silence, activity will accomplish something, but an interpreted silence will accomplish more.

Jesus, I think, must have been very fond of John the Baptist, his cousin. Save the sons of the kingdom, said Jesus, "among them that are born of women there hath not risen a greater than John the Baptist." John was murdered to please a nautch girl, and the disciples came and told Jesus. He did not sit down and talk to them. He did not preach a sermon on the nature of suffering or the place of evil and death in the world. He said, "Let us go out into a desert place and be alone." He knew the significance of silence in the hour of grief.

There is a clue for us again in the intuitive way we try to help others in their hour of grief. Only the fool intrudes with words. We seem to realize for others that in their hour of grief if they possess spiritual resources they will turn to them. If they don't possess them it isn't the time to press them. They must in fact be discovered later when the mind is not so disturbed. No one wants explanations when his heart is broken. He wants the healing silence of God. Even if Christ in the flesh could be present in an hour of grief, I think men would ask him nothing, but in his presence they would find everything. There would be nothing left to ask. He must be so real to us that in the hour of grief we can turn to him and find the healing of a love-interpreted silence in his presence. We cannot receive more than that silent friendship. We don't need more.

I never realized how dreadfully irrelevant and almost vulgar words could be in the hour of grief until an experience befell me in a home where a little girl dearly loved one particular doll. The doll was broken by the carelessness of a person who turned on the little child and said, in words that seemed to sear one's brain as they were spoken, "I'll buy you another." A child's grief is so real and so terrible that it seemed as bad as saying to a mother who has lost her child, "Well, you have other children," or to a man who has lost his dearest friend, "Well, you have other friends." No newly bought doll, however expensive and marvelous, could make up for that dear treasure on whom love had been so lavished that the very paint had been kissed off its face. There it lay in cruel pieces, and nothing on earth could replace it or make up the sense of loss. With the sublime dignity and the spiritual insight that made Jesus himself put a little child in the midst of men, this little girl looked up into her mother's eyes and said, "Don't talk about it, please, Mummy." She wanted only to be quiet. There was nothing that could be said. The heart knoweth its own bitterness, and healing for that heart is silence.

So, in the hour of his men's overwhelming sorrow, he who had insight into human grief did not fill the last hours with advice or reiterated commands or repeated lessons, but simply said, "I have yet many things to say unto you, but ye cannot bear them now."

But look lastly at the significance of silence in the hour of the soul's refusal to come to grips with reality. One of the most awful states of soul into which man can fall is a condition in which no words can do any good. "Come down from the cross," they cried. "Let the Christ . . . now come down from the cross, that we may see and believe." But there was no answer. Only silence. Pilate said unto him, "Whence art thou?" And Jesus gave him no answer. Herod questioned him in many words, "but he answered him nothing." Is there another occasion in history or in literature where silence plays such a significant part as in the scene in Herod's palace when the Master stood before him? Says Luke: "Herod with his soldiers set him at nought, and mocked him, and arraying him in gorgeous apparel sent him back to Pilate." And Herod and Pilate, formerly enemies, became friends over the body of Jesus.

I see in imagination Herod with Christ before him, secretly feeling uncomfortable, as sensual people always do in the presence of goodness, and trying to maintain "face" by breaking Christ's silence. Herod's dirty jests and derisive laughter are directed at the Master. If he had answered, his answers would have been made the basis of more jesting. "But he answered him nothing." The bawdy jokes and unclean innuendoes made no impression at all. It must have been like watching the foul scum of a stagnant pool fall away from the unstainable white breast of a silent swan, who, with proud head and lovely curved neck and dignified poise, sits enthroned on waters whose filth she scarcely deigns to notice. Why did he not reply? Because in the mood in which his tormenters were, there was nothing to be said. He would only have increased their sin by providing it with further occasion for its foul expression.

O my soul, bring not down upon thyself the silence of Jesus! Better his cry of woe such as the Pharisee heard; better his word of appeal such as the sinner heard; better his cry of rebuke such as the disciple heard. It is a terrible indication of a state of soul when Jesus says nothing. "Be not silent unto me, O God," cried the psalmist, "lest if thou be silent unto me, I become like them that go down into the pit," into the final darkness, into the agelong night.

There are two ways of getting through life, and I think we must decide which we shall follow. Some people try one way and some another. The first way is to stop thinking. The second way is to stop and think. A great many people are trying the first way. They rush from this to that. They fill up every hour. They dare not be alone. They give God no chance. They are never silent, never quiet, never utterly relaxed, receptive, submissive, waiting. This method always fails because, of course, one cannot maintain the pace. One cannot travel fast enough. Something happens that one did not engineer, could not foresee, and cannot forestall. Suddenly God *makes* a silence in their lives, or uses one that illness makes, and then they are afraid. Silence is so strange to them. They have never made it their friend and never made it the occasion of realizing the healing friendship of God.

There is a much better way. It is that, from time to time, we should stop and think. I am not going to say to you, "Keep an hour's quiet time every morning before breakfast." If I said that, you would do nothing about it at all and tell yourself that I was talking nonsense and could not possibly understand just how busy you are. But do let me remind you that the old Hebrew word "Sabbath" comes from a root which means "stop doing what you are doing." So may I suggest that once a week, perhaps every Sunday evening, or whichever time you yourself decide, in addition to daily prayers, you should give yourself half an hour—if that is all you can spare—and be alone, quiet, silent, listening, and looking? Perhaps he will say to you something in such a silence that will make that half an hour the supreme experience, not of a week, but of a lifetime. Remember how significant silence is in the hour of the soul's exaltation. So give your soul the occasion of such exaltation by arranging a time of silence for it. Remember that in such a silence he can do something for you so that the hour of grief—and grief must come at some time to us all—may be an hour in which you can lay hold of life's resources, be strong to endure, and able to turn your hurt to the healing of others as well as yourself. And, lest you ever become as those who silence Christ himself by trifling with life, to whom God is remote and unreal, for whom even the eternal and lovely things are cold and dead, stop and think from time to time. Look life in the face. "Study to be quiet." Make time to listen. You may miss him in the wind, the storm, the fire. But in an interpreted silence you will find him and make him your friend. There is only one man whom nothing can finally overwhelm. He is the man who has God for his friend.

> O Sabbath rest by Galilee!
>   O calm of hills above,
> Where Jesus knelt to share with thee
> The silence of eternity,
>   Interpreted by love!

# YOUTH LOOKS AT CHRIST

IF WE ARE TO GRASP WHAT CHRISTIANITY IS REALLY ABOUT, I THINK it is very important that in our minds there should be a picture of Christ that is clear and true. Indeed, I don't think we can successfully carry out the Christian program for society and the world, or enter a rich devotional experience, unless we turn again and again and look at him. You can be a good Communist without a clear picture of Karl Marx in your mind. You cannot make much of a fist of Christianity without looking long and hard at Christ. For Christianity is not a social or political program nor, primarily, a theological system. It is a way of life. It depends not so much on understanding intellectual ideas and working them out with enthusiasm as on a relationship with a Person that has its outcome in a certain quality of life. If Christianity is supremely a relationship with a Person, the more we know about the Person, and the more clearly we see him, the better. Someone has said all that in three words—"Christianity is Christ."

In the various denominations and sects the emphasis is sometimes found to be on matters which I cannot but regard as of less importance. For instance, creeds are important. I should not like to be thought to disparage them. But if we begin with the creeds, we may get lost in the maze of an intellectual theology and see very little of Christ. Ritual and ceremony are important. They were invented, I suppose, to symbolize great truths, to make an appeal through the eye which by constant repetition would assist faith to grasp the truth behind the ceremony. But to begin there might lead some simple souls to bewilderment, and one remembers that some of the best Christians in the world—the Quakers—do not emphasize ritual at all. All the beautiful things that play a part in a service of worship have a valuable place. The architecture of the church, the stained-glass windows, the carefully prepared music are all there to assist faith. But care must be taken lest these lovely things lead us only to purposeless and unchallenging aestheticism. Our picture of Christ then might only be that of a sentimental and unreal Person.

Therefore I should like to ask you to go imaginatively back and start at the beginning where the disciples started: Jesus looking at youth, and youth looking at Jesus. And at the close I shall ask whether you don't think that here is a Leader worth following, here is one who really has the secret we are all looking for—the secret of the art of living—and, indeed, whether or not here is one who can do a unique thing for us, one who can deal with human sin, and who alone, of all the great ones of the earth, is entitled to be called the Saviour. He has done so much with such unpromising material that, if you think for a moment, you must admit that he is likely to be able to do something with us, in spite of all our bad habits and secret sins and overwhelming worries and dark despair. I should like the end of this to be that you really put him to the test to find that he is the Master of life, and that the greatest fullness and the maximum joy can be found by those who embark on the Christian adventure in the strength of his loving friendship. I believe that when Christianity began, when a young man stood up on the green hillside above the blue waters of the Galilean lake and talked to people, they said within themselves, "This is what we have been looking for all our lives." Up till now you may possibly have felt that the church had nothing to say that was relative to your own life. You may have been disgusted by denominational squabbles and quarreling sects. Banish all that from your mind for the moment. Remember that all the denominations of Christendom are one in this, that they seek to bring sin-wrecked lives and broken hearts and wounded spirits into touch with Jesus of Nazareth. Christianity begins there.

I am going to mention five or six things about Jesus which I am sure would appeal to youth. Think them over and etch deeply upon your mind the picture of Jesus.

1. Strange as it may seem to some who have gone a long way in their Christian experience, I want to begin by talking about his physical appearance. To youth, physical appearances are important,

and if we are going to make a picture of Christ, we cannot make it only with nonphysical elements. By deliberately trying to imagine what he looked like, we may correct any picture previously held in the mind which is too effeminate, too much like the stained-glass window, too unreal. We may safely say, I think, that Jesus was physically a very fit man. He lived in the open air. Even the carpenter's shop of the East was in the open air. His love of birds and flowers and grass makes me think that he must often have walked miles over the hills above Nazareth; and since from the hills above his home one can still see the blue waters of the Mediterranean, I feel perfectly certain that he often walked to the coast and bathed in the sea. He was a son of the open air, and his mind was so full of lovely ideas, and his life so full of unselfish deeds, that it is hard to suppose they did not affect his physical form. At any rate, to whatever degree our bodies may depend on our ancestors, the expression of the face, and particularly of the eyes, is some kind of reflection of the soul.

I am quite certain, in my own mind, from the expressions which the Evangelists use, that the eyes of Jesus were very remarkable: "He had looked round about on them with anger"; "Jesus looking upon him loved him"; "The Lord turned, and looked upon Peter." His eyes often flashed with merriment, for his discourse often breaks out into humor. His eyes often blazed with anger. It was the disciple who loved him best who saw him in a vision and said, "His eyes were as a flame of fire." Sometimes those eyes were dim with tears, as when he brooded over Jerusalem. Sometimes they melted in tenderness as he stooped over some stricken form. Sometimes they wore the stern expression of rebuke, as when his beloved Peter tempted him. Sometimes they looked like chilled steel as he turned his face to Jerusalem and the cross outside the city wall. Sometimes they filled with the anguish of suffering, and at least on two occasions we are told that he broke down and sobbed. They were eyes that could win men, but eyes that could wither men. They were eyes that could forgive and eyes that could condemn. They were eyes that delighted in the flight of a bird to its nest, but eyes that could follow the evasions of a fugitive spirit to its farthest funk hole. His eyes were the homes of all men's dreams and could bring life to the dead and hope to the most degraded.

Let us begin there, then, with a picture of one tall and dark like most Easterners, with a body disciplined by hard physical toil, a face lighted up by loving thoughts that dwelt much on God, and whose physical presence has never satisfactorily been portrayed even by the greatest artists the world has ever known.

2. The second thing that would strike youth looking at Jesus would be his inner joy. Deep in his personality there was unbroken joy. You may remind me at once that he was the "Man of Sorrows," but I would remind you that joy and sorrow are not the kind of opposites which cancel one another out, and that the opposite of joy is not sorrow but unbelief. Jesus Christ was not a dull or depressing person, long-faced and melancholy. "Are you a parson?" asked a man in the train of a fellow passenger. "No," said the other, "I've had influenza. That's what makes me look like that." My friends who are of my own profession will forgive me if I say that I don't think Jesus of Nazareth would be very much like the official parson. I think he would talk a great deal about religion, and yet I don't think we should tumble to the fact that he was so talking for some time, for he would not use theological words or ecclesiastical clichés. He would talk about religion as a person who is keen about anything talks about that in which he is supremely interested. His enthusiasm would be infectious, and we should find ourselves listening, with eager eyes, longing for him to go on. We should not feel that religion was something remote from life, or difficult to understand, or something about which men quarreled, or which other men were paid to teach. I think we should feel about religion, while Jesus was speaking, as we feel when a nature lover talks to us about the habits of birds and the joys of the countryside. Religion, far from being difficult and depressing, would stir us like the wind on the heath or a sunny day by the seashore. If the bishop comes to tea, though he tries with all his might to be human and friendly, we don't feel quite ourselves until he has gone; and when the door closes on him, we breathe a sigh of relief and wonder whether we said anything we should not have said. But I believe that if Jesus

of Nazareth came into our homes, he would be the life and soul of
any party, and when he went away we should feel as we feel when
on some summer afternoon clouds suddenly veil the glory of the
sunshine and a chilly wind stirs through the trees. He was such good
company that his fondness for parties and the happiness he brought
to them became a scandal. "A gluttonous man," they said, "and a
wine-bibber, a friend of publicans and sinners." What a strange
thing it is they called him the "Man of Sorrows," and yet he got into
trouble for being the man of joy! I believe that if Jesus of Nazareth
in the flesh could come back to us, his presence would be a revelation. It would be marvelous to be with him. We should wish for
him to stay a bit longer and hate to see the door close on his depart-
ing form. I believe he could go into any officers' mess, as someone
has said, or any stokehold among the crew, or any factory among
the workers at lunch time, or any group of students, or men who
had been working in the mines, and be sincerely welcome, not making folk feel edgy and a little embarrassed as so many good people
do, but making them feel that his life was joyous and serene, as
clean and happy as the dawn, and that theirs might be the same if
they learned his secret.

3. The third thing that would attract youth would be his attitude toward others. If men were hypocrites, really pretending to be
something they never tried to be, his language would blast them out
of their smug complacency, and make them either take further cover
from him, or come into a new sincerity they had never known. If
men were cruel to little children, he would not mince his words; if
they were spiritually proud, his glance and words would strip them
naked. These three sins seemed to him the worst, but the great majority of people are none of these three things. They have their sins,
God knows, but they are not the three worst which he so continually condemned. Men and women who worry about their sins worry
about lust and meanness and bad temper. He would not pass over
these things. He is too good a friend for that, but he would deliver
us from our self-despising and show us that he saw other things
within us besides our sins. So often we label people according to
some outstanding failing, forgetting that very rarely does a label

account for the whole bottle, unless the label says "the mixture."
Jesus had a wonderful way of seeing past the labels that men fix to
others and accept as accounting for themselves. In one who was labeled a grasping little moneygrabber Jesus saw "a son of Abraham,"
and in one whom everybody thought of as the harlot from Magdala
Jesus noticed a woman with a wonderful gift of loving.

I think Jesus' secret of helping people lay partly there, that he
always saw the good in them and acted positively toward it in such
a way as to call it forth into such glorious life that the unclean and
unholy things withered away, having no room to live. What we so
often forget ourselves is that, hypocrisy, cruelty, and pride apart, no
one has ever helped another in this world by giving him mere disapproval. If fellowship is established, there is often a time not only
for criticism but for direct condemnation. But we don't wait until
that fellowship is established. To criticize in such a situation—before fellowship is established—is simply to make a gulf between
yourself and the person you criticize. Very soon you are shouting at
one another across the gulf. The person you criticize, even though
your motive is to help him, shouts back in an attempt to justify himself. If you began with the good in him and allowed yourself to
think well of him because of that good, you would not need to point
out his faults. He would be quick to see them himself and eager to
correct them.

That is what happened to Zacchaeus. The poor little chap was up
a tree in more senses than one. Everybody saw his faults; everybody
despised him and hated him and sneered at him. Nobody had ever
shown him kindness. Nobody had ever sought his friendship. Nobody had ever believed that he had a best to be believed in. It is not
irreverent to glory in the psychological insight of Jesus as well as in
his divine love. Listen to what he said to Zacchaeus: "I must abide
at thy house." Not, "Come and have supper with me," which
would be patronizing and doing Zacchaeus a favor. But, "May I
have supper with you?" making Zacchaeus the host, put in a position to do something for Jesus. What healing for Zacchaeus lay in
that simple difference! As they walked along, Jesus said nothing
about Zacchaeus' faults. He didn't even hint at them. It was Zacchaeus who began to talk about them, and who, before the supper

party began, had himself taken the initiative to put things right. Even to a woman taken in adultery, whom others were ready to stone, Jesus said, "Neither do I condemn you." That does not mean there was nothing to be condemned. It means that there was no need to do the condemning. The woman was condemning herself, and the highest court of authority which ever judges man is the judgment he passes upon himself in the light of the purity of God. The rebuke of Jesus was not condemnation of those who knew they were wrong. It was the silent rebuke of his own unstained purity.

4. I am quite sure that the courage of Jesus would immensely appeal to youth. His physical courage was itself an amazing thing. Has it occurred to you that, when the disciples ran away, Jesus might easily have done the same? No one would ever condemn a person for seeking to escape when an armed mob had set out to kill him. What a terrible rebuke of cowardice his courage was! What would one give to have seen the flashing eyes of Jesus when, before the majesty of his bearing and the sting of his words, men drove their beasts out of the holy place? We need not make much of the whip of small cords. He may have used it on the oxen. He would have no need to use it on the men. In imagination we can hear his voice above the tumult and the din, ringing through the Temple courts, penetrating to the Holy of Holies itself: "My house shall be called the house of prayer for all nations, and ye have made it a den of thieves."

But his spiritual courage was greater still. Everyone to whom he spoke held Moses in the highest possible esteem. Yet the Master had the courage to say, Moses said so-and-so, "but *I* say unto you . . ." To those who regarded it as blasphemy, Jesus said, "I and the Father are one." He longed for friendship, and he had that instinctive longing for approval which is so deep in the heart of every man and woman; but he stuck to convictions and preached them fearlessly, though they made him utterly lonely among those with whom he most desired to be friendly. Let us look at him, and when fear makes us slaves to what other people think and do and say, let us turn back and look at him again.

Yet youth loves the high demand. No church has ever done a

service to youth by watering down the august and tremendous claims which Jesus makes. I feel sick at heart when I hear of a church that, by lowering the threshold, seeks to entice youth into its fellowship. "Come and join the cricket club. We have a good billiard table. There's a social hour, with coffee and buns, after the service next Sunday night. The service doesn't take long; so *do* come." The higher you make the threshold, the steeper you make the path, the more will you attract all that is grandest in youth. When Jesus found an attractive young man, he didn't pat him on the back and press him into his friendship, thinking how useful his money would be in Judas' bag. Because that money stood in the path of the soul's progress, Jesus said, "You will never find life until you get rid of that." I think it is because Jesus makes the demands so hard that we all love him. If the Christian religion were a movement that you could support or not as you pleased, a sort of interest like collecting stamps or playing golf, which some people take up and some people do not, if it made no demands on that which we know to be the finest thing about ourselves, our powers of self-sacrifice, then youth would pass it by. For note this: although youth criticizes the churches bitterly, and in the main thinks little of parsons, and is not much attracted by organized religion, youth never criticizes Jesus Christ; and the severest criticism of us in the churches is that we are not sufficiently like him.

5. One other quality we may glance at—his divinity. Long books have been written on this one subject alone, and I am not pretending to deal adequately with it, save to remind you of his mysterious claims. As we look at Jesus, I want our admiration and love to pass into something else, as it did with those who watched him in Galilee. We too catch our breath and ask with others, "What manner of man is this?" "I am the light of the world," he said. "I am the bread of life." "I am the truth"—the thing all philosophers since time began have sought in vain. "Before Abraham was, I am." "By their attitude to me," he said, "men will be judged." "No one cometh unto the Father but by me." "The world is well lost if I am gained." "Your sins are forgiven you." "I will give to them eternal life." This

is the most monstrous egotism ever seen on earth; or else the truth is that in a unique sense he was God, that all the values of God which humanity can contain were found in him, that I am not merely to obey his teaching or work out his ideas in a movement, but to worship him and find in him cleansing from sin, salvation from such a night of horror awaiting the separated soul that the only word to describe it is death.

Let us glance at the breath-taking contrasts in his nature in closing. He was so human that he is well named the "Son of Man." We feel that this is what humanity ought to be. Yet, if we deny his divinity, his words do not make sense, for his claims are those of one who was either insane or divine. We see a child sitting upon his knee and looking up into his face and laughing, feeling perfectly at home, and then we watch powerful enemies shrinking away from him, plotting together for months before they could encompass his death. I hear him claiming that by their attitude to him men would at last be judged, and then I hear him inviting people to him and, in order to make them at home, telling them that he himself was meek and lowly of heart. He said the most dreadful things that have ever been said about sin, and from his tender lips comes the doctrine of hell; yet he said the tenderest things to sinners that human ears have ever heard, and he made friends with those from whom even the merely respectable shrank back in horror. He claimed to be one with God, and yet he shrank away from all applause. As we saw, he was so joyous that joy bubbled up in merriment and raised a scandal; yet for two thousand years men in the deepest grief and women who are brokenhearted have found that the "Man of Sorrows" alone can understand them. He said at last that all authority was given to him in heaven and on earth, and yet one who knew him best quoted him as saying, "Behold, I stand at the door and knock." He rose from the dead and ascended into heaven and sits at the right hand of God the Father, and yet he will not break into the house of life, or have any violence done to our mental processes, or break down any of the doors of personality, but waits and knocks and loves until we ourselves invite him to be the master of our lives.

I cannot explain him to you. To describe him is an impossible task. I can only try from the gospel records to show you a glimpse of him. All I know is that he holds my heart enthralled and always will. I know I am not worthy to be his friend. Yet, God helping me, though I turn back a thousand times, and wound him a hundred times in a day, I will never desert him utterly, turn my back upon him, and walk out into the final darkness. Having caught even a glimpse of him, I cannot for long live without him. My proud and stubborn and sinful heart may go its own way without him for days together, but then I find that life is becoming cold and bleak, empty and desolate, dull and meaningless. It is as though the sun had gone out of the sky in summertime and winter were back again. I feel depressed unto death, hurting others, breaking his heart, becoming irritable and unhappy. And then I turn back to him again, and find that he will forgive me and restore me and receive me back into his endless friendship; and to be received into that friendship is to be saved. I am not at the end of the journey, but I am back on the road which will bring me at last to that blessedness which is his will, and which, at my best, is my own desire. I don't understand him, but—

> If Jesus Christ is a man,—
>     And only a man,—I say
> That of all mankind I cleave to him,
>     And to him will I cleave alway.
>
> If Jesus Christ is a god,—
>     And the only God,—I swear
> I will follow him through heaven and hell,
>     The earth, the sea, and the air! [1]

I think Martin Luther's words are true: "Take hold of Jesus as a man, and you will discover that he is God."

Youth, you cannot help loving him, and if you will only look at him, you will find that you cannot thereafter be happy for long without him. You will never be able to turn away from him finally again. You will have seen too much. Let me call you back to him now. If you have sinned, he will forgive you. If you are even now

[1] "The Song of a Heathen," by R. W. Gilder. By permission of Houghton Mifflin Co.

intending to sin, he will save you. If you want to be a crusader and build a new world, he will not only lead you in your thinking, but empower you in your doing, and go on giving you power when the power in mere ideas and movements is exhausted by man's selfishness. If you are sad and broken, he will comfort and restore you. If you have no belief in yourself left, let me remind you that he believes in you when you don't believe in yourself any longer, and forgives you when you can't forgive yourself any more. Turn to him now; receive him now. Begin again with him. Keep on looking at him and listening to him. Christianity is Christ. If only I can bring you into living touch with him, he will do the rest. Where he touches, there is healing. Where he beckons, there the light shines. Where he companions, there is peace.

# IS IT REALLY GOOD TO BE ALIVE?

"Life is sweet, brother. . . . there's day and night, brother, both sweet things; sun, moon, and stars, all sweet things; there's likewise a wind on the heath." [1] Yes, in the right mood, and on the right kind of day, in the right place, our relationships right with our fellows, we have all felt like that. Given health of body, mind, and spirit, given youth and joyous high spirits, and contact with the wind on the heath instead of, say, a slum street, an evil-smelling factory, a stuffy office, the sickly-sweet horror of an operating theater, or the smell of the London Underground Railway, we can say "Amen" to George Borrow. There *are* moments about which, in sincerity, we can shout with Wordsworth,

> Bliss was it in that dawn to be alive,
> But to be young was very heaven.

Though even the young, if they stop to think, or stumble on pain in the life of one dear to them, find it increasingly hard to tuck everything into the "life is sweet" philosophy.

For those of us in the second half of life there are still many moments when our hearts echo George Borrow's words, but they would be a very untrue label of life as a whole. For children, yes, but does God really mean it to be so for adults?

Let me make a personal confession. In earlier years I believed that God intended man to be happy in the ordinary sense of the word—free from pain, free from psychological disharmony, which is mental pain, free from insecurity and want and hunger and cold —that God wanted man to have all the things man wants for himself, and that the word "providence" connoted the loving generosity with which God poured out what we call the "good" things upon

[1] George Borrow, *Lavengro*.

41

his children. I labored mentally, as Milton puts it, to "justify the ways of God to men." I sought to prove that when evil does befall, it comes through ignorance, folly, or sin, either in ourselves or in the great human family to which we are so closely bound that, while we joyously receive its assets, we cannot escape its liabilities. Thus the corporate effects of ignorance and folly and sin are visited on the individual in the form of what he calls "evil."

I knew that God was always eager to replace ignorance with knowledge, folly with wisdom, and sin with holiness, and therefore I argued—and still think I argued truly—that the fruits of ignorance and folly and sin could not be God's intention for his children, and were not to be regarded as his "will" in the commonly accepted use of the word.

I now feel that in thus thinking I failed to emphasize sufficiently an important fact, namely, that God *ordained* our slow schooling from ignorance to knowledge, from folly to wisdom, from sin to holiness, and that he *ordained* the family basis of life by which we suffer through others. He may not have willed suffering in the sense of intending it, but he certainly willed the circumstances in which suffering is pretty certain for most of us. Only a few lucky ones escape.

And are they really lucky? I have just used the word "schooling." When I was at school, I heard of boys who, for some reason or another, escaped school. How lucky I thought them! But now I don't think they were lucky. For they had to learn later when it was harder to learn, or else, if they repudiated the discipline of learning at all, they suffered permanent loss. I wonder if that is true spiritually. If by the interplay of circumstances we escape the school of suffering, does it mean that we have to learn later when it is harder to learn, or does it mean that, if even that is avoided, we suffer permanent loss? Probably these words will not reach anybody over thirty-five who has not experienced something in the way of physical or mental suffering, and I think if I could ask you the question, now that the suffering has passed, whether you wish it had been avoided, you would say that you are glad that you passed through it. For as the French proverb says: *"Souffrir passe; avoir souffert ne passe jamais*"—"To suffer, passes away, but to have suffered, never passes." The gain of the experience is ours forever.

Ought the word "providence," then, be enlarged to include those ways of God with his children which *seem* evil, but which promote their highest good? Health, success, material blessings, family happiness, the love of friends, the approval of the community—these we call the good things. "In the providence of God" is a phrase we use when we have received the good and escaped what we call the evil things—sorrow and suffering, bereavement, frustration, poverty, disappointment, and disease. But a thought rises in my mind that will not be suppressed. If the goodness of God to his children is to be measured only by his ability to secure for them what we call the "good" things, then he is strangely unsuccessful in his efforts, for there is probably not one life lived on this planet since life began but which—if lived out to maturity—has undergone a certain degree of suffering. Further, those who have most faithfully done the will of God, and whom we think of as being most like him, seem to have received less "good" things and more "evil" things than the average. And he who perfectly loved God, believed in God, taught the fatherhood of God, and trusted God, was rewarded with the desertion of all his friends, horrible torture, a shameful, revolting death, and the apparent failure of all his plans. Yet so far from railing against the failure of God's goodness, he leads all the saints in asserting the goodness and fatherhood of God, and even in the hour of his keenest pain he gave an unmistakable "Yea" and "Amen" to all God's dealing with him.

After much thought, then, and helped immensely as I have long been by soaking my mind in Dr. John Oman's books,[2] I have come to see how unsatisfactory, and indeed false, my earlier view of providence was, and that God not only *allows* evil things to happen to his children, but puts them into a school, the circumstances of which make suffering almost certain. I see now that God's loving providence is not more manifested in those good things which he

[2] Particularly *Grace and Personality, Vision and Authority,* and *The Paradox of the World.*

loves to give us than it is in those evil things which he allows. I am to avoid evil if I can honorably do so. I am to oppose evil because it is evil and causes suffering to God and man. But concerning the evil that I must endure, either because it is inescapable or because I cannot honorably avoid it, I am to believe that *it can minister to my soul's final good (=blessedness) no less positively and powerfully, but often more so, than the things I call good.*

A true reaction to the good things of life must be *possible*. That is to say, my reaction to them must be *capable* of inciting me to make spiritual progress. "How often would I have gathered thy children together, . . ." says Jesus, "and ye would not!" "If thou hadst known . . . ," but "thou knewest not the time of thy visitation." God *desired* the right reaction to his "good" gifts, and men *might* have responded. When the good things fail to bring the right reaction, he uses evil things. But God cannot possibly *need* evil and depend on it to bring good to the soul. When, however, the appeal of his beneficence fails, he uses the evil which the soul brings on itself, or which others bring upon it, and through it can achieve as great a good. The good things of life may make me thankful and glad, and I may express my humble gratitude in the happy service of a son. But the good things of life may make me complacent, smug, self-satisfied, and slothful. In a book I was recently reading, I came across this sentence: "The Carthaginians had wealth beyond the dreams of avarice together with a commerce which made them masters of the Mediterranean, yet, in the sequel, they became the mere puppets of a soulless splendour, and ultimately they were crushed beneath their weight of golden circumstance." And in another, Arnold Toynbee points out in a chapter called "The Stimulus of Blows" that power and success have always been won by the inhabitants of what he calls "hard countries," not by the dwellers in earthly paradises. The same kind of thing happens in the case of individuals. It is the "good" things that bring them down. On the other hand, while the evil things of life may make me hostile, resentful, and angry, they may also make me respond in terms of heroism, courage, and patience, in such a way as to deepen my character to an extent which unbroken ease could hardly achieve. Indeed, it is difficult to understand how a quality like heroism or courage could be evoked from the human soul in circumstances which made no demand for either.

If this seems a difficult thought, let us ask ourselves one very simple question. Have the good things of life produced the good people? My observation and reading lead me to say "No." The evil things have been the occasion of the goodness of the saints. Does anyone find the finest characters among those who have suffered the least? Is it not a strange thing that we all long for the good things, and yet our pulpit illustrations, taken from biography, are stories of men and women whose splendid characters have been achieved because they were denied the good things? From their reaction to the evil things they have hewn, out of the hard stone of misfortune, characteristics which we love to hold up to others and to ourselves in dark hours.

Here are a few examples written down at random. Catherine Booth in the last year of her life said she could not remember one day free from pain. Robert Louis Stevenson wrote stories of heroism while tuberculosis had him by the throat. Helen Keller was blind and deaf from infancy. Henry Martyn, the Indian missionary, fought consumption of the lungs, while carrying on evangelistic work in incredibly difficult circumstances. St. Theresa endured unending headaches, accompanied by fever and subsequently paralysis. Sir Walter Scott was incurably lame. George Matheson was incurably blind. Beethoven was incurably deaf. Ignatius Loyola, who founded the Society of Jesus, was in lifelong pain. Pascal reported that he had been in pain from his eighteenth year to the year of his death. Cowper and Samuel Johnson suffered from what now would be called chronic anxiety neurosis. They were both in daily fear of insanity. And so we might lengthen the list down to present days.

Must we not, then, relinquish the thought that God's providence involves only his beneficence, and realize that facing the things we call evil is also part of his plan for us and part of his schooling of us? Let me reiterate that this does not mean he *wills* evil. God cannot will evil, but he allows it and uses it as the occasion of our education. We can see this difference in one very simple picture. When a child is learning to walk, his parents will *allow* him to tumble. They do not restrict his adventures to the limits of a padded cell, but they do not *will* that he shall tumble, or they would push him over.

There are two strong reasons why we must relinquish the false thought that providence means only beneficence. The first is that to retain it is going to mean for us bewilderment and confusion of mind if suffering overtakes us, as at some time it probably will. We shall think that God has deserted us, or that he does not exist, or that he has forgotten to be gracious; or else we shall ask silly questions, "Why has God allowed this?" and we shall make foolish statements, such as, "I shan't believe in God any more." Nor will such doubts as then assail us be removed by supposing that God cannot prevent evil from happening to us, or that he puts jam, like endurance, fortitude, and patience, into the bitter mixture which evil makes us swallow. Both such suggestions imply that evil is stronger than he is. It is a poor faith which believes that evil can do terrifying things to us and that all God can do is to help us bear them bravely. The second strong reason why we must relinquish the false view of providence is that only when the false view goes can the true view take possession of our minds and hearts. And the true view, I repeat, is that God can use evil for our final good as powerfully as he can use good; partly because of the way he himself reacts to evil, that is, by suffering love, and partly because of the way we can react to evil. That reaction must not be fatalism—"This is God's will." No evil is that. Nor must it be thought that God is angry—"Thus God punishes me." That statement requires much investigation. I am convinced that the right reaction is, "What does God wish me to learn from this experience? What message is he signaling to me by means of this pain?" I should like to illustrate that by an experience I had on Clapham Junction Station before the war. I forget how many platforms there are at this station, but there seemed an immense number of signals, green lights and red, yellow, and purple and blue. They were confusing and bewildering to me, but an engineer could sit calmly in his cab and drive through the station because those lights, so confusing to me, were a message to him. Many illustrations will occur to you. An aviator signaling in Morse by flashing lights from his plane produces in my mind only confusion, but to one who can read the Morse code the lights convey a message.

Now meaningless pain, I am certain, does not exist. I think it drives the mind to a panic that borders on madness to contemplate the possibility of lonely, meaningless, useless anguish and pain. To suppose that the pain of one child is a lost and pointless experience is to accept a comment on the meaning and nature of the universe that is terrifying in its implications. I admit how difficult it often is to read the message, to understand what God is saying; but if we are patient with him, he will reveal it to us. The action, reaction, and interaction between God and suffering and ourselves can bring us where God wants us to be, and it is God's purpose to use evil to that end.

We are *called* into that co-operation because thus his purposes are forwarded. That word "called" reminds me of the call boy at the theater who taps on the dressing-room door and tells the actor that he must now proceed to the stage to work out the plot a little furher toward that completion which was in the mind of the author. So the "call" of God is the tap on the door that summons us to work out our part in that eternal plot which is his purpose, and "to them that love God all things"—including the evil things—"work together for good, even to them that are *called* according to his purpose." But before this higher faith can be ours, faith in providence regarded as mere beneficence must go. Only when we have parted with the false can we develop a faith which makes us big enough to receive every conceivable evil without allowing it to part us from the sense of God's love and the certainty of his care. I repeat once more that the fact that evil is allowed by God means that it is as friendly to our final good as are those things which we regard as desirable.

The meaning of a verse in Robert Bridges' poem "January" eluded me for some time, but in this context it lives:

And God the Maker doth my heart grow bold
To praise for wintry works not understood,
Who all the worlds and ages doth behold,
Evil and good as one, *and all as good.*[3]

Now all this has an immense bearing on the question whether life is a good thing. If material good is the aim of life, let us cynically plan our lives accordingly. But if the whole universe exists for spiritual ends, obviously the only "good" is that which secures those ends; and if *this* be true, it must be admitted that a lot of people are wasting their time. For their whole energies are set on securing what we call the "good" things of life, and they deny any possible value to the things which by common consent are labeled "evil."

When people ask whether life is a good thing, one wants to ask the next question, "Good for what?" We might consider coal miners working deep in the earth. Is it a good thing that a man, for whatever pay, should work for hours and hours, often lying prone, working, as I have watched him work at the coal face, in dust and noise and heat and darkness? It is not a good thing in itself. It is good only in the perspective of the needs of industry and the warmth of our homes. That is to say, coal mining is not good in itself. It is good only for something else seen later. In the same way, what is the good of plowing the ground? Why the toil and sweat and trouble of forcing that immense knife through the soil? It is good only in the light of something that comes afterward, the harvest. What is the good of a man's breaking stones by the roadside? What is the advantage of spending all that labor and energy to make big stones into little stones? None at all, save in the light of subsequent buildings or roads or cement. Otherwise breaking stones has no more value than tearing up bits of paper, as one may see a patient doing in the corner of a mental hospital.

Is life good? Not, I think, in itself, except at rare moments when we sing with George Borrow and his school. But I am not in any doubt whatever that it is "good" in the light of something else which lies beyond it, *and I do not mean heaven.* I mean the making of a character capable of communion with God; and that goal is

[3] By permission of Oxford University Press.

his glory, our blessedness, and the only thing that will make heaven heaven. I am certain that this point of view is the right one, and that if pleasure is the test of life's worth-whileness, life hardly passes the test—it certainly doesn't for many—and we shall never come to terms with life by supposing that it *ought* to bring us pleasure. But life is "good" in the sense that it is good for something and not good for nothing.

As I see the matter, it is only this truth which justifies a good God in allowing evil to be of such appalling dimensions, power, and influence in his world. He could not justify it by merely following it with good, or by mixing it with good, or by trying to make up to a person in some heavenly life for the fact that his earth life had been filled with evil. "Your sorrow shall be *turned into joy*"—not merely followed by joy. God can justify the widespread presence of evil only by using evil, as truly as he can use good, for something beyond themselves. Faith insists that, in fact, this is what God does; that as man uses plowing and coal mining and stone breaking for something beyond themselves, and as we all value our own schooling for that to which it led, God can use evil as the raw material by which he and man together make man's character such an amazingly wonderful thing that it can enter into communion with the divine and find its blessedness therein. This is life's highest crown, life's final justification, and life's ultimate goal. From the schooling demanded for this great end we shirk. "Let me be alone," we cry to God; "I want only to be happy." How similar it is to the cry of a child, "I don't want to go to school." But we are not here to be happy. We are here to glorify God through a character which has been schooled in such a way that it finds its joy in communion with him. If he left us alone in the elementary, unschooled state which *we* call happiness, it could only mean that he did not think we were worth bothering about. In such a state he has left the birds. Sons can be taken further.

It is only in the light of this theme that I can understand the inwardness of some words spoken to me years ago by one who is still very dear to me, and who died of cancer after three years of suffering. About her a ministerial friend of mine has lately written this:

"I wonder if I ever told you of what your sister's ministry meant to me. She would be astonished if she knew (perhaps she does). I often went to see her during her long illness, and sometimes went from Manchester on purpose. I can never forget my last visit. It was about a fortnight before she went. We had two hours together, and she was full of fun and laughter and a wonderful anticipation. I could repeat today some of the very words she said. *She was like a child going home for Christmas.* I never knew anyone who more completely and literally 'ran up with joy the shining way.' Her influence has lived with me all through the years."

When I myself went to see her shortly after she had received news that recovery was, humanly speaking, impossible, she was in a Liverpool nursing home. It was a dark, dull November afternoon, but when I went into her room, I can only say that it was just as though someone had lighted a beautiful lamp. Nobody had really done so, but the glory in her face seemed to illumine the whole room. I suppose she saw the dismay in my own, because she said, "Don't be troubled at the news. Everything that you preach is perfectly true." And then she added a sentence that is written on my heart in gold forever: *"I am proud to be trusted with cancer."* Now what do you make of that? "I am proud to be trusted with it." Not that she did not fight it. Cancer is not the intention of God. Those who fight it do his will. She fought it and lost physically in the battle against it. She fought it because it is an evil thing, and brings pain to God and to men.

But let me put it in this way. When the gray messenger of cancer knocked on the door of her life, she answered the door and confronted the messenger. She did not turn away and run from him, or seek to hide from him, or cry out in anguish that she could not be asked to face this. Rather she asked for the messenger's credentials, and while she looked through them, she found that the permit of God was attached to them. God did not will it, but God had allowed it, and that was enough for her. By the time it had won a victory over her body, her soul was more than conqueror through him who could use even cancer to bring her where he wanted her to be, to make her soul greater than ever, and to express his own glory in a human life. In that way she came to terms with life. Her

philosophy of providence was not one which welcomed and enjoyed
the good things, and was puzzled, bewildered, or defeated because
the evil things had so great a scope. What we call the evil things did
not deny the nature, much less the existence, of God. They were
God's servants and were allowed to enter human life because in the
end they were made to do his work and serve him in as true a sense
as were the good things. When cancer confronted her, the call boy
tapped on her door and told her that it was her turn now, on the
difficult stage of human suffering, to further the divine purpose and
work out the divine plan.

"To them that love God all things"—the good things *and the
evil things*—"work together for good, even to them that are *called*
according to his purpose." Paul had the right to say that. He had
experienced the good things and the bad things. He knew how to
abound and how to be abased. In one city, Lystra, he was taken for
a god and then almost immediately stoned and flung out of the city
like dead carrion. Two verses further on we read of his reaction.
"They [Paul and his companions] returned to Lystra . . . confirm-
ing the souls of the disciples, exhorting them to continue in the
faith, and that through many tribulations we must enter into the
kingdom of God."

Yes, and he had the right to say to the Galatians: "From henceforth let no man trouble me: for I bear branded on my body the
marks of Jesus." Those marks were made by evil men for an evil purpose, but Paul knew that God used evil for his good, that he used
"all things" in fact. Are we watching a proud man who had been
taken for a god, saved from pride by the blows *inflicted* by un-
friendly men, but *used* by a friendly Saviour? With awe in our
heart and a strange hush in our spirit we hear these wounds, caused
by evil men, called "the marks of Jesus." We can only square our
shoulders and try to follow Paul, and the other saints of God
through the ages, with a faith that sees in the sway of evil the controlling hand of him who makes even the wrath of man to praise
him.

# THE LONELY GREATNESS OF THE WORLD

Behold, the hour cometh, yea, is come, that ye shall be scattered, every man to his own, and shall leave me alone: and yet I am not alone, because the Father is with me.                    —John 16:32

As I speak to you about the loneliness of christ, i would ask you not to try to react to it in terms of pity. I would like to be able to show you the loneliness of Christ as something essential to his greatness—the lonely greatness of the world—as something majestic, as something endured for us, as something which we cannot rightly see in all its significance for us if our reaction is one of pity.

I am afraid the pulpit has often mistakenly represented Jesus. At Christmastime we preach a sermon on the text "There was no room for him in the inn," and people are deliberately invited to register pity for the tiny baby for whom no hospitality could be found and are asked to find him room in their hearts. We preach sermons on the text "He had not where to lay his head," and his loneliness is used to make an appeal to the emotions of the hearers that they should, as it were, take pity upon him and offer their hearts for his home. We preach sermons on the text "Behold, I stand at the door and knock," and the preacher can make a tender, beautiful, and true picture of that lowly suppliant pleading to be let in.

There is some truth in these word pictures, but not much, for it must be remembered that he who descended to be the Saviour of the world, and who entered life as a tiny baby, was "very God of very God." He who had not where to lay his head must again and again have been offered hospitality, and he who stands at the door and knocks is the King of Kings, and his invitation is a royal one. I find it hard to believe that the early church ever offered people sermons in which the hearers were invited to "let Christ in." Their language is rather as follows: "[God] put all things in subjection under his feet, and gave him to be head over all things to the church, which is his body, the fulness of him that filleth all in all." "He must reign, till he hath put all his enemies under his feet." "God highly exalted him, and gave unto him the name which is above every name; that in the name of Jesus every knee should bow, . . . and that every tongue should confess that Jesus Christ is Lord, to the glory of God the Father."

So, as we contemplate his agony and suffering, thinking of his loneliness, I would ask that we banish pity. Let the thought in our minds be of a loneliness which he undertook as an expression of his own endless love for us, a loneliness inseparable from the greatness of his task, and endured, not to win from us our pity, but our adoration of the endless love of God which alone can provide the courage we need in these dark days to live victoriously ourselves.

One of the recitatives in Stainer's beautiful music commemorating the Crucifixion begins with the words: "Is it nothing to you, all ye that pass by? Behold, and see if there be any sorrow like unto my sorrow, which is done unto me, wherewith the Lord hath afflicted me in the day of his fierce anger." I am making no criticism of the music, but I would remind you that the words are nothing whatever to do with Jesus. They were written about a siege which took place nearly six hundred years before Christ, when Jerusalem was threatened by the aggressive tyranny of Babylon. Jerusalem is personified in this lamentation, and the city is crying out in its agony and pleading for pity. These words have been taken from that setting and attached to the Master, but they are as different as anything could possibly be from his spirit. Certain of our hymns unfortunately sound the same note. They are becoming rarer, but one still hears the note:

> All this I did for thee,
> What hast thou done for me?

When we turn from pity-provoking sentimentality to the strong, virile language of the Gospels, we hear what Jesus actually did say. To the women who wept and mourned and beat their breasts on

Good Friday we hear him say, "Daughters of Jerusalem, weep not for me."

There is a comment on all this in one of the sermons of F. W. Robertson of Brighton, who was himself a very lonely man, a man who could write of himself as follows:

> I shall be alone as my Master was. I am hated by some who loved me once, not for what I do, but for what I think. I have long foreseen it. And, knowing that the Father is with me, I am not afraid to be alone, though, to a man not ungently made, there is some sharpness in the thought. . . . I am alone now and shall be till I die, but I am not afraid to be alone in the majesty of darkness which His presence peoples with a crowd. . . . A sublime feeling of a Presence comes about me at times which makes inward solitariness a trifle to talk about.

Such a man has the right to preach to people on the loneliness of Christ, and in a sermon on this theme we find these words:

> There is a feeble and sentimental way in which we speak of Christ. We turn to the Cross, the agony and the loneliness to touch the softer feelings, to arouse compassion. You degrade that loneliness by your compassion. Compassion, compassion for Him! Adore if you will, but no pity.

You will not misunderstand my saying that there is a real psychological danger as soon as we begin to allow ourselves to have pity for Christ, because what happens is that we begin to pity ourselves, although devoutly supposing that our pity is for him.[1] If you have been to a funeral—not to the funeral of one very dear to you, but to the kind of funeral one sometimes attends in order to pay respect to the dead—you may often have suspected that the tears of some so-called mourners are not for the dead at all. By a self-motivated projection, they are really weeping for themselves. They are saying to themselves, "How sad it will be when I come to die and people stand round and weep for me!" I think the tears at some weddings have a similar origin. When the bride's mother weeps, it may be because she is losing her daughter and is therefore sad. But I feel

[1] This point is worked out by Professor H. H. Farmer, *The Healing Cross*, p. 192.

certain that often her mental processes are rather these: "How sad a thing my own marriage has become!" She is weeping over the broken pieces of what was once a lovely ideal.

Pity is not a very positive and constructive emotion in any case, but *self*-pity is one of the most disintegrating emotions in which personality can indulge, and the one can depreciate into the other without our consciously realizing it. Once we begin to pity Christ we do him a disservice, since it is the last thing he asks from us. A great soul does not want his personality pitied. He wants his cause supported, his example followed, and the tasks completed which he has been unable to finish. But we are in a worse plight than ever if pity for him becomes pity for ourselves. It is so easy subconsciously to fall into the subtle psychological morass in which the mental processes run like this: Christ was alone, I am often lonely; Christ was rejected, I am unpopular with people; Christ was misunderstood, I am often misunderstood; Christ's worth was never recognized, I myself am underrated; Christ was persecuted, I am persecuted; until, unaware of what has happened, we are not weeping for him, but for ourselves, and we are the less able to see him because really we are looking only at ourselves.

Recently I heard a broadcast of Admiral Evans talking about Scott, his leader to the Antarctic. It was a manly, virile, majestic note that Admiral Evans sounded. I thought it was one of the most wonderful broadcasts I had ever heard. We were made to feel with great intensity the difficulties and dangers of the expedition, and the courage and tenacity of those who undertook it. But there was no pity, no sob stuff, no tears. We were not invited to look at Evans; we were invited to look at Scott; and although the hardship and the suffering were perfectly described, instead of pity, one felt a kind of pride in belonging to the same race. The proud grandeur of the sacrifice stood out.

It was thus that the disciples saw Jesus. It was thus that they spoke about him. I hope you have realized how restrained are the adjectives about him. The Gospels never say: "Jesus gave a moving address, and great numbers of the congregation were deeply affected." The kind of language used is illustrated by four words:

"He went into Galilee." They do not stay to tell you that that means Jesus went into the area where John the Baptist was arrested for the same kind of "propaganda," and that Jesus said the kind of thing for which John had been beheaded. "He must needs pass through Samaria," we read. But there was no need at all. Every other traveler would have taken a great deal of trouble to avoid that dangerous road when tension was as high between Jews and Samaritans as it was in Jesus' day. This unsentimental restraint is typical of the Gospel writers.

Though they themselves, by their own story, involve themselves in reproach, they show him to us in lonely greatness, the lonely greatness of the world. He must have longed to win the religious leaders of his day. He coveted their support. When they turned away, gathered in dark corners, and plotted his death, *he went on.* It must have been heartbreaking to Jesus that he fell afoul of his own family. No loneliness is so bitter as that which assails the heart of him who finds hostility without and misunderstanding at home. There are no human means left to give his soul its sense of needful security. But though his family openly let it be thought that they considered him mad, *he went on.* There is no doubt that he longed, and for a time expected, to win the populace, but our eyes light on this sentence: "After this many walked no more with him." *But he went on.* One of the saddest passages in the New Testament has been spoiled in its effectiveness by an unsatisfactory way of dividing the text of the Fourth Gospel into verses and chapters. The last verse of chapter seven of John's Gospel is part of the first verse of the eighth chapter. Reading them together, we find these words: "Every man went unto his own house: but Jesus went unto the Mount of Olives." You could hardly find a sentence indicating more definitely the loneliness of Jesus. *But still he went on.* In the Garden of Gethsemane, in the hour of his greatest need, we read this bleak sentence: "They all forsook him and fled." *But he went on.* On the very night before his death, his disciples quarreled. In the Garden of Agony they slept. When he wanted friendship more than at any moment of his life, they had all scattered among the shadows about his cross.

And when he walked along the Via Dolorosa to be crucified,

there was not one person in the whole world who approved of his action. The religious leaders chuckled; he was in the net now. The politicians were glad; they had feared a rising of the people, and a triumphant declaration by Jesus himself of both his position and his power. The disciples thought he was mad. Why didn't he use his supernatural power? The people thought he had been found out. There was not one person in the whole world who approved.

It is probably impossible for us to do more than glimpse such a loneliness. Geographical loneliness is a terrible thing. I have read that in the remote parts of Norway, among the deep fiords, where precipices rise hundreds of feet sheer from the sea, a sailor dare not leave his wife for very long in a tiny homestead alone among the mountains. The majesty of those unchanging hills, the horror of the precipices, the awful storms that sweep the coast, have frequently robbed the lonely of their sanity. I wonder if Admiral Evans could have stood the test of the Antarctic wastes if he had been all alone. What did Mallory and Irving feel on the top of Everest, where, according to the native tradition, devils sported with the lives of men who attempted to force their way into those silent solitudes? It was the awful loneliness that Commander Byrd found hardest to bear. We recall the lines from "The Ancient Mariner":

> Alone, alone, all, all alone,
> Alone on a wide, wide sea!
>
> .    .    .    .    .
>
> So lonely 'twas, that God himself
> Scarce seemèd there to be.

But if it is terrifying to be geographically lonely, to be where man has never set foot before, to climb where strange things happen, where water boils and is not hot, where no dear, familiar landmarks comfort the spirit, or to go where it is dark for six months of the year, where the sky is shot through and through sometimes with queer lights that startle and frighten, what must it be to penetrate spiritually where no soul has ever been before? "He descended into hell." We do not know what the men meant who wrote that down, but I think they were trying to say something of what I am trying to say to you. There are no words to express the utter loneliness of spirit. Where was Jesus when he said: "My God, my God, why hast thou forsaken me?" No one knows. He had gone beyond our power to follow him even in the most daring flights of imagination. He was the lonely greatness of the world.

We can learn something precious from Christ's loneliness:

1. The loneliness of the Master was something he faced for us. He who had dwelt in the bosom of the Father, in a relationship which met his every need, gave it up to be limited, lonely, and outcast on this bleak planet we call our earth. It was part of the sacrifice of the cross. It was not faced by one who was a calm stoic, hardening himself against love—such a person, if he exists at all, is a psychopathic case—it was met by a warmhearted man who longed for friendship and love. He was the more sensitive in regard to his need for love than we can know, because he longed to give love to an extent we cannot measure, and he who longs to give, longs to receive. His loving heart must have been wounded again and again by the cold, sterile, callous attitude, not only of his enemies, but of those he expected to become his friends.

We notice something further. He refused to buy love and so made his loneliness greater. Jesus *need not* have been one who had nowhere to lay his head. Hundreds of homes would have been open to him. Popular preachers can generally find a meal, a bed, and a chat. People who can heal others need not be alone unless they want to be alone, and he could have been, and for a time was, all that. Dr. Farmer says that "one of the greatest tests of character is whether a man is ready to alienate the people who love him in order to bless them."

When life is crying out for fellowship, it is the hardest thing in the world deliberately to pursue a course which you know will, for the time being, destroy it. . . . Jesus wanted these men's fellowship with himself, wanted it more than our egotistic natures can ever conceive, but he knew that there was one thing he must not do to purchase it, and that was to tamper with the truth.

That longing to break loneliness by winning the approval of others is clearly set forth in the life of Florence Nightingale. Sir Edward Cook writes of her thus:

Florence felt that everything she said or did was a subject of vexation to her sister, a disappointment to her mother, a worry to her father. In one of her letters home, when at last, and not until she had reached her thirtieth birthday, the way was opening up for her, she writes to her mother: "I should be as happy here as the day is long if I could hope that I had your smile, your blessing, your sympathy, without which I cannot be quite happy. . . . Give me time, give me faith, trust me, help me. I feel within me that I could gladden your loving hearts which now I wound." But the appeal fell on deaf ears.

Jesus understood that situation. Through his loneliness he did something for us, and let us realize that we should have been robbed of that something if his extremity of loneliness had driven him to pay the price which would have bought the comfort of those who could have given him friendship in return.

2. We may learn also that there is a right kind of loneliness and a wrong kind. There is a right kind of loneliness because loneliness can bring us into a situation in which alone God can deal with us. Some things he cannot say to us unless we are prepared to be alone.

I find that I have to say this to myself again and again. I must be willing to come apart even from the people I love. If we insist always on having our admirers around us, always flying, when trouble and criticisms come to us, to those who are sure to say kind and comforting things, who will protect us by their affection and heal our wounds by their friendship, then there will be some things that God can never get into our hearts. There is something the matter with the person who will never be alone. That "something the matter" may be a psychological illness, and if you are really suffering from a neurosis, let me say at once that this does not apply to you. You ought to have friendship and sympathy until you are better. But, illness of body and mind apart, there is definitely something wrong with the person who dare not be alone, and he would be wise to face the situation.

I think you will know what I mean. The kindness of others can obscure our sins from ourselves. Our friends can be such a protection to us that even God cannot get near us. Our friends will say, "Well, you didn't mean to be unkind," or, "I don't think you should worry about that." Our friends will blacken our enemies and whitewash us, and they have no conscious motive in the matter other than kindness. Subconsciously, they are using our hunger for comfort to creep further into our affection. Men who admire us sometimes do so to such an extent that the ethical situation, with its sharply contrasted blacks and whites, is blurred into a gray; and women, bless them! are worse. They will so minister to us out of their affection and loving friendship that they will lose all sense of ethical justice and call people who criticize us all sorts of names, not because of their sins, but just because they dare to criticize *us*. I am afraid it is true that God wants some of us to be much more lonely much more often, so that we may see ourselves as he sees us, remembering with George Fox that "the light that shows us our sins is the light that heals us."

There is a place for comfort, a time for sympathy, of course; but also there is a time to be alone, even when for us the shadow of the cross falls on our lives, that we may ask God and learn from him all that he would teach us from the experiences we are called upon to go through. Let me write down a sentence about the Master which has often been in my mind: "He went up into a mountain *apart* to pray: and when even was come, he was there *alone*." Through the loneliness of the cross, he achieved a victory which the comfort of friends might have denied him to our everlasting loss.

3. But there is a kind of loneliness that is not right for us, and all I can say to people who are lonely in that way is that you must take your loneliness to Christ, so that he may tell you what to do with it and thus end its overplus.

I am not thinking only of the conventional examples of loneliness—the person who has recently come to a great city, or the person in a strange job, or the like. I am remembering also that the mother of a big family can be very lonely, especially as her brood grows up and becomes independent. The individual member of a family can be horribly lonely, especially if he feels odd or out of it or a failure. Loneliness can even be emphasized by the physical presence of others, even others of friendly disposition, especially when one is bowed down by inward perplexity or secret grief or hidden frustration. Even marriage does not dispel loneliness if love "has turned to kindliness" or, worse, to tolerance.

But this I *have* seen: loneliness to which the right reaction is made can become a wonderful qualification for helping others, and in such a ministry its poignancy is ended. That is Christ's word to those who are under the shadow of his cross.

One thing I must add, in his name: We must never let loneliness drive us in on ourselves so that we descend to self-pitying or eating out our own heart in bitterness. Beware of that dangerous, vicious circle which runs like this: Loneliness can make you bitter, and bitterness can make you more lonely, for no one wants to associate with people who are bitter. Loneliness can make you jealous, and jealousy can make you lonely, for no one wants a jealous person as his friend. Loneliness can make you odd, and then oddness can make you lonely, for people fight shy of those who have lost their sense of humor. Only Christ, I think, can break that vicious circle with the offer of his eternal friendship; and if you take your loneliness to him, it can become a qualification by which you can help others. You will lose your own loneliness because you become one who is positively offering friendship. Let him who wants a friend become a friend. I have noticed in my own ministry that those who are most able to help others are those who, in the depths of their spirit, have known what it is to be lonely. That is one reason why Jesus helps us so much.

Once, when I was little more than a boy, I remember getting lost on the Scottish hills. It was almost dark, and the high mountains were frightening. Then I found a little stream and knew, of course, that it must run to a river. Following the stream I found the river, and on the bank of the river was the village I sought. Through the wild mental country of the past, among all the confusing, bewildering thoughts man has had about God in this great, frightening universe, there ran the stream of the friendship of God. Enoch walked with God. Abraham was the friend of God. "I am with thee," was the message to Moses. "Though I walk through the valley of the shadow of death, I will fear no evil," said David, "for thou art with me." See the stream running through the mountains as man made quest for God! And the stream of God's friendliness led to the great river of divine love seen in the life and passion and death of Christ. Dark may be the night before us, terrifying the mountains; shadowed valleys may be our experience; the power of evil may terrify us, the darkness of doubt and fear seem almost overwhelming. But keep near the little stream of God's friendship till it brings you to the river of divine love, and then you will find that you can say with Jesus: "I am not alone, because the Father is with me."

# THOU SHALT LOVE THY NEIGHBOR

Thou shalt love thy neighbor as thyself.
—Mark 12:31; Matt. 19:19; Lev. 19:18

THOU SHALT LOVE!" WE STOP THERE! OUR MINDS AT FIRST REJECT THE words, for they seem to contradict one another. "Thou shalt!" That is a command. A command is carried out by the will. We can bend our will to any task we are commanded to do. We may not succeed in it, but at any rate we can try. But to say, "Thou shalt *love*," seems psychologically impossible. One cannot *love* to order. Surely love is an emotion and beyond the control of the will. Love rises up of itself without commandment or in defiance of commandment, or it isn't worth calling love. Who, indeed, would care to be the victim of someone's *commanded* love? Would it be the real thing? Would it have the quality of the "divine emotion"?

Love, the theme of endless poets, artists, and musicians, is the loveliest of all things that rise in the consciousness of man, the most perfect flower his personality produces. It does not render obedience to the will. It is called forth by the beauty and truth and love around it. I am thinking not only of the love of lovers, but of the love of friends. In the presence of one who really loves us our minds find rest, our best is called forth, our ideals are shared; wounds are not inflicted; they are healed. In the presence of the loved person by whom also we are beloved we find the maximum happiness, the deepest content, and a relationship entirely free from fear. Such love provides infinite resource against the blows of the hostile world outside; and when the world has done its buffeting, such love is the harbor of the spirit, into which it steals like a battered ship from the troubled waters outside, to be equipped, refitted, and refueled for the next voyage. Love is the gift of God, the sharing of his nature, and the finest quality of human personality. All this I think we mean when we use the word "love."

Surely, then, to say to a person, "Thou shalt love," is almost to commit the crime of seeking to bind two things together which are incompatible. It is like putting together a sword and a rose, a tank and a sonata, a steam roller and a little child's smile—the first, compulsive, forceful, driven by the will; the second, revealing a beauty born from above, kindled by a touch from God, breathing the very nature of the eternal world.

But the difficulty about our text is that it was *Jesus* who said, "Thou shalt love," who gave the commandment, indeed, high place, as the second of all the commandments—and Jesus "knew what was in man." He issued no commands in themselves impossible; and though we may say that the commandment runs back to the Mosaic law, nevertheless Jesus underlined it, reiterated it, and by his words about it gave it still greater authority.

We are driven, then, to suppose that the two are not incompatible; and since we cannot escape the imperious command "thou shalt," we must ask some very important questions as to what "thou shalt *love*" in the New Testament sense really means.

The main answer to this question will be a discovery that to "love" in the New Testament sense means a special way of directing the will. It does not mean that royal emotion we have been talking about. In a sense, it is a pity there isn't another word for it, for it must have confused many minds that Jesus should sanction the command "Thou shalt love." I shall ask you to remember this paraphrase of our text which I believe makes its meaning clearer: *Thou shalt adopt toward thy neighbor a sustained determination to show unbreakable good will in order that the best qualities in the person "loved" may be called forth.*

We had better go on to define the word "neighbor" also; and we shall remember that when Jesus was asked the question, "Who is my neighbor?" he promptly told the Jewish questioner a story about a man who was his traditional enemy, a Samaritan. I suppose if our Lord were still physically present, and a German asked, "Who is my neighbor?" Jesus would tell him a story about a Jew, or an Englishman, or an American; and if an Englishman asked, "Who is my neighbor?" Jesus would tell a story about a German, an Italian, or a Japanese. The meaning of the word "neighbor," therefore, according to the teaching of Jesus, is *anyone whom circumstance puts it in our power to befriend.*

Now let us turn to ask and try to answer the question: What is involved in "loving" our neighbor? And here I must say something in brackets. Whenever I preach a sermon that I think is rather original, whenever I express ideas that I have never seen in print or heard expressed anywhere else, somebody always comes up after the service and says: "Thank you very much for that sermon. *That is what I have always thought.*" Yet when one looks him in the eye, one knows that he is quite sincere. I think what happens is this: he means that ideas which have been lying in his mind and have never found articulate expression have suddenly been clothed in words for him—to his great delight. I felt the same myself recently. Returning from a preaching appointment in Cambridge, I bought Mr. C. S. Lewis' book *Christian Behaviour*. When I read it on the train, I was pleased and annoyed at the same time, for he says so many things that I have thought for a long time! And if now I say these things, you will accuse me of having cribbed them from Mr. Lewis.

I want to offer four points which I think are involved in "loving" our neighbor—two negative and two positive.

1. First, it doesn't mean "liking" our neighbor. Isn't that a relief? "Liking" is something that cannot be compelled. We like a person, or we don't like a person. Sometimes we like a person more if we know him better, but sometimes we like him less! I submit that it really would be impossible psychology to say: "Thou shalt 'like' thy neighbor." Let me repeat, therefore, that the emotion called "love" and the emotion of "liking" are not in the discussion. We are not commanded to feel affection for another. It is the *will* that is to be engaged, the will to show unfailing good will. In the Christian sense, we can "love" our neighbor without liking him, without having anything in common with him, and it would be

only intellectual dishonesty to pretend to "like" our neighbor, or to imagine that "liking" could respond to a command.

2. Second, "loving" our neighbor doesn't mean blinding ourselves to his faults. Obviously if the word "neighbor" is to be understood in the sense defined—namely, anyone whom circumstance puts it in our power to befriend—there may be very many things in the behavior of our neighbor which call forth our definite condemnation unless we are to lose our sense of ethical values. Suppose for a moment that we were thrust into the desperate situation of having to regard a murderer as a "neighbor." We should be bound to hate the beastly thing he had done, but we should still be asked by Christ to "love our neighbor"—namely, to show him a spirit of determined and sustained good will in order that his best qualities might find expression.

Receive, then, if you will, those two thoughts. Loving a neighbor does not mean necessarily "liking" him, and it does not mean overlooking his faults. That is what the old Christian writers inferred, I think, when they told us that we must love the sinner even though we hate his sin. Here Mr. Lewis has for us a very apposite word. He says:

> For a long time I used to think this a silly straw-splitting distinction: how could you hate what a man did and not hate the man? But years later it occurred to me that there was one man to whom I had been doing this all my life—namely, myself. However much I might dislike my own cowardice or conceit or greed, I went on loving myself. There had never been the slightest difficulty about it. In fact the very reason why I hated these things was that I loved the man. Just because I loved myself, I was sorry to find that I was the sort of man who did those things.

Look back at our last two points in the light of that statement. We said "loving" is not a matter of "liking" and not a matter of blinding ourselves to faults. Isn't that exactly what we do about ourselves? Few of us, I imagine, really *like* ourselves. I find that, if I give an hour to honest introspection, I dislike myself for what I have done and for what I have been. Nor, I think, are most of us blind to our faults. We are blind to some of them because we know ourselves so incompletely. We all have many blind spots. But the more we do know ourselves and the more we see our own faults, the more we regard them with a great loathing. Yet disliking our-selves, and conscious of our faults, we go on "loving" ourselves in the sense defined. That is, we go on willing our own good. More-over, we show a sustained determination in this matter; and nothing that happens, though we loathe it and hate it in ourselves, com-pletely takes from us our belief in ourselves or makes us identify ourselves with the rotten things we do and are. The healthiness of this procedure is, I think, emphasized by our delight when, if we have been thoroughly bad-tempered, we overhear someone say, "He isn't quite himself today." We resent the thought of being identified with the meanness, unkindness, cruelty, and all the other kinds of unworthiness which we so frequently show.

Christ, therefore, is only asking that we shall do for others what we habitually do for ourselves—namely, refuse to identify them with the faults they exhibit, and adopt toward them that attitude of good will which rebukes the faults far more powerfully than condemnation, and is the kind of moral sunshine in which the virtues are made to blossom. In other words, "Thou shalt love thy neighbor *as thyself*."

Now look at two positive things which loving our neighbor in-volves.

3. Our third point is that we must act *as if* we "liked" our neigh-bor. This is not a contradiction of our earlier point that we must admit we do not "like" him. Nor do I think it is a farce to try to act as though we liked him. When I search my own mind and examine my own attitudes to people, I find this: if I act as though I did *not* like them, I like them still less and find "loving" them in the Christian sense harder; if, on the other hand, I try to act as though I like them, I find I like them a little more and find "loving" them in the Christian sense easier.

Let me hasten to explain that by acting as though I liked my neighbor I do not mean that kind of servile ingratiation for which I think the slang expression "sucking up" is hard to beat. The man who "sucks up" to another person is not setting out to love others. He is setting out to make others love him, and some will go to any lengths, even surrender their own ethical judgments, rather than oppose the views and feelings of a person whose good will they are seeking to win. "Sucking up" is a neurotic symptom manifested either by those who have been starved of love, or those in whose nature childish fears of offending a grown-up person still sway their conduct even in mature years. "Loving" one's neighbor is not servile ingratiation. It is the sustained determination to show good will, and such determination is bound logically to express itself in acts. The acts will reflect the determination, but they will at the same time manufacture the emotion of liking.

One might express it by looking at the opposite. Not to "love" one's neighbor is to withhold good will. That increases the dislike, and the dislike is likely to be expressed in deeds which still further deepen the dislike and turn it into hate. If you hate people, you do yourself much harm—indeed, more harm than you can do to the person hated—and you will express the hate in cruelty and deepen the hate. In such an attitude you are widening the gulf between yourself and another, breaking the fellowship which it is God's plan to strengthen, and obviously you are landed in definite sin.

It is right to *hate* evil. No tepid disapproval is sufficient. It will not fire the energies of personality against that which must be ruthlessly fought. But let us not hate people. Let us believe in them. We hate only what evil people do, because we have seen a better way of life. If we hate the people who do evil, we shall never win them to doing differently; we shall antagonize them and make between us and them a gulf harder and harder to cross. Hate is a right reaction to evil but a wrong reaction to a person. To express the emotion of hate against evil is to purge the soul. To express the emotion of hate against a person is to poison the soul.

4. Our fourth point—the second positive one—is that we are helped to "love" our neighbor by remembering how God loves us. The sooner we part with the thought that God loves us because we are worth loving, or because of our moral achievements, or because of any of our qualities, the better.

Have you ever looked around a crowded bus and amused yourself with the whimsical thought that God actually loves all those funny-looking people? One can hardly withhold the thought: What funny taste God must have! They do look such a queer lot, and of course we look the same to them. Whenever I look at a crowd, I say to myself, "What queer taste God must have to love every one of these people!" And there isn't a person that he does not love. But he doesn't love us because we are clever or beautiful, or have a good figure, or a good brain. He loves us because we belong to him and because we are part of him. Indeed, if I may break into the subject of this sermon, his loving us is his only way of realizing his own God-ness. If he excluded you from his loving, he himself would be incomplete. In the two priceless parables of the lost sheep and the lost coin, both sheep and coin are quite content to be lost. The picture is that of the person who owns them dismayed by his or her sense of incompleteness, and the joy is the joy of a completeness recovered. God loves us as the poet or the artist loves that which he has himself created and which is part of himself.

We shall be helped to love others in the New Testament sense if we realize that God loves them, and that although God has the advantage over us in seeing perhaps lovable qualities in them which we cannot see, we are to act by faith where he acts by sight. Since we believe that there are lovable things deep in us—though the world may see few of them—we are to suppose that there are lovable things in everybody, and we are to act in such a way by sustained good will as to bring to obvious and glorious life the imprisoned splendors.

I love the familiar story of Michelangelo walking through the builder's yard and seeing in the corner a misshapen block of rough marble. When asked by the great sculptor what he was going to do with it, the builder said that it was useless. But Michelangelo made the famous reply: "It certainly is not useless," he said; "send it around to my studio. There is an angel imprisoned within it, and I must set it free." This will be the result of "loving" our neighbor. Sustained determination to show unbreakable good will is rewarded at last, I believe, by our being allowed to see from the unpromising natures of other men and women like ourselves the release of hidden beauty.

I have read somewhere that in the process of making the Kingsway, which runs, as you know, between Southampton Row and Aldwych, the excavations were so deep for the immense buildings of that thoroughfare that soil was thrown up to the surface which had not been exposed for many years. In that soil were seeds which, it is alleged, the Romans must have brought over with them. I did not know a seed could live so long. But, it is said, strange flowers bloomed in that upturned soil, flowers never seen in England before, though common enough in Rome. If the story is true, it is another illustration of the kind of thing that happens when men love their neighbors.

As I was writing down these thoughts, there came to my memory the verse of an old hymn I had not heard since childhood. You may know it:

> Down in the human heart, crushed by the tempter,
>   Feelings lie buried that grace can restore.
> Touched by a loving heart, wakened by kindness,
>   Chords that were broken will vibrate once more.

And with the memory of the verse came this most liberating thought: there is no quality in any of the greatest saints that is not present in every human life. Some qualities, perhaps, are as seeds. The state of development may be immature. Some may feel that the lovely things of life have become covered over, like the seeds under the Kingsway, by the bricks and mortar of materialism and even cynicism. But let me say it to you again: there is no quality exhibited in the lives of any of the saints that is not present, at least as possibility, in every human life. You may have a reputation for being all kinds of things which men despise—mean or gossip-loving, grabbing, conceited, or unclean—but you are also much more than that.

The attitude of Jesus to men and women shows us how well he himself fulfilled the command he lays upon us. Do you ask me to believe that Jesus "liked" everybody? I wonder. With his insights he would see something to like which would elude us. But I believe he "loved" everybody in the sense we have defined: that he would adopt toward everyone a sustained determination to show good will, and that, in doing so, he would call forth the best.

The flowers that had wilted and died, that seemed shriveled up and withered forever, would bloom again for him. To everybody else Matthew may have seemed a crusty old taxgatherer, and Zacchaeus a mean little moneylender. Neither of them seemed of any use to anybody. But in both cases deep under the soil were the seeds of saintliness. I wonder if Matthew knows today that in church we read from the Gospel according to *Saint* Matthew. If so, I think he smiles quietly to himself as he recalls the miracle of love which made his goodness blossom on the bleak soil of his earlier character. There was Mary Magdalene, her hair down on her shoulders, the sign of the prostitute, the woman of the street, spurned by everybody except one, who did not blind himself to her faults, for he said, "Her sins are many," and then added, "but she loved much." Indeed, I should imagine that often the harlot falls into the pit just because she loves much and wants to be loved, and, not finding the real thing, sells herself for a substitute love to those who "love" her body but stamp unheedingly upon the lovely things of the soul. One watches Jesus pushing away the rubble and stones and broken bricks, so that the seeds of the beautiful flowers of real love may have the wind and rain and sunshine of his friendship. He saved men and women like that. It was not his teaching; it was his loving. It was not the fulfillment of a ritual; it was just caring.

There cannot be the new world of dreams, can there, until in the New Testament sense we learn to love? And what a wonderful world it will be when men and women, frustrated and thwarted, cynical and unhappy, hating sometimes, indifferent sometimes, are brought through the grace of God to believe in one another and to love one another.

Some of you have said that you don't see any part that you can play in making the new world. I think the message of Jesus for today would not be that we should begin by "loving" the people in foreign lands, but that we might begin with the people in our own homes and in our own offices, the people whose lives touch ours every day. Everybody can begin there. You can.

"Thou shalt love thy neighbor as thyself."

# THOU SHALT LOVE THINE ENEMY

*Ye have heard that it was said, Thou shalt love thy neighbor, and hate thine enemy: but I say unto you, Love your enemies.  —Matt. 5:43-44*

THAT SOUNDS A VERY STRANGE TEXT TO ANNOUNCE, AND SEEMS A FOR-midable subject to discuss during wartime. You might even think it a dangerous subject and one likely to undermine the morale of our people. It might be easier conveniently to forget that Jesus ever said those words. I should not be at all surprised if someone felt immediately cynical, saying in his heart, "Do you expect us to love the Gestapo? Are you seriously asking us to love those who run concentration camps, persecute the Jews, lock up little children in filthy railway cars and send them to unknown destinations, tearing them away from their parents? Have you forgotten already the Nazi atrocities, the inhuman brutality, and authentic records of bestiality? The foul deeds of our enemies are proved beyond possibility of doubt, and you have the cheek to stand there in that safe pulpit and tell us to love our enemies. We bomb them night after night as hard as we can. Do you suggest that on an eight-thousand-pound bomb we should tie a label, 'With love from Britain'? Surely it would be better if you forgot these words for the time being. At any rate, I'm not going to listen to such nonsense."

If anyone feels like that, I entirely understand. It is a natural reaction to such a text. But since Jesus did say these words, and since it is sheer cowardice to put them in cold storage and drag them out again after the war, when perhaps it is easier to love the people of hostile nations, let us quietly think together about them, reminding ourselves of two important facts:

1. We shall not fight any better by hating people. Hate is an emotion which disturbs cool judgment and blurs good motives.

If those in command were moved by feelings of hatred of persons, they would speedily become unfit to command. Anyone who knows the British soldier can safely leave the matter of hate where it is. There is less hate shown among those who actually do the fighting than among those who stay at home, lose their loved ones, and are forced to remain inactive.

2. At this moment we are moved to a more generous mind because the war is going the way we want it to go. It is easier when we are winning to have a right attitude to those we are compelled to fight than when we are depressed or made savage by military reverses.

I can assure you quite sincerely that I am myself convinced that we must carry the war through to a successful conclusion. If there were a criminal band in our city, disturbing the peace, bringing sorrow and pain and suffering to innocent people, maltreating the aged and the poor, driving little children from their homes, prejudicing the peace and happiness of our city for years to come, then I think most of us would agree that that criminal band should be tracked down, punished, and its activities brought to an end. As I see the war situation, we are engaged in the same task, though the criminal gang is a large one and the methods we must use to bring the criminals to book are bound, in the nature of the case, to be far removed from the dispassionate mechanisms of justice which would accomplish the task in this one city. One of the most terrible entails of the attack of an international criminal gang is that the only way we can prevent it from having its evil way is the dreadful method we call war.

In dealing with the text "Thou shalt love thy neighbor" we made it clear that, since the word "love" is linked with a command, it cannot be a matter of the emotions, but must be a matter of the will. Let me remind you of what was said on that subject: When the New Testament commands us to love one another, the appeal is not to the emotion, but to the will. Romantic feeling is irrelevant. What is enjoined upon all who would call themselves Christians is a sustained determination to show unbreakable good will in order that the best qualities in the person "loved" may be called forth.

An emotion is not sufficiently within the control of the will. Therefore it would be nonsense to say to anybody, "Thou shalt love," if we were asking him to produce that warm emotion which generally goes by that name. "Thou shalt love" in the New Testament means, "Thou shalt adopt a sustained determination to show unbreakable good will." If you remember, it has been shown that loving your neighbor does not mean liking him, which again is a matter of feeling, not will; nor does it mean blinding yourself to his faults. It does mean acting *as if* you liked him, for acting *is* within the control of the will.

I want now to work out the same idea in regard to our new topic: "Thou shalt love thine enemy." It cannot mean liking our enemy, for no one could be expected to like the typical Nazi. Yet I do want to say that I not only like, but have a deep affection for, many friends I made in Germany. They have been silenced by Nazi tyranny and find no means of expressing themselves, but I am sure that they must hate the evil that has seized the high places of power, and that they still love and worship our Lord Jesus Christ. At the same time, no one who holds as precious the values for which we are fighting can possibly *like* those who have set themselves to destroy them, and who would fain practice a ruthless domination over the rest of the world.

Further, no one can possibly blind himself to the enormities that the Nazi regime has brought to literally millions of innocent people. In my view, the Allied governments are quite right in demanding punishment, in demanding that after the war, by legal courts duly constituted, those who are responsible shall be brought to justice. To say, "Thou shalt love thine enemy," does not mean letting him off. Such punishment will deal more charitably with the evildoer than the lawless revenge of Czechs and Poles would mete out to him.

We are now ready to try to express simply the positive implication of our Lord's words. Loving our enemy means acting toward him in the spirit of good will. Before you dismiss that as impossible while we keep fighting him and dropping bombs on his cities, let me show you two ways in which we still have to practice the spirit of good will, which is what the New Testament means by loving.

1. We must refuse to identify the crime and the criminal. I have tried to show how we must do that in regard to our neighbor, and how, indeed, we do it in regard to ourselves. When we have done something about which we are ashamed, we say to ourselves, truthfully and valuably, "That's not the real I," or, "I didn't realize what I was doing," or, "I'm ashamed of what I did"; and we are deeply relieved if somebody in charity says, "He couldn't have been himself." In other words, we make a separation between our real self and the things we do. Showing good will toward the enemy, that is, loving him, means a readiness to believe that the enemy is not expressing his real self in the foul deeds that he does. Years and years of evil teaching have made him accept false ideals. The inferiority which the crushing defeat of 1918 thrust upon him made him ready to clutch at any method of scrambling out of the abyss. The element of vengeance has swayed many German hearts, and Germany once more is trying to impose her aggressive, dominating spirit on the world. But hard though it may be to do so, we shall never make progress in the task of restoring good relationships after the war unless we can do, to some extent, what our fathers called "loving the sinner and hating his sin," that is, believing that the German is capable, as indeed he is, of making a contribution to the family of nations which is of immense value.

Some of us have studied German philosophy; others have studied German music; others again have read German literature; and still more have benefited by German scientific research, especially in the realm of medicine and surgery. I appeal to you never to identify the word "German" with all that is evil in the Nazi regime, but so to separate the evil from the people that have committed it that you are ready to show good will to the German, believing that what he has done in the past, in the way of contributions to culture, he may do in the future if only we do not identify him with the crimes of those who dominate him, and do steadfastly believe in his possibilities for good.

2. A second way in which we must show that good will to our enemies which Christ demands is by refusing to exaggerate their

crimes. As Christian people we must take a strong line here. Remember those great words of Paul in his first letter to the Corinthians, of which Moffatt has given us so excellent a translation: "Love is never glad when others go wrong; love is gladdened by goodness, always slow to expose, always eager to believe the best." One of the marks of a Christian is that he never exaggerates the evil of another. He admits it and is honest-minded about it. He doesn't whitewash it or pretend it never happened. But if a Christian gets one into a corner and almost licks his lips with satisfaction as he tells one the horrors that the Japanese or Germans have perpetrated, one knows that his Christianity is being undermined by the war.

Into the psychology of all this we need not enter now, but you will realize that to blacken another's character is to feel a little whiter oneself. We feel a little bit better when we have made others seem a little worse. The moral glow which a man feels when he reads in the newspaper of the fall of another is a glow he gets from the fires of hell, not from the stainless beauty of heaven. And anything which makes us feel, "I should never sink so low as that," rather suggests the machinations of Screwtape than the sanctity of the saints. The Christian attitude would be one of sorrow that members of a race—German, Italian, or Japanese—which has contributed so much to world happiness, and will continue to contribute so much more, could have been so deluded and bemused by those who have seized power over them as to do such unworthy and despicable things.

Let me summarize in one paragraph my message as I have developed it so far. Loving our enemies means a determination to show them good will. It does not mean liking them, or whitewashing them, or blinding ourselves to what they have done, or sentimentally refraining from punishing them. It does mean acting as though we still believe in them, and acting in two ways: (1) by not identifying the doer with the deed, as though they were inseparable—since we refuse to do that in ourselves—and (2) by refusing to exaggerate the evil in order to stir up hate or to feel better ourselves.

Now let us adopt a device which I have always found helpful in a difficult situation. When I am interviewing people in deep distress, people who ask the question, "What ought I to do?" I always test my advice by asking what would happen if they did the opposite. If, therefore, you are still critical of my repeating the words of Jesus, "Love your enemies," look for a moment at the opposite. If you decide that you cannot act toward the enemy in good will, then you will decide to act toward the enemy in bad will. If you don't "love" in the sense defined, you will hate; or, in other words, you will seek to bring about not ultimate good to the enemy— which I shall try to show in a moment is one of the great purposes of the war—you will seek to bring about ultimate evil.

You will be unable to seek ultimate evil for the enemy without hating him, and such hate is always a faulty psychological reaction.

> When I am dead, what I have guessed so long,
>   My soul shall know in clearer, purer light:
> That where I loathed and hated, I was wrong;
>   That where I loved and pitied, I was right.

The hatred of people is always a poison. I would commend, especially to my medical friends, the evidence contained in the book called *Disease and Integration,* by Dr. Newsholme, the medical officer of health for Birmingham, in which evidence is gathered and cases quoted to show that personal hate definitely manufactures toxins in the body.

I am not taking a lofty attitude of condemnation to the emotion of hate, as though I never entertained it myself. The tendency to hate people is a normal—and a non-Christian would say inevitable —result of the denial of desired love. If A loves B and wants all the love B can give him, and if B gives extravagant love to C, then A tends to hate both B and C. A hates B because he or she has given away love which A thinks belongs to him, and A hates C because C has been a party to the fraud by receiving the love which A thinks is his alone. It is very hard for A to stop hating both B and C. He can do it only by the grace of God, acknowledging meanwhile to himself the desire to hate and be revengeful, but acting as though he still loved both B and C, realizing that if he gives vent to his hate, he will spoil his chances of attaining his goal, that of winning love. He can win love only by giving love; and if he cannot give the emotion, he must give the good will, that is, he must love in the New Testament sense. Once he gives rein to his hate, he will harm himself more than he can possibly harm the person he hates. If, therefore, you say to me, "I shan't listen when you tell us to love our enemies," I shall reply, "Beware of the opposite, for by hating you will harm yourself more than you can hurt your enemies."

Further, this hate will bring about a permanent dislike, and the dislike will mean that you steadily refuse to see any good at all in the person hated. Once you do that to Germans as a whole, you postpone the very thing for which we are fighting, a world of new relationships. If we exclude Germany from this, we only sow the seeds of another war in another twenty-five years. I should like to bear witness, with pride, to the spirit of most British people, even those who have lost their loved ones. There is nothing like the hate in this country which I remember in the last war. During the last war, in some places, German music could not be played at a religious service. People were commonly heard saying, "There is no good German but a dead German." Such sentiments are rarely heard today. Sometimes the emotion of hate sweeps over a person who makes some such unguarded statement as I heard a lady make in a train, that every German should be exterminated. But when I suggested to her that she should be given a sword and invited to start on a class of blue-eyed, golden-haired little German children, her face told me that she would be the last to carry out her expressed desire. The hate was in the emotional part of her mind for a moment. It had never gained access to her will or her thought. To hate the enemy would be sin, for it would be making an unbridgeable gulf in international relationships, while knowing that the purpose of God is to make of all nations one family. It would be fighting against God.

"But," you will say, "how can you use the word 'love,' even in the New Testament sense of showing good will, when night after night you are bombing the enemy?" Well, let's go back to the earlier illustration of the criminal gang. Supposing, we said, that there were in this city a criminal gang, it would be the duty of the state to end its activity, even at the cost of human life. Granted that war is a faulty method of dealing with international criminals, yet—and the blame of this lies upon all our hearts—it is at present the only method of achieving the desired result. I hold, therefore, that it is justifiable. Though the method is a bad method, as compared with police activity in dealing with the crime of a city, the goal we have in mind may still be the same, Thus, the goal which the state has in mind is to make every criminal a good citizen. The goal the Allied governments have in mind is to make the Axis powers good neighbors. We desire the good of the enemy, though he himself, plus the sin of all the nations, has driven us to terrible methods of securing this end.

Let us make it clear to ourselves that the state, again and again, has to use a method which would be sin in the individual. For example, if somebody offended you personally, and you, with the help of a friend or two, tied him up in your cellar for six months, then I am afraid you would get into trouble, even though you could prove that you had fed him and given him some degree of comfort. Yet the state is rightly approved for passing a sentence of six months during which a man's liberties are restricted in probably a more austere way than the individual would adopt. In the same way, what would be murder in the individual may still be justified as the activity of the whole state, if it is the only way the state can find of achieving its end.

It may be that the state must even take life, and the Bible seems to me to approve that principle. For it is very important to point out that, when you read in the Old Testament the ancient command "Thou shalt not kill," you are reading in a bad translation. The Hebrew original means thou shalt do no *murder,* which is a very different thing. Murder is sin. It is an act in which the individual assumes an authority that may belong only to the state. And in the New Testament, when Jesus repeats the commandment, we find that the word used is not a word that means "kill," but "murder." Jesus does not say, "Thou shalt not kill." He does say, "Thou shalt do no murder." If the state finds that the taking of human life is the lesser of two evils—the other being the spread of international crime—if the taking of life is the only way by which an international criminal gang can be put down and the highest human values preserved, then I claim that the state has the right to take life, *and in doing so is not denying her purpose to show good will*—and to show good will is, in the New Testament sense, to love. Therefore there is no necessary conflict between loving your enemies and killing a sufficient number of them to make the rest desist in their attempt to spread evil.

Some of you may remember that shortly after the war broke out, when we were all trying to think our way through these things, I told a story of some Chinese pirates. I was rather amused afterward to find that somebody who heard me tell that story quoted it in Hyde Park as an answer to a pacifist speaker. The speaker, who is a great friend of mine, made fun of the story, supposing that I had invented it to substantiate my own argument. Actually it was not a made-up story at all. It was true, and if you turn up the files of the *Daily Telegraph* for February 2, 1935, you will find the details. What happened was this: Some British and American children were on board the steamer "Tungchow," on their way from Shanghai to school at Crefoo. They were set upon by pirates in the China Sea. With those facts in our mind, let us imagine that we were in charge of the children. If the pirates would not listen to reason, would not discuss the matter, would not do anything else than take the children off to their lair in the mountains for immoral purposes, do you think you would be justified in sending a radio message for a destroyer or an airplane? I am quite sure in my own mind that it would not be wrong to send such a message. Let us at once admit that it is wrong to risk drowning a pirate. But if your daughter of sixteen or seventeen had been on board, would you not feel it was a better thing to risk drowning pirates, or bombing them, than that an innocent girl should become a prostitute in a Chinese camp for perhaps a dozen years in some remote mountain fastness? In the actual case I am quoting the children were rescued by planes from the British aircraft carrier "Hermes," supported by the British destroyer "Dainty."

To my mind the international situation is not dissimilar. As we engage in war, there is no joy in our hearts at the terror and destruction it causes. For my own part, even the news of successful engagements gives me no feelings of hilarity, but only a kind of grim satisfaction that the end of the war is that much nearer. I have stayed in the Christian homes of some who lived in the area inundated by the floods released through the breaking of the dams in the Ruhr Valley. I think of one German Christian home in which I stayed for several happy days while attending a Christian conference. It consisted of a Christian father and mother, two girls, and a rosy-cheeked boy. Probably they were all carried away by a wall of water thirty feet high sweeping down upon them, and I am not ashamed to tell you that I cannot feel that it is a matter for rejoicing. All that one can feel, amid the conflicting emotions of sorrow, sadness, and grim acquiescence, is that probably only by such means can we save the remaining cities of Western civilization from the horror which befell Belgrade, Warsaw, and Rotterdam. One recalls, for example, that, *before war was declared on Holland,* and meeting with very little, if any, resistance, the Germans slaughtered thirty thousand people in Rotterdam, with not even the pretense of destroying only a military objective.

Again and again, life presents us with the difficult problem, not of deciding between the perfectly right and the obviously wrong, but of deciding the kind of question to which I have made reference. For example, shall the lives of the pirates be destroyed, or shall the British and American schoolgirls be made prostitutes? Even when one lifts the question to the highest court and asks what would Jesus do, there can be little doubt about the answer. For when we remember the perfection of Jesus, it does seem important to remember that Jesus was not a perfect man working in a perfect world, but a perfect man working in an imperfect world. If the former had been true, there would never have been money-changers to turn out of the Temple, or proud Pharisees to receive the lash of his words. But Jesus was the perfect man working in an evil world, and could do only that which would achieve his end in the circumstances thrown up by evil. I feel confident, therefore, that the war must be prosecuted to its end and that we may even pray for the victory of our arms because, far from perfect though we may be, we have to use the only method to achieve our end which the evil in the world allows.

I know how deeply the thought of taking the life of the enemy troubles the consciences of some. I know how hopelessly inconsistent some feel it to be to talk about loving your enemy and trying to kill him at the same time. But think over this problem: Imagine that you yourself were about to commit the most horrible crime you can imagine yourself doing. I will not cite any imaginary horror, for there is no point in harassing your feelings. But then imagine that, before you committed this dreadful crime, you were shot. I wonder, if in the life to come, you would not be glad that you were shot before the crime was committed. You might even, in the next world, go up to the person who pulled the trigger and say, "Thank you very much. You did me a service." Jesus said a man was better dead than cruel to a child. This argument does not mean that you should go around shooting people here and there lest they commit a crime they will regret! Remember what we said about the state's being morally able to do that which is denied to the individual. But, in the light of the illustration, ask yourself the question again: Is taking life necessarily inconsistent with showing good will? I think it might be the highest expression of good will to Germany to stop her, even by killing, before bestial horrors have turned the whole world into a jungle. War, I claim, is not a denial of good will unless it makes you hate, and that is in your own hands.

I have referred in this sermon to enemies as though the Axis powers were the only ones. I must leave to you the application of the interpretation of the text in terms of your own personal and private enemies, but I will leave with you a picture which I saw lately in the press. A group of our men had been fighting fiercely and heroically in North Africa. They had been definitely trying to encompass the death of the enemy. Then, suddenly, the word went round that all resistance in North Africa was over and the campaign was ended. The very men who had been trying to encompass the death of the enemy are seen in a press photograph giving the same men—now German prisoners—chocolates and cigarettes. Now that is a parable.

As soon as the enemy ceased to be the personification of the evil we are trying to destroy, as soon as it became untrue to say that the only way of destroying the evil was to destroy the people who practiced it, as soon as the identification of evil with the people who committed the evil no longer needed to be made, then our determination to show good will was able to take a new turning, and our men are seen, not killing, but handing out chocolates. But please note this: *the determination to kill and the offer of chocolates came from the same motive,* the motive of good will toward the enemy. That good will had to express itself in killing first, because that was the only way of stopping the evil which the Nazi regime embodies. When that evil offered no further resistance, it was possible to separate the sin from the sinner, the evil from the people who *had been* doing it; and chocolates and good fellowship became the new expression of good will.

Such a picture made me wish that those who arrange the terms of peace should be those who fought the enemy. At the end of the last war we handed over the making of peace terms to politicians. I will make no comment on that save to say that the men who fought in the last war would never have imposed the terms which politicians imposed.

Love your enemies! Never let yourself hate! You may have a desperate task to break the evil which threatens the world, and the only way may be to fight and kill. But though we fight to the death, let us maintain unbroken good will and have the highest welfare of our enemies, as of the whole world, clearly in our minds, as the goal toward which we move. Those enemies also—possessed though they may be at present by evil demons—are the sons of the same Father who hates evil more than we do, but who loves all his children. When Jesus said, "Love your enemies," he added this: "that ye may be the children of your Father which is in heaven: for he maketh his sun to rise on the evil and on the good, and sendeth rain on the just and on the unjust."

A prayer that shows the true Christian spirit to our enemies was offered by the chaplain at the Sunday morning parade service on board the battleship "The Prince of Wales" on Sunday, August 10,

1941, at the historic meeting off the coast of Newfoundland between Mr. Churchill and Mr. Roosevelt, the meeting that gave us the Atlantic Charter:

Stablish our hearts, O God, in the day of battle, and strengthen our resolve, that we fight, *not in enmity against men, but against the powers of darkness enslaving the souls of men,* till all enmity and oppression be done away, and the peoples of the world be set free from fear to serve one another as children of one Father, who is above all and through all and in all, our God, for ever and ever. Amen.

# THOU SHALT LOVE THY GOD

WE COME NOW TO THE THIRD OF THE TRILOGY OF SERMONS OF WHICH
the first was from the text "Thou shalt love thy neighbor," the
second, "Thou shalt love thine enemy," and now the third, "Thou
shalt love thy God." The order is not accidental. It is hard to love
one's neighbor. It is harder to love one's enemy. For many people it
is hardest to love God. In regard to the neighbor and the enemy,
we can put on them part of the onus of the difficulty of loving. We
can say, "My neighbor"—even if we use the term in the widest sense
—"is difficult. In any case I don't get on with strangers very well."
In regard to the enemy we can say, "It is particularly difficult in
these days to love one's enemy, and if I don't succeed, it is partly his
fault." But in regard to God we cannot put the onus on him. If
God is the perfect being and we fail to love him, the reflection is on
ourselves.

Yet I cannot feel that we are entirely to blame. On a lovely spring
morning, if health is good and spirits are high, and our loved ones
are near us and our relationship with them happy, and none of
them is ill or in danger, and we know of no people with whom we
are out of harmony, and business or professional cares are not
worrying us, then with Browning's Pippa we may go out into the
sunshine and say:

> God's in his heaven—
> All's right with the world.

It is easy then to tell ourselves that we do love God.

But there are days when God seems far off, vague, and unreal.
There are days when the spirit is half dead within us, and all the
wheels of being are slow; "when the burdens we carry chafe our
shoulders and weigh us down; when the road seems dreary and

endless, the skies grey and threatening; when our lives have no music in them, our hearts are lonely and our souls have lost their courage." There are days when the soul is stunned by bad news: illness threatens those we love better than life, or news of bereavement turns our hearts to lead and drives the sun from our sky. God's ways seem so confusing. It is hard to understand what he is doing and difficult to love him as one recalls the things that he allows. Many men, weighed down by the suffering and sorrow of the world, would confess that they do not really love God. If they were honest, they would say that they were critical about God and sometimes hostile to him. They are made unhappy only by being told that they *ought* to love him, for "ought" and "love" don't go together.

No true father says to his sons or daughters, "You *ought* to love me because I am your father," and it would be wise if we honestly recognized that in many families there is a good deal of insincerity in this matter of loving relatives. To suppose that brothers really love one another merely because they are brothers is to live in a realm of pretense. The frequent quarrels of sisters point the same way. Husbands and wives are frequently supposed to love one another, but in many a home love has given way to kindliness and to the desperate attempt to keep up appearances by making the best of a bad job. To call the relationship by the same name as that which binds two people who never chafe one another, always call out one another's best, find rest of mind and kindling of spirit in one another's company, wanting to do everything together and each finding himself or herself incomplete without the other, is indeed a misuse of words.

Those who carry out psychological treatments frequently find that relatives hate one another, and neurosis has often been set up by pretending to love and repressing feelings of antagonism and even hatred. Many a patient has suffered in childhood from some tyrannical and dominating parent who happens to have been labeled "father." Such a patient has never admitted to consciousness that she does not love him, because all the conventional shams of modern life and the Christian ideal she supposes she ought to hold conspire to tell her that she may admit to consciousness only the word "love," since the person concerned is her own father. Were he not her father, she would readily admit that she hates him and despises him, and she would find at any rate the beginning of some degree of health in labeling the emotion with honesty instead of with sham. Such a patient frequently breaks down at her father's death, especially if she has nursed him through a long illness. For she has a new conflict. She is really relieved and glad he is dead, but convention demands she should be sorry and show the signs of grief. She frequently develops the obsession that in some obscure ways she is responsible for his death. It is much more important for our mental health that we should be honest than that we should be conventional; and, as we said, "ought" and "love" don't go together. The teacher can say to the naughty schoolboy, "You *ought* to be sorry." If he could look into the schoolboy's heart, he would learn a good deal of psychology at once. He may proceed to cane the schoolboy, and then he does make him sorry, but he only makes him sorry that he was caned or that he was found out. To make him really sorry for the fault demands a different approach altogether. The only teacher who can make this approach is one who has an insight into the nature of things and who realizes at least the fundamental principles by which an emotional response of a true order may be evoked.

Now we always get a glimpse of the nature of God's ways with us by thinking about an *ideal* family. Jesus himself again and again argued thus from the ideal in man to the ways of God. The ideal father does not command that he be loved emotionally. He realizes that the fact of being a parent does not give him any right to demand love or even loyalty or even respect. These must be won. (In parenthesis, we often notice that a father realizes that he must win these things from, say, the little boy next door, and he sets himself out to do so when the little boy next door comes to play. But to his own little boy he is frequently brusque and demanding because he supposes his own boy *ought* to love him.) In the two previous sermons about loving our neighbor and our enemy, we found the key that opens the door. We said that, when we talk about loving our neighbor, the *feeling* of love is not meant, because an emotion cannot be commanded, but that loving means a determination to show unbreakable good will. When we talked about loving the enemy, the only way in which we could make sense of the command was to understand by it that we were to show the enemy an attitude of good will, and we proceeded to show that even fighting him might be an expression of that good will. For we are not fighting the German people as such; we are fighting the false ideas which have become their ideals, and with which at any rate the Nazi Party has so identified itself that the only way of overthrowing the ideas is to fight those who express them in their activities. Such fighting shows more truly an attitude of good will than a complacent indifference which allowed Nazism to spread over the world, to damn the souls of those who practiced it, and to victimize those who suffered through it.

When, therefore, the text says, "Thou shalt love the Lord thy God," it cannot mean, in my view, a feeling of warm emotion. That cannot, in the nature of things, be called forth by a command. What we have to show to God is good will. The father in the family, we said, cannot command emotion and, if wise, does not try to do so; but as the head of the family he has the right to command good will so long as his aims are directed to the welfare of the family as a whole and to every member of it. The family will fall to pieces if everybody is sabotaging the unity of the family and its purposefulness toward a high ideal. Thus the father has the right to say to his sons: "Do show me good will. Here are my purposes. These are my plans. This is what I am out for. Do co-operate with me. The unity of every family is essential in society. It is the basis of the happiness of the whole state. Don't, therefore, behave in a way that is hostile to those interests which we all have at heart." It would be a heavy father indeed who delivered himself of such a lecture to a young family, but, roughly speaking, I think that would be the attitude of an ideal father's mind. And I think that is the kind of thing God asks when in this commandment, which is underlined by the authority of Jesus, we are told to love the Lord our God with all our powers of heart and mind and soul, and thus of all our strength.

There will be many times, as we said at the beginning, when we have no warm emotional feelings about God; but, unless we are disloyal, there need not be any times when we sabotage his purposes and run our lives in opposition to his will. We may not be able to give God our feelings on many an occasion, but feelings do not matter, and feelings are not asked for. There need be no occasions when we cannot offer God our will and good will, and ask that, even on our dullest days, we may help, not hinder, his holy plans.

So to serve him by the offering of our will, even when feeling seems dead within us, is a truer expression of loving God than sitting in a deck chair in the garden *feeling* that we love God because the sun happens to be shining and the birds are singing, but never turning our hand to those great enterprises which we know to be his will. We are to love with all our strength. Strength is not expressed in feeling, but in the directed will. If that purposefulness is fired by feeling, so much greater the strength. But feeling alone doesn't get things done.

Even the phrase "loving with all our heart" is not, I think, an appeal to the emotions. Suppose that for twenty years you had set your heart on great literature, so that you knew the great poets and dramatists and prose writers and could quote them and communicate their magic to others. Suppose then, with a crowd of other people, you found yourself in a prisoner-of-war camp. The welfare officer sought you out and asked you whether you could give a few talks on literature to relieve the tedium of the other prisoners. I think you would be persuaded into helping. After all, literature is the thing you had *set your heart on,* not in feeling only, but in purposefulness. Your twenty years' enthusiastic study fitted you for a piece of service which no one else could give. Doesn't God say to us, "Set your heart on my kingdom, on the welfare of my world family. Study my ways with men; come into close fellowship with me. Then, when the moment comes, I can use you"? Emotion plays a part, of course, for it is impossible to separate thinking and feeling and willing. But loving God with all your heart does not merely refer to the flow of warm emotion. I think it means purposefully turning your whole being to the contemplation and study of God's ways with men, that, entering into the joys and delights of his kingdom, you may further his purposes in the world. As a boy sets his heart on stamp collecting, as a man sets his heart on being a great lawyer, as a girl sets her heart on being an able violinist, as a mother sets her heart on making her home a place of rest and recreation and renewal, let us set our hearts on the things of God and love him with all our hearts.

Loving God with our mind is such an immense subject that I hesitate to embark on it. It seems to me to mean a readiness to think things through with absolute honesty and untiring industry. I know that Christianity is a simple thing in one sense, but it is necessary that we should use all the powers of mind that God has given us to try to understand his ways with us. Fortunately, to be a good Christian one can be simple-minded and without high intellectual power. Indeed the man of simple faith often has insights into divine things that take him further than the theologian. At the same time, fearless and honest thinking would do a great deal for us, especially when we are confused and distressed by the things that happen to us. To have *thought out* a philosophy of life before calamity happens, as well as to "have faith," is to find shelter in the day of storm. Not to have done so, to have clung to an untruth or half-truth, even with much faith, is to find that the shelter breaks in upon one in the hour when one needs it most.

"Thou shalt love the Lord thy God with all thy mind." Thou shalt be willing to think things through. People hate to be made to think. In religion many seem to prefer magic and the mumbo-jumbo of meaningless words. Others seek to make themselves believe by repeating words instead of understanding them. But loving God with the mind means a fearless determination to follow truth wherever it leads us.

I was pulled up violently in this matter in India by a student with whom I attended a service during which the Creed had been recited, including the words, "I believe in . . . the resurrection of the body." He asked me what the words meant, and I replied that I meant by them a belief in the survival of personality after death. "If so," he replied, "why don't you say so?" The phrase "the resurrection of the body," if words are taken at their face value, means that the particles buried in the grave will be gathered again in some future state, and no one believes that now.

I am not making any cheap jibe at the creeds. They were set down, not to express final truth, but to combat immediate error. It is a matter for discussion whether they should continue to be used when, concerning their phraseology, one continually has to make mental reservations and odd interpretations involving making the words mean what those who wrote them down certainly did not mean. For everybody to say the same creed, but to mean something different by the words used in it, is to attain a spurious unity by a species of intellectual dishonesty. Some think the creeds should be restated every few years. Others argue that it is enough to keep the traditional words if modern explanations are made. But it is certainly wrong to allow room for so much misunderstanding that people hug words to their bosom when the strength of the truth has gone out of them. Many people today do not lack faith; but, not having been taught to love God with their minds, they "wander in perpetual twilight among shadowy ghosts of former faiths" which they do not really understand and cannot intellectually embrace, but which, for lack of clearer alternative, they cannot expel. In an attempt to rethink our way through Christian belief, we may have to reduce the number of beliefs very considerably, but it is better to have a few simple truths which carry intellectual conviction than to seek to embrace the whole theology of Christianity by mumbling words which we do not understand or cannot accept. I cannot help feeling that God loves the fearless, questing mind, even though there are many things which cannot yet be accepted because of the honesty of that mind.

"Thou shalt love the Lord thy God with all thy mind." Thou shalt not say words that mean nothing or mean something that cannot be accepted by the mind. Jesus opposed the hoariest traditions in order that he might satisfy the august claims of the truth. Somebody has asked what the condition of the nation's health would be if, in the days of Henry I, somebody had written down thirty-nine articles to be followed by all physicians for the rest of time. But our spiritual health is in peril partly because we are using words which the man in the street does not understand, which lead him astray if he takes them at their face value, and concerning which we have to give elaborate explanations which amount to admitting that the words mean something very different from what they say.

I must not attempt to work out all the meanings of loving God with the soul. I think it means turning our spirit to him, seeking to find harmony with him, being undismayed by the things that seek to lure us from him, never accepting defeat through sin, but turning back to him again in obedience and renewed dedication, and maintaining, by every means we know, our sensitiveness to his guiding voice. We may not have the ecstatic experiences of the mystics. We may not be very clever and be able to argue for our Christianity. I find that, more and more, it means for me putting one step down in front of the other, doggedly going on and trying to give God obedience and loyalty, setting my heart on the things of his kingdom, setting my will to obey his commandments and my mind to understand his ways and my spirit to look up to him in prayer. Feelings and mystic experiences are not for me to demand, as they are not in my power to engineer.

There is some kind of summary of my theme in the simple words of a song written by Maude Louise Ray:

> To love someone more dearly every day,
> To help a wandering child to find his way,
> To ponder o'er a noble thought, and pray,
>     And smile when evening falls;
>
> To follow truth as blind men long for light,
> To do my best from dawn of day till night,
> To keep my heart fit for His holy sight,
>     And answer when He calls,
>
> This is my task.

# ON HAVING A RIGHT SENSE OF VALUES

ONE OF THE MOST IMPORTANT THINGS IN THE WORLD IS THAT WE should have a true sense of values, and that, in spite of all the hostile forces that threaten to destroy it or undermine it, we should be able to maintain it.

What do we mean by our sense of values? We mean our assessment of those things which are of greatest worth. It is interesting to recall that the word "worth" and the word "worship" come from the same root, and that the origin of the word "value" is the same as that of the word "valor." Our sense of values, then, is our appreciation of those things which are really the valorous things, the strong things, the lasting and dependable things.

The importance of having our sense of values right is seen in this, that nothing would make the life of the whole community deteriorate more quickly than the abandonment of the "values," or the substitution of false values for true ones. Obviously if wealth is a "value," if one supposes that making money is the most worth-while use of time and strength, one will be dominated by the pursuit of wealth, and possibly spend fifty or sixty years of one's life with that quest as its main aim. Every energy will be bent to that end, and so dominating can be the pull of our sense of values that we can become ruthless in yielding to its pressure, and we can rationalize—or unconsciously give ourselves plausible reasons for—deviations from truth and honesty and kindness while we pursue our goal.

Pleasure, having a good time, squeezing selfish happiness out of life, constitutes for many life's main ambition. In other words, pleasure is a "value" in their estimate of things. They seek to obtain selfish happiness, becoming increasingly indifferent about the needs of others and blind to the more worth-while things. The more this "value" is given prominence in their lives, the more they miss a much greater happiness and much deeper joy. For the highest type of happiness is never gained when it is the *object* of our search; it comes to us as a *by-product* of a search for something else—namely, a truer value like unselfish service, or friendship, or artistic creation.

I traveled on the train recently with a girl of twenty-three, fair-haired and blue-eyed and attractive, who boasted to the man sitting opposite her, after he had offered her a cigarette, that she was making the journey from London to Bradford in order to attend a party. It was impossible to avoid hearing their conversation. She boasted that on the previous evening, which happened to be Sunday, she had taken so many neat whiskeys before dinner that she could not tell what she was eating. I was rather pleased when the man opposite said, "I am very sorry to hear it." She evidently thought to impress him with the story of her vulgar orgy. The train was crowded, and soldiers were standing near us. I thought of this young girl, on the one hand, and young men, on the other hand, who have given up their careers and are offering their very lives to make our land safe and free, and to build a new world for girls of twenty-three as well as for future generations.

But turn to more enheartening pictures. When some of our soldiers and airmen who had been prisoners of war in Germany came home in the recent exchange, they left behind them a certain doctor, an ophthalmic surgeon, who elected to stay in a German prison camp. When the fact that he was entitled to come home was pointed out to him, he said something like this: "While I have been in the prison camp I have been able to treat blinded prisoners, and in some cases to restore their sight. Others in similar need will come to this camp, and I want to remain to help them." He did not attach supreme worth to personal comfort and selfish happiness, but he valued more highly the chance to serve others in their need. In other words, his sense of values was different from that of the girl; so it was *worth* staying. When a man says, "It's worth it," he reveals his sense of values. I think of that boy whose story I have told elsewhere, who went out during the last war into no-man's-land where the shells were falling to save his wounded friend. His superior officer gave him permission, but added, "It isn't worth it. Your friend must be dead, and if you go out there, you will be wounded or killed yourself." However, the boy went, hoisted his friend on his shoulder, and carried him back to safety. But he was terribly wounded himself, and his friend appeared to be dead.

"I told you it wasn't worth it," said the officer. "Your friend is dead, and now you are mortally wounded."

"But it was worth it, sir," said the hero.

"Worth it? How could it be worth it?" The officer almost snapped the question.

"It was worth it, sir," said the boy, "because when I got to him he was still alive, and he said, 'Jim, I *knew* you'd come.'" The high claims of friendship were a value that made the sacrifice worth it. Our whole life depends on, and is governed by, our sense of values —our estimate as to which things in life are worth while and which are not.

Modern life has made it increasingly difficult for us to keep our sense of values from being confused. Dr. Temple, the late Archbishop of Canterbury, in one of his addresses to Oxford students in 1941, said this striking thing: "The world, as we live in it, is like a shop window in which some mischievous person has got in overnight and shifted all the price labels round, so that the cheap things have the high-price labels on them and the really precious things are priced low." Then he added, "We let ourselves be taken in." Oh, my soul, heed that word! "We let ourselves be taken in." Getting on in the world, having a good time, making money, chasing fame, seeking beauty, indulging in sex expression without thought to the cost to others and to our own better nature—how we follow these aims with unwearying purposefulness! Let us find time today to sit down quietly and ask ourselves these questions: On what am I really setting my heart? What goal do I seek to reach? What am I really looking for in life? Have I got my sense of values right?

Since the blitzes started in London, I have noticed many people who have been pulled up in their quest for life's prizes and who have begun to think that perhaps their sense of values has gone wrong. A faith that is a real anchor in the day of storm, a deeper communion with God, a habit of rewarding prayer, the secret of inward serenity, a heart cleansed and freed from besetting sin—how they wish now that they had these things! In calm, happy, successful, healthy days, these things never seemed to matter. They were priced low. But in the hour of crisis and danger we know that they are the real gold of life, and we wish we had more of such gold with which to meet the immense spiritual expenditure which these days demand. People are in the mood now to mark those things at a high price, but they didn't think much of them in the carefree, easy days before trouble fell, and now they have got their sense of values muddled up. As Dr. Temple said, "We let ourselves be taken in." We said, "What shall I do to be comfortable? What shall I do to be happy? What shall I do to be well off? What shall I do now so that I shall not have to do anything later on?" We never said, "Which is the way that leads to true life?" or, "How can I achieve the integration of my personality?" or, "Who can show me the way to inner satisfaction?" or, if you like it better, "What must I do to be saved?"

We leave so late the questions that matter, don't we? I sat with another minister in the home of a charming and wealthy layman who was entertaining us both. The talk turned on Wordsworth's poetry, and our host said, "You two make me jealous talking that way. I have always thought I would like to read a lot of poetry, but I have never had time. When I have made my pile, I shall take it up." He was quite sincere about it, but he never did take it up. A sense of values is not a thing you can switch over, like turning the dial of a radio. You cannot engineer an interest in it, let alone attach dynamic purposefulness to it. It becomes harder and harder, as the years pass, to direct your life by a new star. Self-discipline is both more necessary and more irksome. If you spend fifty years with the dominating aim of making money, you can't suddenly say to yourself, "Now I will like poetry." You lose your taste for the lovely things, or, worse still, they don't seem *worth* so much. Your sense of values alters, or perhaps some tragic thing happens. You say, "I will turn to this or that one day"—but you never do. Procrastination and the absence of self-discipline play the devil with our values. "He who stays in bed on Sunday morning," said Dr. Selbie of Mansfield College, Oxford, "may not be committing a great sin, but his sense of values is being filched from him. He is putting the value of comfort higher than the value of self-discipline and worship."

There is more than fun in the story which Mr. Winston Churchill used in a recent speech, when he told of the sailor who dived into the waters of Plymouth Harbor and saved the life of a little boy. Two or three days afterward the sailor came across the boy and his mother in the streets of Plymouth. He saw the boy nudge his mother, and the mother then stopped the sailor and said, "Are you the man who pulled my little boy out of the water?"

Expecting some kind of gratitude, the sailor smiled, saluted, and said, "Yes, madam."

"Then," said the mother, with mounting anger, "where's his cap?"

We smile at the story, but our sense of values has in some cases gone as far astray.

How can we test our sense of values? I want to suggest these three ways:

1. A real value would remain if all that could be taken from you were taken.

2. A real value would not be rendered worthless by any situation that could possibly arise.

3. A real value is recognized by the kind of satisfaction we get when we acknowledge it in action.

Now all three points can be illustrated by reference to the three ultimate values of truth, beauty, and goodness.

Think of truth—dependable, eternal, which (1) no persecution can take from you, which (2) no circumstance can debase in value, and (3) to assert or defend which gives us a kind of spiritual satisfaction. Men have been glad even to die for the truth. Take a look at Andrew Melville, the Scottish reformer, threatened with violent death at the hands of the Earl of Morton, and saying, "Tush, my lord, make these threats to your courtiers. It is all one to me whether I rot in the earth or in the air. It is not in your power to hang or exile the truth."

Take a look at the scene almost at the end of Masefield's play *Good Friday,* when the old man who is selling lilies musingly says to Christ:

Friend, it is over now, the passion, the tears, the pains,
Only the truth remains.[1]

Or turn to beauty. Isn't it a lovely thought that, however trying
and horrible the circumstances may be through which we still have
to pass, no device of Hitler, no power of hell, no bestial atrocities of
Nazis, no sorrow or loss or pain can take the glory from the dawn,
or silence the singing of the birds, or annul the judgment which the
beauty of a starlit night delivers on the hateful ways of little men?

On one of those dreadful days in 1914 when the lights were going
out in Europe, Viscount Grey sought composure at Lady Glencon-
ner's house, where Mr. Campbell McInnes sang to him some of
Handel's songs. Afterward Grey wrote to Mr. McInnes these words:
"Europe is in the most terrible trouble it has ever known in civilized
times, and no one can say what will be left at the end. But Handel's
music will survive." Beauty is a value, eternal, indestructible, un-
debasable, spiritually satisfying.

Then turn to the strange appeal which goodness makes. A little
while ago in London a man rushed into a blitzed and blazing house
in the night to save a little girl whom he believed was trapped
inside. In truth she was standing behind him in the darkness, and
he did not know it. Yet who will say he threw away his life? At the
close of Meredith's story *Beauchamp's Career* the hero is drowned
in rescuing a little riverside boy who has fallen into the water. The
contrast is drawn between the great gifts and brilliant promise of
Nevil Beauchamp and that for which he gives up his life—what
Meredith calls "the insignificant bit of mudbank life remaining in
this world in the place of him." The book leaves us with the question, "Was it worth it?" But those who have their sense of values
right can answer the question.

Truth, beauty, and goodness—and their derivatives, like kindness, friendship, love, sincerity—what a strange appeal they have
to us! What responses they call forth from us! Having seen them,
we could not deny them their authority even if we would. They
have secret allies in every heart, often sleeping, but often awakened,
and if awakened, making us respond in a way that seems almost
independent of, and above, ourselves, carrying us to an acquiescence

[1] By permission of the publisher, The Macmillan Co.

with the true, the beautiful, and the good that startles us by its glorious authority and compelling power.

How can we maintain our sense of values?
1. By reminding ourselves of what we are.
2. By reminding ourselves of what we cost.
3. By reminding ourselves of where we are going.
Let us look at those three points a little more closely.

1. Someone has aptly said that it is not so true to say that man is a body and has a spirit, as that man is a spirit and has a body. It is with this in mind that I have used that familiar but lovely phrase of Augustine: "Thou hast made us for thyself, and our hearts are restless until they find rest in thee." Man the spirit may maintain his sense of values by reminding himself that, *because* he is spirit, he will never be happy by pretending that he is only a body and a mind.

One of the distressing things about some modern novels is that they almost suppose that man is not even a mind, but is only a body. I shall not spend time now reminding you of the immense dangers and difficulties into which we are drifting through following one of the demands of the body. Venereal disease is only one symptom of those vast dangers. I will only say that in thirty years' experience in the Christian ministry I have never found that any of those alleged short cuts to happiness, such as free love and promiscuous sexuality, lead to anything but illness, both of mind and body, to psychological maladjustments, to tears and unhappiness. Listen to the concluding sentences of a modern novel, the name of which I shall not give:

I came out of a cloud of thoughts to discover the narrow compartment with its feeble lamp overhead and our luggage swaying in the rack, and Isabel, very still in front of me, gripping some wilting red roses tightly in her bare and ringless hand. For a moment I could not understand her attitude, and then I perceived she was sitting bent together, with her head averted from the light to hide the tears that were streaming down her face.

Passion was a value. Its falseness was proved. The end was tears. Yes, if only we could remember what we are!

2. And if only we could remember what we cost. "Ye are not your own," said the apostle. "Ye are bought with a price." At our Friday Fellowship somebody said something like this: "If only we could realize all that it cost God to save us, we should never sell ourselves again for either lust or gold!" What a true word that is! When we look at the cross and are in the right mood and have humbled ourselves to look with understanding, dimly and faintly there dawns on us something of the agony of God himself in that greatest act of all human history, when through the precious blood of his dear Son he gave to the uttermost because, in his loving estimation, we were *worth* it. If we knew *that* and could realize *that,* we should maintain our own sense of values. I never expect to be able to put the little measuring tape of my mind round the mystery of the Atonement; but if from time to time, looking at the cross, I can say, "That is what it cost him; he thought I was worth that," then I think I shall not be able to sell myself for the worthless things. As Faber said,

> That thou should'st think so much of me,
>   And be the God thou art,
> Is darkness to my intellect
>   But sunshine to my heart.

3. If we realized where we were going, it would help us to keep our sense of values right. My friend Dr. Sangster in one of his books has an excellent illustration here. When the "Titanic," he tells us, was going down, a certain titled and wealthy woman who had been allotted a place in one of the boats rushed back to her stateroom and snatched up, not her jewelry, but three oranges. An hour before the accident diamonds were more valuable than oranges, but not now—not on a journey when diamonds could do nothing, but when oranges could satisfy both hunger and thirst.

Well, we are on a journey too. Where we are going diamonds won't buy anything—nor money, nor fame, nor sex, nor beauty. Let us ask again the questions we asked at the beginning: What do we seek most in life? What do we value most—remembering that we are off on a journey to a world completely spiritual? It would be hell to be at an endless concert and not to be able to appreciate music, or, perhaps, even to hear. The only thing left is music, and the only way to enjoy it is through appreciative hearing. It would be hell to be at an everlasting banquet and not to be able to eat anything. It would be hell to be in heaven and never to have developed any taste for the things of the spirit, when the things of the spirit are the only things that remain. How many people in hell, both this side of death and the other, must say, with an anguish that deserves the word flame, "If only I had kept my sense of values right."

The late Lord Stamp, one of the greatest authorities in Britain on economics and finance, and also a local preacher, once broadcast a talk on "The Gold Standard." It was technical and abstruse, but listen to the magnificent witness of his last paragraph: "Before I finish, I should like to say one other thing, and it is this. I have not the slightest interest whatsoever in any scale of values excepting only as it may subserve that other scale of values introduced into this planet by Jesus of Nazareth. That is the only scale of values which ultimately matters and which no man now listening to my voice can ever afford to ignore on peril of his soul."

"I do nothing," said Socrates, "but go about persuading you all, old and young alike, not to take thought for your persons or your property, but first and chiefly to care about the greatest improvement of the soul." That sounds very much like the word of another in whom all the true values were gathered together and harmoniously realized in action. "Don't worry overmuch," he says, "about the things to eat and the things to wear, and don't spend your money on that which is not bread. Don't let your lives be overcome by the trifling or the tawdry or the tinsel treasures for which men seek so passionately and for so long. Get yourself into the right relationship with God. Seek ye first his kingdom. Hold on to the lovely things, and everything else will fall into the right perspective."

I wonder why it is that the true values have such final authority over us. It is not because they pay. Men feel a satisfaction at telling the truth, or discovering it, when it means pain and loss to tell it or to know it. Many have died rather than deny the truth. Beauty often has for us in certain moods the stab of pain. And as to the good, let me quote the late Archbishop Temple again. This time the quotation comes from his book *Christus Veritas*: "There are some forms of good deliberately chosen in which the element of pleasure is almost non-existent, while pain is very prominent. Of such good we may say what George Eliot's Romola says of the highest happiness: 'We only know it from pain by its being what we would choose before everything else because our souls see it is good.'" Why *have* the values such power over us? Whence their high authority? Why are there things which we would rather die than do? Why is it that everybody *knows* that kindness is better than cruelty, and love is better than lust, and truth is better than lies? Can it be that the true values are the very attributes of **God**, sign posts pointing to him, voices calling us home?

# WHY PEOPLE DON'T GO TO CHURCH

THIS SERMON HAS ARISEN FROM A STRANGE BUT VERY DEFINITE FEEL-
ing that I must speak, not to the members of the church and the
regular worshipers, but to some who, I have been led to feel, have
desired to worship God after perhaps a long absence from church,
during which they have given him little chance in their lives. Even
if it reaches only one person who is in the condition I have described, "my voices"—as I sometimes call such intuitions—drive
me with a compulsion I often resist to speak to him. So the word
"you" in this sermon means specifically you who have drifted away
from God, given up all attempt at prayer perhaps, kept away from
his house, shut yourself off from his love, and left him out of your
life.

First of all, I want to say to you a sincere word of welcome. We
who are in the church want to know you. We want you to come into
fellowship with us. We do not pretend to be in any way superior.
We stumble and make mistakes. We go back on our vows, and
we let Christ down. But we really do love him. We believe that he
stands for the highest things in life; and we believe that if you, and
all the other people who secretly admire him, would join in fellowship with us and with all those who want to see his spirit working
through the world, then the evils that we all hate would go down
before us, and in our personal lives we should find, as a by-product
of finding him, that rare, incredible happiness in which the soul
finds its deepest satisfaction and its truest life.

I wonder if you know how often you have set us a problem, you
who seem so much better than your creed. Again and again in our
Friday Fellowship I have been asked the question: "How is it that
so many people inside the churches seem difficult, hard to get on
with, often mean and petty and unloving, and yet so many people
outside the churches seem broad-minded, tolerant, and generous?"

Possibly you would be the first to recognize that a tree may flourish because its roots go down to an underground stream, the presence of which few suspect, and its leaves are lifted into a sunny air which it shares with the trees around it. A great many people never go near the churches and almost boast that religion plays no part in their lives; but when they were little children, their devoted parents saw to it that their roots went down to the rivers of God, and those underground rivers below the conscious levels of the mind still bring strength and nourishment. Life for all in this land, whether churchgoers or not, is still lived in the atmosphere of a Christian country; for, although the phrase "Christian country" is mocked and scorned and is the object of an easy sneer, Christ's influence is in our statute book, and his sunshine plays upon the lives of men and women, whether they recognize his power or not. It is true that many of us who are in the church need Christ's influence to spread more powerfully and widely through our lives. Some of us *are* mean, intolerant, unloving; some of us, all our lives perhaps, have had less promising material to deal with in our own make-up than you have had; and you perhaps have escaped any severe times of testing; but, at any rate, we should be far worse without Christ, just as you would be even finer with him.

May I suggest four reasons which have kept you away from church? In enumerating them, I am not going to utter criticisms against the church. I know that many church services are dull, that religion seems irrelevant, that membership is too lightly held, that ecclesiasticism repels you, that doctrines seem intricate and difficult to understand, that ritual seems bewildering and confusing, that we parsons are this and that, and that the church is still divided within itself. These factors count, but you can't do much about them. I am going, rather, to try to speak more personally to *you,* to endeavor to look into *your* mind and lay bare the real reasons which I think account for your keeping away.

The first and, as I think, the greatest is the fear of hypocrisy. Jesus hated hypocrisy, but I do not think he hated it more than the modern person does. The trouble is that the modern person does not understand what hypocrisy really is. The word that Jesus used for "hypocrite" means an actor, one who is never a real person, but is endlessly acting in a play, and who therefore never *intends* to square his real character with his acted part. What is a hypocrite? Not a person who does not live up to his ideals, *but a person who does not try to,* who has no intention of squaring his behavior with his profession. The modern businessman subconsciously argues like this: "Hypocrisy is the blackest of all charges that can be brought against one: Therefore, in order not to be charged with falling below what I profess, I will profess nothing. Then I can be consistent; and, whereas I shall be scorned if I fall below my profession, by professing nothing I can obtain merit by occasionally living above my profession." He therefore steers as far away as possible from contact with religion because it would make him a marked man. Thousands of people listen to broadcast sermons who would never be seen in a church. They even write to the minister. They know their letter will be treated in confidence and answered carefully, and yet they will never have to meet him or run the risk of being identified with religion. They have not been seen leaving a church, and no one knows they wrote to a minister. There is even psychological insight in calling some of the places in great cities where men and women worship "central halls." You will find that the entry is on the pavement level, never up steps. There may be steps inside but never outside, lest a man be *seen* going into church. He can slip in and slip out of a central hall unseen; and, indeed, if he is unfortunately encountered, it is a "central hall," not a church.

This terror which men have of becoming marked men, of being thought religious, is mirrored in the general dislike of ministers. If one wants to be sure of a corner seat in a train, it is a splendid idea to wear a dog collar. Even if the train is filling up, the minister hears a voice say: "Come on, George, there's room farther up. There's a parson in there." During the last war, one of my greatest friends, now a minister but formerly an engineer, gave several days a week in the engineering shop of a shipyard. On these days he was seen, not in a dog collar, but in his blue overalls. On one occasion he made a considerable journey dressed in overalls and got into conversation about religion with a man opposite. So friendly did they become that my friend offered his card, saying to his new acquaintance, "Come and look me up one day."

The man glanced at the card and, seeing the title "The Reverend," handed it back to him, saying, "You've given me the wrong card."

"No," said my friend.

"What," said the other, "are you a parson?"

"Yes," said my friend. "Why not?"

"Well," said the other, "you're the best ——— parson I've ever met, but if I had known that you were a parson, I wouldn't have been seen talking to you."

It is strange to find that a man who is a university graduate, welcome in any society, hail-fellow-well-met by all the world, should, within a month of entering the ministry, be regarded as something not quite human, and be avoided wherever possible. I remember clearly during the last war how soldiers would come to me, quite ready to discuss religious matters, but always prefacing a sentence with, "I'm not a religious bloke, Padre," terrified lest you should think that they were "coming over," always intent to hold aloof.

Can I affectionately suggest to you that it is not very worthy to decide in advance that you will never even attempt the heights lest you be scorned for falling, that you will only set yourself to walk along the level mud flats, where achievement is easy and safe? "Let him practice what he preaches," shouts the man in the street at the parson. If he is worth his salt, he tries to practice what he preaches, but don't ask him to preach only what he practices, or you will get worse sermons than you do get; for he would have to scale aspiration down to achievement. The minister with his people form a fellowship of those who are together seeking the highest things in life, and they call you to join them and to put away that unworthy fear of being called a hypocrite.

The second reason why people don't go to church is that religion is not "the thing." All around us there are still men and women who, as tiny children, were *compelled* to go to Sunday school and *had* to go to church. Too often they saw, in the lives of those who directed them, little of the gladness and joy and radiance of the true

Christian. Religion was a dreary duty which had to be carried out in obedience to adult command. Little wonder, then, that when these youngsters grew up to the point where adult tyranny could be thrown over, they threw over religion without ever discovering what it was. They lost the baby with the bath water, but as the baby had never lived, the loss seemed small.

We may say, and often do say, that we don't care what other people do or what other people think. Whenever I hear a person say that, I feel certain that quite recently his armor has been pierced and that he is feeling very sensitive at that moment about what other people do and what other people think. There are few things in peacetime that we fear more than the opinion of others. So much so that a number of my friends dare not suggest to those who linger at a tea party on Sunday afternoon that the company should adjourn to church. Going to church is not "the thing to do," and they dare not suggest it even when they would like it. Every psychologist realizes that a man may be six feet tall and proportionately broad and pass as a man of the world but emotionally still remain a little boy. We remember from memories of our school days what torture it was to be different from the other boys, and in our hearts we are little boys still. The ladies will not mind my saying that there is not one of them who would have a hat exactly like another lady's hat, but—even more—there is not one who would be seen out in something that looked nothing like any hat ever constructed. Would it be unfair to say that you are still a little girl, and that fashion sways you with a dictator's might? I am challenging all popular men and all beautiful women. It is you who so greatly determine what *is* "the thing to do." If you are popular enough, or charming enough, you can even do the odd thing and not only get away with it but persuade others to do the same. The church could do with more people who make religion popular and who dedicate their popularity, charm, and influence to the highest cause in the world.

I was recently invited by an important firm to take a service for their employees at nine o'clock on a workday morning. It was a privilege to spead to that congregation of all denominations and of none. It was gratifying to think that an important firm hauled their colors to the top of the mast and made that public act of witness. It would

surely be difficult in that particular business for a foreman to bully
his men, for a departmental manager even to suggest that any practice should be followed which was not quite on the straight. I have
accepted an invitation to take a similar service with the employees
of another firm, and I am glad to record these evidences of the fact
that businessmen of weight and influence are prepared to help make
religion "the thing." The best definition I know of a saint is this:
"A saint is one who makes it easier for others to be good." If there
were more saints, more folk would come to church and join in the
fellowship of those who seek the heights.

The third reason why people don't go to church is the oft-heard
dirge that someone who professed much has done some unworthy
thing. We who are church members and regular worshipers must
take this to heart, for in a very real way Christ has committed his
cause and his honor into our hands. Wherever we go, we are
watched with a penetrating scrutiny. Men make decisions based on
our reactions to life, out of all proportion to the importance of
those reactions.

I can never forget a terrible story of Mr. Gandhi's early life. It is
said that when he was a rising lawyer in Bombay, hearing that native laborers in South Africa were being unjustly treated, he made
the voyage to South Africa to plead for them in the law courts, because no white lawyer would take up their case. One Sunday evening he made his way to worship in a Christian church, but was met
at the door by a white-faced but black-hearted official who said,
"This church is not open to niggers," and directed the would-be
worshiper to a native mission hall in another part of the town. I
have read that Mr. Gandhi registered a vow that he would never
attempt to enter a Christian church again, and Gandhi has a way of
keeping his vows.

But when all that has been said, the logic of the person who says,
"I will have nothing to do with the church because I know a church-
warden who ran away with somebody's wife, or a deacon who stole
the collection, or a vicar who diverted gifts for the poor to his private pocket," is strangely at fault. It is just like saying, "My doctor
is a duffer. I shall not seek health any more." If religion is what I

believe it to be, spiritual sunshine, fresh air, and abounding health, what fools we should be to miss it because there is a parson in Dartmoor who stole the collection! The logic is absurd. It is like saying, "I have finished with music because the girl next door can't play Beethoven's sonatas."

The question is: "Has Christianity power to change men's lives or has it not? and, if it has, do we want it or are we prepared to miss it and dismiss it?" I was speaking only recently with a distinguished agnostic who appeared to hold the mistaken view that the main evidence for Christianity was intellectual evidence for the truth of its theological dogmas. With his first-rate brain he realized the difficulties of accepting the story of the virgin birth. He weighed the problem of the Trinity as it appeared to a thinker. But thousands of simple people have found new life in Christ who have not the mental apparatus to appreciate the fine points of an intellectual argument. The evidence for Christianity is not intellectual; it is the lives of the saints. It is the true stories of people who have entered into an experience comparable with exchanging winter for spring, or passing from darkness into light, or from bondage into freedom.

I always wish that I could take the doubter to an Indian village untouched by the power of Christ and take him back some years later after that power has had the chance to make itself felt.

A little while ago one Hindu said to another, "I hear that funds have given out and the English missionaries may be withdrawn."

"Well," said the other, "they have accomplished one of the miracles of history. They have brought it about that the name of Jesus is honored from one end of this land to the other."

At the present time five thousand people a week are pressing into the Christian church in India, and a high authority of the London Missionary Society, Dr. Chirgwin, tells us that at the present rate all the people in India will become Christian within the next hundred and fifty years. During the last ten years the number has grown from six and a half million to nine and a half million.

I see in imagination the Indian jungle village untouched by Christ. Infant mortality is 50 per cent; illiteracy—by which I mean inability to sign one's name—is 94 per cent; girl babies are thrown into the jungle for the wolves and the jackals, because it is believed

to be a shame to have girl babies—they mark the anger of the god.
A woman prays for a child and is told to attend the temple at a certain hour in the night. She is told that the god will visit her. The
truth is, the priest rapes her. In that village men sell their children
as slaves to the landlord before those children are born. There is
tyranny, darkness, superstition, terror, cruelty, ignorance. But visit
that village again ten years later. A young girl has left England,
with all that England holds dear. Probably she holds a university
degree. She is quite content to sit in a mud room, without any of
the apparatus of the modern educational institute, and teach little
Indian children—not for education's sake, but for Christ's. That
building over there is a hospital. A brilliant youngster with his doctor's degree sacrifices all prospects of wealth and reputation and for
a mere pittance is spending the best years of his life healing Indian
natives of their many diseases—not for health's sake, but for
Christ's. Fear and tyranny and terror are banished. Love and light
and joy take their place. Has Christ power or not? Is Christianity
worth while or not? C. F. Andrews, the missionary, after obtaining
a first-class degree at Cambridge, spent scores of years in India and
died almost penniless. Why? Was he a fool? Was he mad? If that is
madness, it is more attractive than our sanity. And I could not help
pointing out to my distinguished agnostic friend that a world full
of men like C. F. Andrews would be a lovelier, happier, nobler place
to live in than a world full of agnostics.

Don't let us miss the greatest transforming power in the world because some reprobate lets religion down.

4    The last reason we can give now as to why people don't go to
church is the hardness of the Christian way.

It is sometimes said that Christianity has failed. No! Christianity
has been tried, found difficult, and thereupon given up. Of course
one of the great troubles within the churches is that a great many
people have given it up and don't know it. They offer service to
Christ. They attend many services. They listen in to innumerable
religious talks. They even engage in religious discussion. But they
are spiritually dead. Their character doesn't show that attractive-
ness, that joyous sense of power, that inner serenity which mark the

true Christian. Frankly, they don't intend to take Christ seriously. They like to stimulate their minds with the beautiful thoughts in which Christian truth is expressed. There is something about a Sunday evening service, with shaded lights and subdued music, which gives them what they call a thrill; and they falsely suppose that that frothy emotionalism is somehow healthy for them and pleasing to God. In fact, of course, it is neither, unless it has its counterpart in objective living. Few things undermine the real health of the soul more than to hear continuously words describing great experiences, or expressing mighty truths, without ever *intending* to bind one's will to carry them out; and few things can be more displeasing to God, for we are all the time coating ourselves with an armor of familiarity that blunts the sharp arrow of his word to our souls.

I cannot say, and would not say, any word which would seem to make the Christian way easy. It is easier in the long run than the way of sin, because from the latter you have to come all the weary way back, but many of us won't believe that until we have found out where sin leads us. And, to use a common phrase, some folk need a long run for their money. Until that dreadful moment of self-revelation comes, most of us who complain that we cannot find God are not really seeking him; and when we say we have not time for our prayers, we really mean that we have no taste for his company.

The Christian way is a hard way and, like everything else that is worth while, will always remain so.

But let me leave you in a different atmosphere. Put away from your mind all accretions that have gathered around Christianity, some of which have become substitutes for it and others of which destroy its truth or blunt its cutting edge. Go back to the very beginning of things. Make an imaginative picture now of the beach at Galilee. Over there are the green hills, before you the blue, blue sea. You are alone—not even with your best friend. You are not in a hurry. You are not rushing to catch a train or fulfill an engagement. You are walking thoughtfully and quietly along the edge of the water, where the fret of the tiny waves runs up the sand at your feet. Now imagine that Jesus overtakes you and slips his hand into the crook of your elbow and walks along with you. You are silent for a time. You know that he is reading your innermost thoughts, and you are not very proud of them. I think within a few minutes you would be telling him your story—how sick to the very soul you are with yourself, with the poverty of your efforts and your failure to reach your ideals. I know that is just how I should feel. And I think for a moment that you would really feel very sad, almost heart-broken. He is everything we long in our best moments to be, and yet we seem to be hopelessly beaten by failure and sin.

But I am quite sure that, in a very short space of time, a little fire of confidence would begin to burn in your heart, because he would talk to you. He believes in what you may become, whatever you are now, and however grievously you have failed. And before he had walked a mile along the beach with you, he would make you feel it too. There would be an exultant confidence within your heart saying: "I can. I *know* I can become the kind of person I want to be." And when he left you—if, indeed, you felt he ever did leave you— you would know that in another sense he was always there, the available friend who, knowing the worst, believes in the best, who lifts up the fallen to new faith in themselves, who heals the broken spirit and leads men on to fullness of life. Did he not promise this himself? "Lo, I am with you all the days until the end of the age." So, go out now with Jesus, for Jesus is with you. That is Christianity. The church exists first and foremost to offer Jesus Christ and the new life he brings to men and women like you.

# WHY PEOPLE DO GO TO CHURCH

WE HEAR A GREAT DEAL OF COMPLAINT IN THESE DAYS THAT PEOPLE
don't go to church, and in the preceding sermon I discussed some
reasons for this. Let us look now at the reasons for which people
*do* go to church.

Half a century ago it might have been true to say that many people went to church because it was the conventional thing to do. The
men put on terrible frock coats and top hats, and the ladies were
appropriately garbed—I will not attempt a fuller description of
their dress—and they would have been shocked at the very thought
of not attending church at least once on a Sunday. That is certainly
not true now. I don't suppose there are many persons today who attend church from a purely conventional motive. There may be one
or two reluctant husbands dragged by their wives, but that kind of
compulsion doesn't account for much churchgoing these days. The
truth is that those who now attend, though fewer in number, are of
more sincere motive. They are truly seeking something or Someone,
even if the goal of their quest is a little uncertain even to themselves. Let us ask ourselves why we attend, for if we are clear about
what we are seeking, we are much more likely to find it.

Here, then, are four reasons why people go to church:

1. The first—and by far the most important—is that you go to
worship God. You do not, I trust, go to hear a preacher, or to hear
lovely music, save as both do what they are meant to do, help you to
worship God. And what does worshiping God mean? It means all
that prayer means—adoration, thanksgiving, confession, petition,
intercession, meditation, dedication—and we cannot, of course, discuss them all now. But I do feel very sorry for a person who has excluded God from his life, who neither in joy nor in sorrow has any
sense of "otherness" about his life, who as he wakes up after a

113

night's refreshing sleep and finds himself healthy in body and mind has no one to thank. I pity even more a person who in the depths of sorrow has no one to offer him comfort, and still more the person who, crushed beneath a burden of sin and self-loathing, has no one to whom he can turn, no philosophy of life except a bleak humanism, no resources of strength save his own. One of my friends was driven to a belief in God by the sheer intolerableness of supposing that man was alone in the universe with no outside help whatever and with no hopes at all save those which arise from man's self-born striving.

I came across two sentences in my reading lately which express that forlorn attitude. Here is the first: "Man is a low form of cellular life on his way to the manure heap." Here is the second: "Man is fighting a lone fight against a vast indifference."

I believe that you go to church, in spite of all the alluring voices calling you elsewhere, because you believe in Someone, strong, loving, serene, and holy, who is the personification of all those qualities which you believe matter most to man. They are of priceless *worth,* and I need not remind you that the word "worship," the word "worth," and the word "worthy" all come from the same root. As you look up from your humanity to God, your spirit is already climbing up to realize that in him there are, and that in you there may be increasingly, those qualities in life which are of greatest *worth.*

It is not my intention to go into that vexed question as to whether God is so self-sufficient that he does not *need* our worship at all. I think, if I were pressed, I should say that, of his own ordaining, he has decreed that his entire perfection lacks something if it is denied human response. But I cannot, at any rate, escape the belief that God is *pleased* with our worship. Suppose that you had enough money and time to make a very lovely garden. You would set it about with trees and lawns, flower beds and shady pools, and you would welcome into it little children. It would be true to say that every flower in the garden was already yours. But if some little child whom you loved plucked a flower and brought it to you and said, "I picked this for you," would you not be pleased? You would not say, "They are all mine, anyhow." Of course they are all yours, but if you loved the child, it would give you joy to think that he picked something that was beautiful and gave it to you. You would be delighted that his little mind linked up together the beauty of something and the desirability and suitability of giving it to you. God has made a lovely spiritual garden in which are thoughts and feelings and acts, as well as the translation of his thoughts into the things we see and hear and touch. All are his already. But if you go into this garden of thinking and feeling and willing and offer him your little blossom of worship, saying, "I have brought this to you," he will not say, "I need it not." The offering will bring him joy, and, if the figure of speech may be pressed, he will wear your flower in his bosom. Said Tennyson, "Our wills are ours to make them thine." So are our thoughts and feelings and every power of our personality.

But apart from that, apart from what worship may mean to God, I am quite sure that it can mean something very important to us; and it is because of that that we do go to church. Our minds lay hold on those qualities which we believe he not only possesses but *is,* and as our minds lay hold on the thought of what he is, to some tiny extent we become like that ourselves. "As he thinketh in his heart, so is he." I suppose the psychology of it runs somewhat thus. Whenever you express an emotion, you strengthen the emotion. When, therefore, you express the emotion of admiration for those things which God is—and worship is partly such an expression— admiration for the qualities concerned is increased, and it is a commonplace to say that we tend to become what we admire. In a more profound sense than perhaps the words have sometimes meant to us, man is made in the image of God. The man who looks up to God in worship is constantly being *remade* in the image of God. The sneer has often been uttered that man makes God in his own image, and I admit the danger and comparative truth in the sneer; but in worship, as our hearts go up to him in adoration, God remakes us in his own image. To some tiny extent we become like the God we worship. Even, therefore, if a man goes to church in a bad mood, the music, the hush, the beauty of the building, the grandeur of the hymns, the majesty of God's word, and the message of the preacher may so remind him of the things of God in whose image he is made that, as it were, he will put out the hands of his spirit and draw down into himself something which his best self has always admired, and he will strengthen, not only the emotion of admiration, but the will to possess the admired quality. That, then, is our first point. People go to church to worship God.

2. People also go to church to find forgiveness. Don't be shocked if I say that nine times out of ten that doesn't make sense at all. They don't find pardon, because they don't seek it. They have such a faint sense of sin. How many people even notice the petition in the monotoned Lord's Prayer, "Forgive us our trespasses"? It is no good pretending. We just let the petition slide over us. Unless we have a real sense of sin, felt either as a personal burden or a share in the corporate guilt for the evils in the world, we find no reality in the offer of forgiveness. And the truth is that, more and more, the modern man tends to give sin a more attractive title. It is not *sin;* it is his inhibitions or complexes or perversions. It is his heredity or environment or the treatment of his nurse in infant days. It is moral disease, for which, it is said, he is no more to be blamed than for measles. It is due to evolution, the legacy of the jungle for which he cannot be held responsible. A friend wrote me recently of a girl for whose illegitimate baby he wanted me to find parents. The father was unknown. The girl wanted to be rid of the baby. But, in the writer's view, the girl hadn't sinned. She had, in his phrase, "slipped up." She had been "unlucky." It was a mere peccadillo, a youthful adventure that turned out badly. There was no thought of a little life pushed out into the world with neither father nor mother, of a holy thing made cheap and shameful—no case needing forgiveness. There was no sense of sin.

If there is not even a sense of guilt in regard to the gross sins, when will men wake up to a sense of sin in regard to the evils Jesus condemned, such as unkindness, spiritual pride, the unforgiving spirit, gossip, failure to do our duty to those who pay us to do it, the neglect of the suffering of others, and causing the weak to stumble? Forgiveness is unreal because, in the main, the sense of sin is weak, and, even where it exists, God is thought of as a sentimental indulgent father who will pat us on the back and say, "There, there, I'm sure you didn't mean it."

But sometimes there steals into the place of worship some burdened spirit, some depressed heart, some crushed soul, writhing sometimes in a torment of agony and self-loathing; and then what has been a truth of the intellect becomes what Shelley called "a truth of the emotions." A truth to which the reason assented becomes a truth that burns in the heart like a living flame. We might use the illustration of the automobile and say that the energy expressing itself in the revolving flywheel suddenly becomes geared in so that the car moves forward. Something that has always been true becomes a power to drive and to satisfy. When that happens, we are caught up into that unity with God which is one of the most amazing experiences we can know. I am not talking now to anyone who has no sense of sin at all, who is not burdened in that way—though I would in parenthesis suggest that truly to look upon the spotless purity of God would, if we let it do so, produce a deep and healthy sense of sin. I am talking to the one who feels unworthy, overburdened, sick of himself; and I am offering in the name of Christ that miracle, much more amazing to me than many of the miracles in the Gospels, by which we can be rid of the burden. It really can fall off our shoulders. We can reach that unity of God which the birds, who have never known sin, express; which the flowers, that worship in unblemished splendor, reveal; which the stars, shining in a majesty unassailed by evil, manifest—a unity deeper than they can ever know, the unity of the sons of God. We can be caught up joyously, gladly, volitionally, into that perfect harmony with God. There is no greater experience in the world than that. You may have "known" all your life that God forgives sins, and then in a time of worship "know" it in a completely different sense. I am aware that you may find this pardon outside the church, but every part of the worship of the church is there to remind you of God and of the endless offer of his forgiveness.

I remember this happening to me during the last war. I wasn't a chaplain then, but a staff officer riding from one Arab sheik to another on government business. I had not been able to attend a service for weeks. One Easter Sunday night I remember going into a crowded

Y.M.C.A. tent to a service. I cannot remember a word of the sermon or who preached it, but we sang that great hymn "Christ the Lord is risen today," and suddenly his presence became a fact. His forgiving love became real. I think I felt something of what John Wesley felt when, having *known* the fact of forgiveness for years, having preached about forgiveness, having gone as a missionary to Georgia and offered forgiveness to others, he afterward sat in a little room in Aldersgate Street and *experienced* forgiveness for himself. "I *knew*," he wrote, "that Christ had forgiven my sins, even mine, and saved me from the law of sin and death."

The rapture of this experience no one knows until he has had it. It was of this that Masefield was writing when he made Saul Kane say:

> O glory of the lighted mind,
> How dead I'd been, how dumb, how blind.
> The station brook, to my new eyes,
> Was babbling out of Paradise;
> The waters rushing from the rain
> Were singing, "Christ has risen again."
> I thought all earthly creatures knelt
> From rapture of the joy I felt.
> The narrow station wall's brick ledge,
> The wild hop withering in the hedge,
> The lights in huntsman's upper story,
> Were parts of an eternal glory,
> Were God's eternal garden flowers.
> I stood in bliss at this for hours.[1]

Our second point, then, is that people go to church to restore a broken relationship, to find the forgiveness of God, and that they should go out, whatever they may have done in the past, looking up into the face of God and saying to him, "There is nothing between us now."

3. Men go to church to find fellowship. One of the things that used to please me most about the City Temple in the days when great crowds thronged it was the fact that people would write again and again—not only our own members and regular worshipers, but

[1] "The Everlasting Mercy," *Poems*. By permission of the publisher, The Macmillan Co.

visitors—to say something like this: "As soon as I crossed the threshold I felt that I was among friends." If we church members pray more and love more, if we gossip less and find fault less, eager, not to see where others are wrong, but to see and draw out their best, if we go to church determined not only to get good for ourselves but to make it easier for others to find God and to find love and friendship, then even strangers and wayfarers will find something worth coming to seek. I am quite sure that the synagogue at Capernaum was quite different when Jesus was present. I do not mean when he was preaching or reading the Scriptures, but when he was worshiping there. If we go to church in the right spirit to pour out our hearts in prayer and intercession, to ask God to unite us with all others present and give us loving thoughts about them, then the whole service can become a unity of fellowship, so that the downhearted and unhappy, the lonely and the sad, the mentally tortured and the spiritually dead, will be caught up into fellowship and thus into the life of God.

I have been rather disturbed in my correspondence lately because so many people have talked about taking their own lives. I know that my correspondence is unusual and that I am therefore liable to get a distorted view of life, which for the great majority is probably still happy. I know that I spend most of my time with people who are ill in either body or mind or else unhappy and in some kind of distress. The war has something to do with it, not because the war can destroy the Christian faith, but because so often it proves that we have no real hold on the Christian faith, that what we thought was faith was merely assent, or else faith in something false. But, insanity and nervous illness apart, people would never talk about taking their lives if they had the security that comes from belonging to a fellowship in which one is loved. One can be desperately unhappy, worried, and restless, but a fellowship should be strong enough to hold one, however great the individual agony. I think the suicide is the person who, at the dread moment, believes that nobody cares or that nobody cares enough. The Christian church should offer a fellowship that goes down underneath that tendency toward disintegration, as though to say, "We love you, and we will hold on to you."

I believe that the very memory of what Christian fellowship can mean can become a strong factor in a man's life. A man I know had been a victim of sex temptation and had successfully resisted it over a long number of years. Only his very best friends knew what a battle this particular problem was for him. One evening he found himself on business in Berlin with time on his hands. As he strolled down the Friedrichstrasse, his attention was caught by a large framed photograph of nude women. You can guess the kind of place that was thus advertised. He was greatly tempted to go in. No one would have known. His character would not have been damaged in the eyes of his friends. His respectability would have been unsoiled at home. Then suddenly, with great resolution, he walked away. A hundred yards from the place he had an immense sense of relief and spiritual power. When asked how he had found strength to make that great decision, he answered without hesitation, "My church at home." Even the memory of the fellowship, even the thought that he belonged to a company of people who loved him and who, with him, were seeking together the high and the lovely and the true and the beautiful things, strengthened him in the hour of temptation.

But the fellowship of the church involves not merely "my church at home." It is a fellowship that goes right across the world into all lands, where men are worshiping in jungle villages, in desert towns, in ice-bound solitudes, in tropical forests. It is a fellowship that goes back throughout all the centuries, a line of witnesses in an unbroken chain, so that as we imagine it we note that the last man in the chain has his hand in the hand of Christ in a little upper room at Jerusalem. It is a fellowship indeed that goes not only across the world and back through the centuries but up into the unseen. "Therefore with angels and archangels, and with all the company of heaven, we laud and magnify thy glorious name, evermore praising thee, and saying: Holy, Holy, Holy."

Our third point, then, is that men come to church to find fellowship.

4. Lastly, people come to church to find power—spiritual power for this difficult task of living. Here again I suppose the psychology of it is this: power is released in the will through the emotions

whenever the mind takes hold on truth. I would ask you to ponder that statement. Whenever the mind is really possessed by truth to such an extent that we *feel* it to be true as well as give it our intellectual assent, then power is released in the will. The will alone is not enough. The feeling alone is not enough. One might risk the illustration that feeling is to the will what gasoline is to the machinery of an automobile.

It is all very well for people to tell us that everything depends on will power. I was reminded, by a sermon of Dr. Fosdick, of the following hymn:

> Awake, my soul, stretch every nerve,
>     And press with vigor on;
> A heavenly race demands thy zeal,
>     And an immortal crown.

Philip Doddridge wrote five hundred hymns, including "O God of Bethel," but "Awake, My Soul" is not one of his best. Certainly when he wrote it he was not in any deep trouble. I can imagine very few situations in which I should wish it to be my message. The people I talk to are not much interested in an immortal crown. They are wondering whether they can get through today and tomorrow without defeat, and I for one would not dare to say to anyone, "Stretch every nerve." The people I deal with have their nerves stretched to the breaking point.

I know a young woman who wanted very badly to be a surgeon. She took the long and arduous medical course necessary, passed with distinction in surgery, and was ready to set out on that grand career. But in a bomb explosion glass was flung in her face, and for a long time it seemed as though all hope of her ever being able to see had gone. She has had thirty-five operations, and there is left to her only the glimmer of sight in one eye. Shall I say to her, "Stretch every nerve, and press with vigor on"?

In a family of my acquaintance there are two daughters, one fifteen and one twenty. The girl of fifteen is what a girl should be at that age, healthy, happy, full of life. But what shall I say about a lovely girl of twenty, at the very threshold of life, whose brain has been infected by germs which have destroyed her controls so that she cannot be left day or night? I have consulted a specialist on her behalf, and his opinion is that there is no hope whatever. Twice she has tried to take her own life, and there always exists the danger of her attacking others. The sentence of the most eminent medical opinion is that she must remain in a mental hospital for the rest of her life. That may be fifty years. Yet for periods she is entirely sane and pleads to be taken home. Shall I say to her and to her stricken family, "Stretch every nerve, and press with vigor on"?

I will not harrow your feelings by talking thus. If you and I were meeting in a little room, you would say to me, "Yes, I know a case where . . . ," and I would only have to open my own diary at any week in the year to tell you of case after case of deep human need, so deep that no human resourcefulness is an adequate reply. All last winter, when the horror of bombing went on night after night, I found it almost unbearable to listen to some new story each day. There are many people to whom I minister who have lost their boys, lost their home, lost their business, lost everything except their faith. I would not like to ask them to say to themselves:

> Awake, my soul, stretch every nerve,
> And press with vigor on.

I would not presume to offer them the petty shallowness of any word of human wisdom, the pagan triviality of being told to endure, the irritating irrelevance that others suffer similarly, the heartless torture which falsely teaches that all suffering is punishment for sin.

But I think I know why such people go to church. Those people go to church because the only comfort for them is God—not God explaining himself in arguments, for no explanation I have ever met satisfies the need of the mind, let alone the hunger of the heart; not God remote and far away; but God coming down into human life and into human suffering; God who is himself crucified and who still remains serene, calm, loving. That God, who doesn't try to answer our questions, answers our need; and I believe in a God who brings his children through their dread sufferings with finally nothing lost, but with something gained which is of immortal worth.

Since I have criticized one hymn, let me offer you another:

> See, from his head, his hands, his feet,
> Sorrow and love flow mingled down:
> Did e'er such love and sorrow meet,
> Or thorns compose so rich a crown?

Those who go to church and find the real God answer for themselves the question with which we started, "Why do men go to church?" They go to worship; they go to find pardon; they go to enter a fellowship; they go to get power. No! No! We need not divide it thus. They go to find all their deepest longings satisfied when they find God himself. He is the goal toward which our spirits move. He is the reality behind all men's dreams. He is the answer to all our prayers. Jesus, who was the supreme Master of the art of living, could not live without God. Can you?

# WHY SHOULD I READ THE BIBLE?

Let us begin by being perfectly frank with one another about the Bible. We really should like to find in it those treasures which other people are alleged to find there. We should feel it a serious affront if anything cut us off from the reading of the Bible. We have learned that it is still the best seller of all the published books the world knows. Pious people, again and again, have told us to read the Bible and say our prayers. Probably if we were going away for more than a few days we should put a Bible in our luggage. We might leave it on the bedside table when we unpacked, and there it might remain to impress the lady who made our bed. During a holiday, it probably lies unopened, but it is at least something that we take with us. It was not difficult to persuade people to give a considerable sum of money so that Bibles might be sent to the troops at the front. I was once in a party of people who were discussing what books they would take with them if they had to live on a desert island for two years. A number of volumes were discussed, and then one young person, with a candor and honesty which made us laugh, said, "Well, I suppose one of the books would have to be the Bible, wouldn't it?" I recall a friend of mine saying to me, "I do read the Bible every night in bed, but I must confess that I am glad to put it down and pick up a novel."

All this shows that we feel somehow that the Bible is important, and yet we cannot be said to relish the reading of it. Let us face some of the difficulties.

1. The Bible has been spoiled for a great many people because it has been made part of a subject which had to be "got up" for examination purposes. Many of us have had to remember the order of the kings of Israel. We have bullied our minds to recall all the places at which Paul stopped in his missionary journeys, and we have cherished the secret wish that his missionary ardor had not led

him so far from home. For thousands of people a love of Shakespeare has been killed by making Shakespeare a subject to be "crammed" at school. I fear that the same is true about the Bible. Modern methods in Sunday schools seem to me to make the teaching of religion the thrilling thing it ought to be, but in olden days the Sunday-school lesson was not a very inspiring half hour. I remember vividly one of my own Sunday-school teachers who used to make us read around the lesson verse by verse, and then *he* turned with relief, and I can assure you we did also, to the thrilling subject of how to make an electric battery. Thus, except for the scripture reading, the time of the Sunday-school lesson passed pleasantly away!

2. When we were exhorted to read the Bible because it was supposed to do us good spiritually, we found in adolescence that the Bible was rather like those puddings which are served in boarding schools. They are called "plum puddings," but the plums are often so far apart that one used to wonder how far away from the pudding the cook stood when she threw the plums in. We read chapter after chapter of dull matter, and then come to some very fine plums, full of beauty and value and meaning; but countless thousands who have made a great resolution to read the Bible through and have started valiantly with the book of Genesis have found their enthusiasm failing before they got to the middle of Exodus, and they generally perished in the barren desert of Leviticus.

Without doubt the Bible is uninteresting compared with the kind of thing which a great many people are constantly reading in these days. We must at least remember that we are spoiled in this matter. There was a time when people crowded into the churches to get near the Bible—the time when first it was opened up to ordinary people—but in these days of exciting films, thrilling detective stories, and "Penguins," it should be admitted straight away that the reading of the Bible will demand discipline. But, after all, is there anything in life really worth while which does not need a measure of self-discipline? No one plays a violin, or learns a language, or is familiar with the names of flowers and birds without some kind of disciplined reading. Are we willing to impose upon ourselves the discipline of giving half an hour a day to the reading of the Bible?

3. Another difficulty about the Bible is that it is unattractive. As a rule it is unattractively printed in two parallel columns. But this is not its only unattractiveness. It is made unattractive by being flourished by unattractive people. I hope that that is not unkind, but it is as well to be truthful and honest and face facts. Suppose you found that you had to share a room with another man or girl and that you were to live together for a number of months. If your bedroom mate unpacked from his luggage and sat down to read a novel, you would not be at all surprised; but if he took out a Bible and began to read it, I think you would say to yourself, "Good heavens, I wonder what sort of a fellow I have to live with now!" I suppose somewhere in the corridors of the mind there still lurks the ghostly memory of the old, pious humbug who always walked about with a Bible under his arm. Yet let me put over against all that a quotation from a letter received from a member of the City Temple, a young lady whom no one could charge with being dull, conventional, or stodgy. Here it is. She says: "I am quite excited about one thing. I have been given a Moffatt and the Scripture Notes on the Daily Portions, and it is so helpful, and I am finding it really something to look forward to every day."

4. A further difficulty which most of us have felt at some time or other is that so much of the Bible is irrelevant to life as we live it now. A great many parts of the Old Testament seem remote indeed. During my last summer holidays I was present at a little village church in the heart of a Kentish valley, at which the vicar spent an extraordinary time in reading what I suppose was the lesson for the day, a long chapter from the book of Kings. I looked round at the simple village people worshiping with me, and wondered whether they could make any sense of it at all. It seemed to me to have nothing on earth to do with the kind of life that one is called upon to live in these days. Frequently the Old Testament lessons take us immediately from our modern, scientific world into one which is entirely strange. From this world of science we are transported into a world where axes float, where the sun stands still, where bushes burn and remain unconsumed, where a person is carried to heaven in a chariot of fire, where food drops out of the sky for hungry people. No doubt the scholars would be able to give us rationalizations

of these things, and make sense of these happenings; but we live in a world where we have to pay for all our things, where we see few exciting manifestations of the power and presence of God, and where the sky is much more likely to drop bombs than manna on hungry women and children.

5. Then there is the real difficulty that so much of the Bible is frankly quite unsuitable to be read in a modern place of worship. For instance, in Joshua 8:26 I read: "Joshua drew not his hand back, wherewith he stretched out the spear, until he had utterly destroyed all the inhabitants of Ai." And in I Samuel 15:3 I read that Saul was invited to "go and smite Amalek, and utterly destroy all that they have, and spare them not; but slay both man and woman, infant and suckling, ox and sheep, camel and ass." The story goes on to say that Saul sinned by failing to carry out the order of Heaven, and God rejected him from a kingship as a consequence. I am not making a plea that such matter should be struck out of our Bible, because it is interesting to note the development of thought; but to me it seems something approaching blasphemy to read it in public worship, at which men seek help for the daily task of living. One somehow wishes that the parson reading it would preface it by saying something like this: "Please don't take any notice of what I am about to read, except to note how far the spirit of Jesus Christ supersedes the bloody massacres of the Old Testament, which people thought God liked before they understood him and saw him in Jesus." Some of the Psalms touch a peak of devotional purity which makes them the fit expression of human aspiration for all time; but, quite frankly, some of the Psalms sound like a complete antithesis of Christian teaching, for example, Psalm 137:8-9.

6. A final difficulty which most of us have found is that which scholarship itself provides. I welcome the light which modern scholarship sheds on the Bible with all my heart, but I cannot conceal from myself that the ordinary layman who is asked to read the Bible may feel something like this: "I don't know how to find my way in the Bible these days. I am told that this may not be an authentic part of the book, that this has been added by a scribe, that, although the English version says this, the original version means something altogether different, that probably this person never said the words

attributed to him. I have not the time or scholarship to enter into these problems. Scholars themselves have disputes about the meaning of some of the most important passages in the Bible; so I simply give the matter up."

Now what are we to say to all these difficulties? I want to say two things. First, the Bible is the word of God—and one must go on immediately to say what this means. To me it means supremely that *God matters*. Let us remember always that the Bible is not a single book; it is a library of books. The writers number over a hundred. They were men of different outlook, education, and temperament, and the period covered by their writings is well over a thousand years. No intelligent theory of inspiration teaches that God spoke through them as though they were machines, overwhelming their own personality. So we find incorporated their prejudices, their beliefs, their background of cosmology and astronomy and philosophy. We find in the Bible history, legend, drama, poetry, prophecy, story, parable, mystic vision—almost every kind of literature there is in the world.

Even so, we must not imagine that there would be any close parallel between this and putting together the writings of Blake, Shakespeare, Trevelyan, Bunyan, Shelley, J. R. Green, Oliver Wendell Holmes, and D. H. Lawrence. For throughout the Bible runs a golden thread, as a thread runs through a necklace, making all the separate beads into a unity; and I would call that thread "God matters." The biblical historian is less concerned with accuracy in our sense than to show God at work. The mystic vision has not art for its end, but the glory of God. The parables and the poems are not offered as works of creative genius, but to show something of the truth of the nature of God.

Let us just take one of the forms of literature used—the poem. It seems to me that Shelley would have been almost offended if one had asked him whether he wrote a poem with any moral purpose. He was simply enshrining the beauty which he had seen in his own soul. If I remember rightly, in one of his essays Shelley protests that moral purpose would ruin poetry. Yet when you read Psalm 139, which is one of my favorites, you find that the art of the poet is subordinated to one tremendous theme. He is attempting to "get over," as we say, the fact of the presence of God. It is alleged that someone said: "I don't know why anybody writes poetry, for everything he wants to say could equally well be said in prose." But it cannot be said in prose in a way that gets over to the reader. I might say to you coldly, "God is everywhere," and I might offer arguments for that view, but listen to this:

> If I ascend up into heaven, thou art there:
> If I make my bed in hell, behold, thou art there.
> If I take the wings of the morning,
> And dwell in the uttermost parts of the sea;
> Even there shall thy hand lead me,
> And thy right hand shall hold me.

On the wings of beauty you are transported into the very fact of the presence, and feel it, as what Shelley himself called "a truth of the emotions." If I could so present the nature of God that you could *feel* how great God is, I should do you a much greater service than if I argued you into a belief about the greatness of God. The poet in the Bible is trying to say: God matters; God is like this; God is like that; and nothing else matters but God and your relation to him. It could be said in prose, but you would not receive it.

All this is true, not only of poetry, but of history and legend. The Bible begins with a beautiful legend about the beginning of things. The whole legend is summarized in the first four words, "In the beginning God . . ." In that lovely legend of the Creation the editor of Genesis is not trying to write a book of science. If he is still in heaven and takes interest about the things of earth, he must often have laughed at the wrangles of our great-grandfathers as to whether every word was literally and scientifically true. He wasn't interested in science. The word meant nothing to him. He was writing that lovely parable to say that every beautiful thing we find on earth comes to us from God.

Even when we read the strange history in the Old Testament, with its tale of dreadful slaughter, yet the spirit of the Bible, if I may use the phrase, is saying to us: "I know you feel that this is crude and gruesome; but, after all, you are being shown that men thought that God was working out a plan, even through their bloody battles. They followed the light they had. They responded to those meanings of God which they could see, and you would be a lot better today if you did the same. You can't say very much about the bloodshed of the Old Testament on the part of men who had never heard of Jesus, for your world is drenched with blood, although you have learned his name. If you lived up to the light you have, as they did, you could make a world more after God's own plan. You can't throw stones at the blood-stained warriors of the Old Testament. They were working out God's plan as far as they could understand it. You understand it so much better that you scoff at them, but you are not working it out."

The second answer that I should like to make to the difficulties we admitted a few moments ago is that God is mediated to men in the Bible. When we read the Bible we say to ourselves: "This concerns me." Let us agree that this is not so convincing in certain parts of the Old Testament, and yet if we took the proper point of view, we could find the spirit of God speaking to us almost in every part. For instance, to turn once again to Psalm 139, when we read the challenging words, "Search me, O God, and know my heart; try me, and know my thoughts," I should think not one reader in a hundred is thinking that this is a psalm of David. Indeed, he finds that it doesn't matter to him whether David wrote it or not. The "me" in the first sentence is not David. *It becomes the reader.* A great deal depends, of course, on how we read the Bible, but I would conclude by saying this: It is a lovely starlit night. I am going to imagine that I have a fine telescope and that I invite you to come with me, so that, looking through the telescope, we may view the stars. I should be very surprised and disappointed if, instead of looking through the telescope at the amazing miracle of the night sky, you criticized the telescope, and told me that its brass wanted cleaning, and its bearings wanted oiling, and that it was almost unfit for use. The use of a telescope is that you should look through it, not at it. You may need a little help in focusing and manipulating the telescope, but he who looks too closely *at* it wastes his time.

I like to think that the same thing is true about the Bible. Its supreme value is that you should look through it to the nature of God. If you look too closely *at* it you will miss its message. After all, what more powerful and convincing answer can be given to the question, "Why should I read the Bible?" than that Jesus himself is offered to us in it. If you look through it and see him, you won't ask the question, "Why should I read the Bible?" any more. You will become part of the answer to the question yourself.

> Teach me to love thy sacred word
> And view my Saviour there.

# HOW SHOULD I READ THE BIBLE?

THESE WORDS ARE ADDRESSED TO THOSE WHO WANT TO MAKE A BEGIN-
ning, or a new beginning, in Bible reading. Concerning most books,
quite a good place to begin is at the beginning! But in the case of
the Bible it is the worst place to begin. I think you will agree with
me that we must begin with Jesus. All that was written before him
was preparation. All that was written after him is comment. Therefore begin with the earliest book in the Bible about Jesus, and that
is the Gospel according to Mark. I have always held that it is best to
begin with Mark's Gospel, and I am pleased to notice that in the
excellent book by E. R. Micklem, *A Book on the Bible for Every-
man,* the advice given is the same.

I regard Mark's Gospel as the loveliest and most precious docu-
ment in the world. The real Gospel, of course, is from the first verse
of the first chapter to the eighth verse of the sixteenth chapter. You
may draw a line after the eighth verse of the last chapter, for the
rest has been added by another hand. Probably Mark's Gospel was
in the form of a roll which was passed round from church to church,
and from reader to reader. It was very popular, and the end of it
became tattered and worn and finally lost. No one knows how
Mark's Gospel originally ended.

Before you begin to read, try to have a little picture in your mind
of the person who wrote it and roughly the conditions under which
he wrote. John Mark was probably only a boy of seventeen or eighteen when he became the friend of Peter. We may imagine that Peter
was his hero, and both of them, of course, were great lovers of our
Lord. Probably Mark's Gospel was practically dictated by Peter.
Mark was the boy who followed Jesus into the Garden of Gethsemane from the house at which the Last Supper was celebrated. The
supper room was probably in Mark's father's house, and I always
imagine it to have been built on the flat roof. Mark I imagine to

132

have been resting on the flat roof just outside the door of the upper room, so that he might be ready to warn the disciples and their Master of any danger—the secrecy with which the supper was arranged shows how great the danger was. The disciples were to come in separately, and they were guided to the house by a friend of Jesus, a man carrying a water jar.[1] Mark was also there in case the guests wanted anything. He did not intrude upon their privacy, but he was there to serve them if he was needed.

When Jesus and his followers went out about eleven-thirty to walk through the silent streets of Jerusalem into the Garden of Gethsemane, Mark saw a look on Jesus' face which made him want to follow; and since the Garden of Gethsemane was probably Mark's father's olive orchard, there was no difficulty about Mark's going with them. Indeed, the disciples seem to have gone to sleep, and it is probably to Mark that we owe the record we have of the agony in the garden, which Mark's eyes were the only human eyes to see, and Mark's ears the only human ears to hear. Mark was probably the young man in the tomb on the resurrection morning. The First Gospel seems to show a decided preference for angels, but Mark speaks of a young man, and there is a good deal of evidence to suggest that he was the young man who greeted the women on the first Easter with the triumphant words: "He is not here. He is risen."

Mark was probably greatly loved by the early Christians. We see this in the tradition that he was called the "stump-fingered." It is supposed that in the scuffle in the Garden of Gethsemane Mark either put out his hand in protest against Peter's flashing blade, or somehow got injured in the melee, for he is called "Mark, the stump-fingered." He was almost certainly the young man in the linen cloth who fled away naked (Mark 14:51).

We note that Mark has an eye for detail. We note that he tends to emphasize the human nature of our Lord. We note that he does not soften things down for the credit of the parties concerned. In these trying and difficult days it is interesting to recall that Mark almost certainly wrote this Gospel in Rome, shortly after one of the

[1] Women, of course, usually carried the water. The cleverness of the device is seen in that a man would be noteworthy if he carried a water jar and yet not so conspicuous as to cause comment, since a man living alone might be seen fetching water.

most awful times through which the church passed, the persecution by Nero. This quiet Gospel was written at the time when women had been thrown to the lions, men dressed in skins soaked in oil and set alight to illumine Nero's gardens. It was written at a time when Nero had done everything he could to persecute the church. Nero had tried, you will remember, to fix the blame for the great fire which broke out in Rome on the Christians; and it is possible that during the very time that Mark was writing out his Gospel, his hero, Peter, was put to death. I have sometimes wondered, though it is only a fancy, whether Peter did not charge Mark with the task of writing down the facts about our Lord's life. The Gospel was written down between A.D. 65 and 70. Jesus died in 29, and the time gap is probably due to the fact that the early church thought that the end of the world was at hand, and the return of Jesus imminent. As this great consummation seemed to be delayed and delayed, a generation of Christians was growing up that did not know at first hand the facts about our Lord's life and death. One imagines that Peter said to Mark: "Don't bother to write my life. That is very unimportant. But do write down all the facts I have told you about Jesus, for those who are growing up did not know him as I did."

I should like to suggest three ways of reading in answer to our question, "How should I read the Bible?" (1) Read uncritically. (2) Read imaginatively. (3) Read devotionally. Let us look at these a little more carefully.

1. Read uncritically. A young friend of mine, a medical student, told me how much it had meant to him to take the Gospel of Mark and read it through in order to get a sense of the whole picture which the book presents. That is exactly the kind of uncritical reading that I wish to suggest we should do. I am not, of course, trying to put you off from any critical inquiry you may care to make; but if you allow your mind to stick, say, at the miracles, or at some interpretation of a difficult passage, you will not get the message of the book in the way I want you to get it from a first reading. In a sentence, you will not see the forest for the trees.

I know very little about art, but I am quite sure that at the first sight of a picture one should not go very close to it and concentrate on some detail; one should stand away from it and let the picture as a whole make its impression upon one's mind. So I suggest we should read Mark's Gospel right through, if possible at a sitting, glossing over the difficulties, just letting some things remain *sub judice*. Say to yourself concerning them, "I will come back and examine them later," but first of all read uncritically, so that you see, not details, but a Person at work in a human setting, dealing with men and women like ourselves.

After all, just because the Gospels are human documents, we may expect that in details there will be matters which we shall never be asked to take as evidence of divine inspiration. Remember that Mark himself was trying to remember what Peter told him. Peter was trying to remember what Jesus said and did. Now Jesus spoke in Aramaic, Mark wrote down his Gospel in Greek, and for us the Greek has had to be translated into English; so we shall not expect to have the kind of accuracy which a shorthand transcription would give us. No doubt in Mark's Gospel we are very close to what Jesus said, and anyone clever enough to make up what Jesus said would have to be another Jesus. At the same time, when you come to study the difficulties of detail, you must make allowance for the human factor. All the Gospel writers have their peculiar prejudices. For instance, the First Gospel seeks to see very many things in terms of the fulfillment of prophecies which really do not bear that interpretation at all. When Jesus is carried back from Egypt by his parents as a tiny little child, Matthew says, "Thus it was fulfilled that was spoken by the prophet, 'Out of Egypt have I called my son' "; but when those words were originally spoken they had nothing to do with an infant Messiah returning from the south. In a similar way, in relation to the woman with the hemorrhage, one of the Gospel writers says that she tried many doctors and, instead of getting better, spent all her money and only grew worse. But Luke was a physician; so we find that he is not going to be a party to such a slur on the profession, and he conveniently leaves that out!

In your first reading don't let questions or criticism crop up in your mind. Just try to let the whole picture of Jesus which Mark gives us make its own impression upon your mind. That is of tremendous importance, because afterward you will judge all your

Bible reading by your picture of Jesus. You will not, if you are wise, judge Jesus by the Bible; you will judge the Bible by Jesus; and so it is all-important to have your central picture of Jesus clear in your mind. As Mr. Micklem says: "If we are perfectly sure of Jesus, we can be content to be uncertain about a lot of other matters."

2. Then I want to suggest that we read imaginatively. There is a great word of John Ruskin which runs: Let us when we read the Bible try "to be present, as if in the body, at each recorded event in the life of the Redeemer."

When I say, "Read imaginatively," I mean: Imagine that you are there watching. Use any travel you have been able to have, or any reading you have been able to do, to make a vivid picture of the setting of the incidents about which you read in Mark's Gospel. See Jesus, not as a stained-glass figure, unreal and remote, but a sun-tanned, healthy man, standing there on the pebbles of the beach of Galilee, with the blue waves breaking on the shore and the green hills behind him and the lovely azure sky above his head, dressed, I suppose, in a blue robe, with dark, long hair, with flashing eyes and kindly face, the kind of person to whom little children would run. See him standing there, with his fearless eyes, his strong, attractive, serene personality, and then read the story as if you too had crept up behind the crowd, and were peering over someone's shoulder and listening to his voice. Don't be afraid of the humor of the Gospel story. Again and again Jesus made the people laugh, as when he told the story of a Pharisee drinking soup and straining out a gnat and then swallowing a camel, or of a man lighting his lamp and putting it under the bed, and so on. Try, if you will, to pretend that you have never read the story before, and let it make its own impression upon your imagination. Then you will find that Jesus presents you not with arguments but with pictures. I am sure it is legitimate to read imaginatively, for Jesus almost always spoke in pictures which demanded the use of the imagination.

A certain lawyer comes to him and asks the question, "Who is my neighbor?" Jesus gives no definition of what a neighbor is, let alone a definition in legal language, but at the end of the interview the person who asked the question knows what a neighbor is, and he

gets it from a picture story. A certain man went down from Jerusalem to Jericho. It is the most dangerous road in Palestine. You
can still get held up on that road. He fell among thieves. . . . The
story unwinds itself. A certain Samaritan . . . So you see, when
Jesus was asked the question, "Who is my neighbor?" his answer
was the story about a foreigner, and, moreover, the most despised
foreigner of all, a Samaritan, a word a Jew would not use.

3. My third point is that you should read devotionally. You are
not asking for information. You are trying to meet a Person, who
wants to meet you. There are all sorts of way in which Jesus can
come through to us, but I think this is one of the most wonderful.
If you read, for instance, in Luke's Gospel the story of Zacchaeus,
you will find at the end, if you have read uncritically, imaginatively, and devotionally, that you have not been reading so much a
story about Jesus and Zacchaeus; you have been reading a story
about Jesus and you. Here is this little man, despised, with a dreadful inferiority complex, such as little people often seem to have.
This little man is hated by all kinds of people. He is a taxgatherer.
He takes money from his own countrymen and passes some of it to
Rome. He is despised and possibly despicable. Then he hears about
Jesus. He stands on the edge of the crowd. He cannot see through
them and cannot push through them. You know what crowds are
like. You know how people hate you if you try to push through a
crowd. Try now to feel their hatred for this little renegade.

So Zacchaeus goes into a garden behind the crowd and climbs up
into a sycamore tree. How the little Jewish boys must have laughed
at him! What an undignified and ungainly business it must have
been! Then Jesus comes down the road with his disciples. Here is
the only rabbi in all Palestine who does not despise taxgatherers.
He looks up, stops, calls to Zacchaeus. You can almost imagine Zacchaeus, with his heart beating more quickly, shrinking back among
the leaves; and then the most lovely voice in the world says, "Zacchaeus, I am going to have dinner with you." They walk away together, and the lovely story proceeds. Jesus makes no criticism of
Zacchaeus. It is Zacchaeus who says, "I must do something about
the extortionate demands I have made in the past."

But if you are reading in the proper way, you are in the crowd too; and, having read, you put down your New Testament, and you begin to meditate. Here is a person whom the rest of the world, inasfar as it knew him, hated and despised, but Jesus loved him and believed in him and won him. It may occur to you that there is no one in the world whom Jesus would scorn, or for whom he would show contempt. He would have dinner with Hitler. Jesus must hate the atrocities of the Nazis more than we hate them, but has it ever occurred to us that Jesus loves the Nazis as much as he loves us, because he loves all sinners even while he hates their sins. Then as we meditate on our scripture reading, it begins to dawn on us that if we are nursing resentment against another person, however despicable his conduct may have been, we have really never seen Jesus. If I may put it this way, we have never seen Jesus with Zacchaeus. If we think God loves an Englishman better than a Nazi, we have never seen Jesus with Zacchaeus. We may have read the story again and again and again, but we have never read the Bible in the proper way. For this is not merely a historic story of Jesus and Zacchaeus; this is the word of God to all men for all time.

Further, my friend, if you hate yourself and despise yourself and think that you are of no use to anybody and that nobody loves you, go read the story of Zacchaeus again, and you will hear Jesus say to you, "I want to come and live with you," and you will perhaps be wise enough to open your heart to him. For he loves you when you hate yourself. He forgives you when you can't forgive yourself. He believes in you when you no longer believe in yourself and don't know anybody that does believe in you. You will catch hold of self-respect again. You will hold your head up—as indeed you well may —because Jesus loves you and cares for you, and his touch upon your life can heal you and bring you back to healthy ways of living, new ways of loving, definite ways of serving. You can become the kind of man he means you to be, because, however despised or despicable you may be, Jesus' hand is on your shoulder, and he is saying to you, "I am coming to live in your house."

So we might take story after story in the New Testament. For myself, I love the story of old Nicodemus going to Jesus by night.

Here is a chance for you to let your imagination paint a picture—the moonlight, the old man stumbling along. He does not think that Jesus can tell him much, but if there is any more to be learned, he is willing to learn. A fine type of old religious teacher. I imagine those two sitting in an upper room at the house where Jesus was staying in Jerusalem. I imagine the evening breeze rustling the vine leaves on the trellis that is fixed up outside the house. I imagine Jesus telling Nicodemus that, for all his learning, he has got to start all over again, like a little child, and begin at the beginning. Then I think, as the evening breeze sweeps past the house, Jesus flings open the window and says, "The wind bloweth where it listeth, and thou hearest the sound thereof, but canst not tell whence it cometh, and whither it goeth: so"—as he flings the window open—"is everyone that is born of the Spirit."

Why, if you are reading uncritically, imaginatively, devotionally, you find yourself saying: "My word! I must open a few more windows in my life. I find that knowing the facts about religion is nothing to do with it. I have to experience the breath of the Spirit in my heart, and I have been keeping a great many windows closed. My business life could do with the fresh air of the Spirit blowing through it. I find that I am a good Christian everywhere except in my home, and that's no sort of good at all. I find that I have never let God in on my prejudices. I have never let the Holy Spirit of God blow away my hatreds and resentments. I find I've never let God in on my sex life." And so as you read the story of Nicodemus you will find that he fades into the background, and *you*, in some quiet, imaginative upper room, are sitting there talking to Jesus yourself, and Jesus is looking at you with eyes full of love, and he is telling *you* just where *you* must begin all over again. If you are a wise man, you will finish that hour of Bible reading on your knees, and you will be saying, "O God, show me how to open all the windows of my being, that thy healthful Spirit of love may sweep into my stuffy heart."

Who said that reading the Bible was dull and uninteresting and unattractive and irrelevant and unsuitable? We can be changed men and women if we will only read the Gospels uncritically, imaginatively, and devotionally.

Let me conclude with a true story. A little boy said to his father, having worried for long in secret about this question: "Father, has anybody ever seen God?" His father answered in a way so curt that the laddie could ask no further questions. As it happened, the minister was coming to tea that day, and the little boy thought to himself, "Well, he ought to know. I'll ask him." So, very shyly, when he found himself alone with the minister for a few moments, he tugged the latter's sleeve and said, "Has anybody ever seen God? How can you see God?" In a very pompous voice the minister said, "No one can see God and live." Poor little chap! He slunk away and went out into the garden and cried a little out of sheer disappointment.

The boy used to go fishing with an old man. One day his father said to him, "Who is this fellow you go fishing with? Is he all right?" The little boy said, "I think he is all right, Daddy. The other evening when we came back down the river I noticed that as he looked at the sunset his eyes filled with tears." His father made no comment, but at any rate no criticism.

One evening, as the old man and the boy were returning from a fishing expedition, the sunset was even more glorious than ever. They drifted slowly down the river, both completely silent.

At last the little chap nudged the old man and said shyly, "I never meant to ask anybody else this question, but I want to ask you: Can you see God?" The old man turned to the boy a face shining with joy, his eyes full of tears. After a pause, he said, "Laddie, sometimes I thinks as I never sees anything else."

If you have been exhorted to read the Bible and have either never made a beginning or else given it up, may I suggest that you go back to Mark's Gospel, read it uncritically, imaginatively, and devotionally. The boy in the story I have just told saw God through the eyes of a fisherman with whom he spent much time. That is what happened in Mark's case. He was just a boy. He spent much time with one whom he greatly admired, who was a fisherman called Peter. He listened to the stories Peter told. He watched Peter's face. He saw God. Mark has a message for you. There will come a moment, sooner or later, when you will see God, the God that Jesus revealed, and that will be the most wonderful moment of your life.

# THE SECRET MINISTRIES OF GOD

The Lord will perfect that which concerneth me.                    —Ps. 138:8

He which hath begun a good work in you will perform it until the day of Jesus Christ.                                                    —Phil. 1:6

So is the kingdom of God, as if a man should cast seed into the earth; and should sleep and rise night and day, and the seed should spring and grow up, *he knoweth not how.*                          —Mark 4:26

ONE OF THE GREATEST FACTS ABOUT THE GRACE OF GOD IN DEALING with our souls is commonly overlooked. We stress, and rightly, the necessity on man's part of opening his life to God, of "accepting Christ as his Saviour," of spiritual discipline, of daily readjustment. We stress, on the other hand, God's endless grace through the Sacrament, the worship of his house, the response of God to our private prayers, the reading of the Bible, and, above all, the power that comes to human lives through the loving companionship of Jesus Christ.

But beyond all this there is an agency at work, silently and secretly, when once the spirit of man has been opened to God, and indeed often when no conscious response has taken place, which seems to me to be the spiritual counterpart of the *vis medicatrix naturae* of the body and the mind, the healing force of nature, the secret, integrating work of God to make the human organism perfect and complete.

A man who is cured through a doctor by means of a treatment or a surgical operation will commonly say that he was cured *by* Dr. X. It is a convenient way of speaking, but it is wholly untrue, and most doctors—all sensible ones!—would agree. All doctors would do well to take to heart a pregnant sentence of the most distinguished physician of antiquity after Hippocrates, the famous Galen, the devout Greek doctor who practiced in Rome about A.D. 164: "I bound his wounds, but God healed him." No one has ever healed another. Where would any healer be without the secret force by which severed tissue is united, disease overcome, and by which the body and mind move toward the restoration of health?

The passage from the psalm before us is a plea that God will "perfect" or—a better translation—"complete" the work begun in the psalmist's soul, that the Divine Artist will not "forsake" or—again a better translation—"discard" the work of his own hands that he has begun.

The psalmist, could he have heard it, would have been greatly comforted by Paul's unequivocal assurance to the Philippians, that "he which hath begun a good work in you will perform it until the day of Jesus Christ."

A charming story is told of the painter and sculptor Sir Hubert von Herkomer, who founded the Herkomer school of painting at Bushey in 1883. His aged father, who had brought his son at the age of eight from their Bavarian home, was persuaded to spend the last years of his life with his distinguished son. The father, also a sculptor, asked for clay that he might while away the evenings in modeling. But, what with age and enfeeblement and failing sight, the old man would put aside his work at night almost in despair. He could not make it what he wanted to make it. The actuality was so distressingly far below the vision that the old man would go to bed quite sad. But after the father had gone to bed, his son would go and work secretly at the clay. In the morning the father would look at his work of the previous evening and, never knowing that another hand had touched it, would exclaim with delight: "Why, it isn't as bad as I thought!" "The Lord will perfect that which concerneth me." "I shall be satisfied, when I awake, with thy likeness." We can say these comforting things to ourselves, for God has secret ministries which carry on the work on our own nature which we would fain do but cannot.

1. Here is one of God's secret ministries, which, like the loving toil of Herkomer, operates during the night when we are fast asleep. It is grand to see in a law of psychology a secret ministry

of God. This law states that the dominant idea of the mind before sleep ensues goes on working, like yeast in dough, through the depth of the unconscious mind when consciousness has closed down for the night.

How tremendously important, then, is it to determine what our last thoughts at night are! What wise, if unconscious, psychologists were our parents and grandparents, who told us to say our prayers the last thing at night! How sound was the intuition which led Paul to write to the Ephesians: "Let not the sun go down upon your wrath." Sundown was sleepy time. Don't let anger fill your mind at bedtime!

I have read of a professor who was trying to work out an abstruse mathematical problem and wakened one morning to find to his own amazement that during sleep he had taken pencil and paper and gone on with the problem to its final conclusion. A bank manager once told me that he went to sleep repeatedly turning over some problem relative to his accounts and frequently found that the missing figure or entry was immediately apparent on awakening. Wise preachers know that if they go to sleep over their sermon on Saturday night they can keep the people awake with it on Sunday morning! It has gone on working and seems to have soaked itself into the very fiber of the preacher's mind.

There is the danger of evil's being done by the law's working as is the case with all law. The law of gravity which brings down the beneficent rain to our fields will bring about the death of him who walks over the cliff edge. And this law of psychology, by which the mind is stained the color of its last dominating thoughts before sleep, can bring us near to hell. Don't let the mind brood on lustful thoughts, or lust will color area after area of your thought life and lead to immoral action. Don't let the mind brood on anger, resentment, jealousy, hate, or the thought life will become embittered. Remember: "As he thinketh in his heart, so is he." Don't let fear, pessimism, or doubt hold the mind in tyranny just before sleep, for those thoughts are seeping into the very nature all night long.

Note rather how the right use of this law is one of the secret ministries of God. For a time some of us at my home made a practice, at the end of the day, of definitely calling to mind the most beautiful thing we had seen or heard that day and making it the closing thought. It might be a vase of snowdrops, or a bird's song, trees against the sky, the sunset light reflected on the snow, an old woman feeding the grocer's pony, anything that was beautiful, unselfish, brave, kind, holy. "Whatsoever things are true and lovely and pure," said Paul, "*keep on thinking* about these things." Your mind then is stained that color, steeped in that quality. Remember that your whole reaction to life depends on the state of that mind.

So during the night God, working through his own law—for all law is his—is molding your character as Herkomer molded his father's clay; and when you wake up, you will be a better man than when you went to sleep. You will prove in your experience the truth of a sentence of the psalmist which is grievously mistranslated. We read: "He giveth his beloved sleep." He does; but the correct translation is even more significant: "So he giveth *to* his beloved *in* sleep." (Psalm 127:2 R.V. margin.) Offer the mind, the last thing at night, that positive affirmation which is the soul's deepest need, and which may be the very opposite of your present condition, and in the unconscious hours the mind will move toward it and lay hold of it and gradually capture the quality you desire. It is one of the secret ministries of God.

2. Here is another, though each should form a separate sermon. In "A Death in the Desert" Browning makes St. John say that he

> . . . patient stated much of the Lord's life
> Forgotten or misdelivered, and let it work.

Some people are very troubled because there is so much they forget. What we must not forget is that forgetting is the highest function of the memory! Sanity is maintained by the forgetting power of the memory! I am certain that my own sanity would go if I could not forget some of the stories of human misery that I have heard. But sometimes we are distressed because we cannot remember. People read a book or hear a sermon or pick up some helpful thought, but they cannot remember it, cannot bring it all back again to consciousness, and they imagine its influence is lost.

Now a good memory must be a very nice thing to have, and I favor all methods which improve it. I believe in jotting things down which I want to remember. But one of the most interesting discoveries of modern psychology is that once the mind really lays hold of an impression it never lets it go. It may fall into the deep mind so that, operating from the surface, you cannot reach it and recover it to consciousness. But it is there in the mind, and it is influencing the mind and therefore influencing behavior in all those situations relevant to the thought received. Experiments in hypnotism show that under certain conditions of deep hypnosis a patient can bring back to conscious memory incidents that happened in the first year of life. In my own work it was found that a very susceptible patient actually went back gradually in memory to her own birth and described the whole happening.

Now see how important that law is when we think of spiritual things. After all, it can be illustrated from the physical plane. You don't *remember* what you had for dinner a fortnight ago, but it did you good. It mingled with the tissue of the body and was dealt with in that amazing laboratory and turned into energy and power, including the power to think. What an intriguing thought that rice pudding last Tuesday helped to make this sermon!

So the truths which your mind accepts may be forgotten, but once really received they pass into the substance—as it were—of the personality and, *even if never consciously remembered again*, determine the kind of personality you are and, what is more, determine the kind of reaction you make to life. You can't find the sugar and catch it in your spoon after a very few moments, but the tea is sweet. That is what God wants—"truth in the inward parts." The whole mind remains sweetened with the eternal truths which have the power to make us true men and women, even long after the particular form in which those truths were presented to consciousness is forgotten and may be never recovered.

How important, then, becomes what we read, what we hear and receive. One of the greatest obstacles to the making of a new world is that German youth has become the incarnation of the ideas on which German minds have been fed. But that is the misuse of God's law. One of his secret ministries lies in the fact that *truth* admitted to the personality goes on working silently and secretly, making the personality gradually the incarnation of itself.

3. I believe that the way beauty is similarly absorbed is another secret ministry of God. We may not be able to recall a single picture on the walls of our childhood home. But those pictures have affected us. I would counsel newly married people to buy pictures slowly and buy one good picture rather than fill the walls with rubbish. The pictures on schoolroom walls have a much more profound influence than we commonly imagine.

The hillmen of India are quite different from the rice coolies of the plains—tougher, more tolerant, with a keener sense of humor and a steadier bearing. I find it hard to believe that the glory and majesty of the Himalayas have had nothing to do with character. Gardeners, farmers, shepherds, and country folk who work in the open and hear the birds all day long, who tend flowers or sheep, who see God's open sky and watch wind-driven clouds, seem different in outlook from the city merchant driving the close bargain, living out of sight of everything that God has made, letting business success bulk far too largely on his horizon and take from him so much energy that there is none left for God and the true enjoyment of simple things. Even the first snowdrop moves him less than a fall in the price of lard. What a tragedy it is when anyone, rich or poor, is so obsessed with the means of life that he loses sight of the meaning of life! Many people are not really *living*. They don't know how to. They are *earning a living,* that's all.

He who keeps a little place in his life for beauty will find that it does something for him and in him, and that something is a process that goes on when the beauty is no longer before his eyes and ears, like a seed growing secretly in the dark. God, by a secret ministry, can turn the sight of a snowdrop into hope and the sight of the dawn into courage. A concert can do something spiritual within us as well as a prayer meeting. Slip into St. Paul's one day and look at the original of Holman Hunt's "The Light of the World." It will do as much for you as many a sermon. One of the finest services held in the City Temple was a service without a sermon or address, when a large congregation one Good Friday afternoon heard the choir interpret Stainer's *Crucifixion*. When Jesus called men out into the wilderness to rest, it was not for sleep and lethargy so much as to see the birds and flowers and sky and sea, to have, after the demands of a hectic multitude, time to experience the secret healing ministry of beauty.

4. Let us now consider one of the greatest of God's secret ministries. Have you ever tried to analyze just what it is in friendship which is so utterly satisfying? Was it not Carlyle and Emerson who forgathered for an evening together and sat utterly silent for hours until one rose to go and said: "We've had a grand evening!" It may be with one closely related to us, or it may be with one who is—as we stupidly say—"just a friend," but we have all, I hope, had hours of communion when something from our friend's very nature has passed into ours, and perhaps from us to him or her, bringing strength where there was weakness, comfort where there was distress, hope and courage where there was despair or even defeat. There is something mysterious about friendship. You may walk for an hour with a person and say certain things, and the hour may be one of boredom and fatigue. You may walk with a friend over the same ground for the same length of time and even say the same things, and at the end of the hour be exhilarated and refreshed. Through the friendship a hidden ministry of God is at work, integrating and building up the personality.

We can go further. We get strength from a friend who is far away and whom we rarely, if ever, see or even write to. The very *fact* of the friendship, the thought that you *have* that friend and that he is *there,* is a secret ministry of God to your spirit, one of the ways in which God's spirit operates on our lives. As Browning fearlessly puts it:

> Hush, I pray you!
> What if this friend happen to be—God?

God is ceaselessly at work on our lives. There is the pull of "original sin" the other way, but God loves us, not only as a Father, certainly not only as an assessor of morals, but as a great artist who will not leave creative work unfinished. He will perfect that which concerneth us. Deep in our nature his secret ministries are at work, like the mystic power that makes a seed grow; and it will be well if we remember that God is far more eager and constant in his desire for perfection in us than we have ever been.

Much we must do ourselves. The frail barrier of our misused will can hinder him. But if at last we become what we in our best moments desire, and what he wants us to be, it will be not through our own efforts, but through all the varied ministries of his grace, and not least those secret effects of the laws of our own being by which we assimilate and partake of the divine.

Let me close with some appropriate and beautiful words from a pamphlet by Dr. W. R. Maltby called *God in Everything—The Letters of Miriam Gray*:

In His mysterious humility He tends the last smouldering lamp in every rebellious heart. He is, we find, the friend of every hard-pressed generosity in a base heart. It is He who defends the last strip of territory against the invasion of passion when all the rest is gone, and raises mysterious defences about beleaguered virtues whose doom seemed sure. When He is denied or unrecognized in His own person, He still lingers about a man, dimly apprehended as a sense of duty, or as some indestructible principle, some notion of what is "not cricket," some code of thieves; or He returns upon us in some New Thought, some shadowy Infinite, some impersonal Life-Force, some half-crazy system worshipping its fragment of truth; and so men entertain Him unawares. These vast tracts of the unbaptized human life we make over to poets and novelists and dramatists, who explore them with inexhaustible interest and sympathy. Yet that interest and sympathy come from God, who loves this human life of ours, not only as a moralist approving where it is good and disapproving where it is bad, but as a poet or an artist loves it, because He cannot help loving a thing so strange, piteous, and enthralling as the story of every human soul must be.[1]

[1] By permission of The Epworth Press.

# THE GOD OF DETAIL

To the religious man there is no such thing as a detail, if by detail you mean an incident which is so trivial that it cannot hold spiritual significance.

Imagine a professor of philosophy sitting down to his desk to work at his lecture for the following day. Like some other people I know, he cannot work at an untidy desk. So he proceeds to clear away the papers strewn upon it, papers which have been put there probably by a lady who, like someone else I know, acts on the principle, "When you don't know what to do with pamphlets, magazines, handbills, and the rest of the clutter that gets pushed into the mailbox, put it on father's desk." The professor picks up a magazine published by the Paris Missionary Society. He is about to throw it into the wastebasket, when on mechanically opening it he catches the title of an article, "The Needs of the Congo Mission." The professor reads it through and puts it down. In his diary that night, he writes the words, "My search is over."

The professor was Dr. Albert Schweitzer, and the "chance" reading of a missionary report took one of the most scholarly and gifted men in Europe to study medicine at the university in which he was a professor and then spend his life in Equatorial Africa. Though he has a doctor's degree in philosophy, theology, medicine, and music, his best years have been given to a mission station, Lambaréné, in French Equatorial Africa.

I wonder what the person thought afterward who left the magazine in Schweitzer's mailbox. I wonder whether he was a bit tired that afternoon and nearly decided not to bother with the remaining houses in that street. What a detail seems one magazine more or less! Yet see what an immense issue depended on it. It makes one want to do one's best down to the last detail, doesn't it? For there is no such thing as a detail with God. And the more we share his mind and see his world as he sees it, the less ready we are to say concerning anything, "Oh, that's a mere detail." So often a detail decides a destiny.

Readers of the life of Grenfell of Labrador will remember that his admirers saved up to give him a motor boat so that his fine service to the people living in the islands off the coast might be facilitated. Soon after the boat arrived, Dr. Grenfell received an urgent summons in the night. It was dark and foggy, but since he had his good motor boat and its compass, he started happily enough. To make a thrilling story very short, long after the time had elapsed when by all his reckoning he should have reached the island he sought, his men saw looming up in front of his boat a dangerous rock which they knew was miles down the coast and quite in the wrong direction. After the harassing night—in which a mother lost her life—examination was made, and inquiries were set on foot; and at last it was found that a young lad who had been entrusted in Liverpool with the task of fastening the compass to its wooden base had lost one of the brass screws and used a steel one. The compass apparently was not tested after fixing, and the lack of one brass screw cost a life, and nearly cost the life of one of the finest men of our time.

As we say to the children, "For lack of a nail a shoe was lost. For lack of a shoe a horse was lost. For lack of a horse a rider was lost. For lack of a rider a message was lost. For lack of a message a battle was lost. For lack of a battle a kingdom was lost."

After all, what is a detail? I was once asked by a friend with whom I shared a bungalow in India to deliver a note to a girls' boarding school in Madras. It was a mere detail to make a short detour on a journey I had to make in any case. But the lady who came out on the veranda that sunny morning, and whom I then met for the first time, is now my wife!

But my message is not merely that we must do our work thoroughly down to its smallest detail because we never know what might hang upon it. That *is* a message and an important one, which I hope may help those whose whole lives are spent in what others miscall details—such as making beds, cooking meals, washing up, tending a machine, adding up figures, wrapping up purchases, and the like. That message is a by-product of what I think is a deeper message still, and one which it is most important to understand.

It is, in brief, that we must be careful not to affix the label "detail" to anything, since nothing is "a mere detail" to God, and he uses what we call detail in such a remarkable way.

It is very human and, I suppose, inevitable that we should use the word "detail," but to do so in regard to God is to fall into the mistake of anthropomorphism. Anthropomorphism is the mistake of thinking of God in terms of a man—a very powerful, wise, loving, and, indeed, ideal man, but still a man.

Now Jesus himself taught us thus to think. Again and again when he was telling men what God is like he began a story thus: "A certain man had two sons. . . . " "If you want to know what God is like," said Jesus in effect, "think of a perfect man, and your picture will be as true as you can make it." But Jesus always made it clear that God is like man *in the realm of moral values, not in the realm of creative power*. The truth that God made man in his own image is no authority for man's limiting his thought of God to the purely human concepts.

Man obviously cannot do the sort of thing God does in the realm of power. Man cannot make stars or the mechanisms by which a baby laughs. God, on the other hand, is not like man; he requires no rest, no information. He is not—as man is—located only in one place. He is not imprisoned in time or space. So we might go on. Let it be sufficient to sum up in inspired words: "My thoughts are *not* your thoughts, neither are your ways my ways, saith the Lord."

The editor of the book of Genesis fell into the mistake of anthropomorphism when he wrote, "God rested the seventh day" —save, of course, that such a phrase was part of his parabolic way of speaking of creation. To think of God "resting" is really as foolish as thinking of God sitting back and drinking tea. Infinite activity knows no rest. He "shall neither slumber nor sleep." If he did, the whole universe would disintegrate at once and be no more. In him all things consist or hold together.

It follows, therefore, that nothing is "hard" to God except winning men whom he himself has given the free will which they use against him. But even there the "hardness" is caused by man. It is not caused by any lack of power in God. The words "hard" and "easy" are man's words. If God can do a thing at all, that is, if it is a normal function of infinite power and wisdom and goodness to do a thing, why then God can do it. Not without *cost*—for every expression of love is costly. Not without what we in our prison call time. But certainly *without exhaustion*.

"With God," said Jesus, "all things are possible." There are many things God *must* not do. There are many things that would deny his own nature, remembering that perfect wisdom is included in his nature. There are many things that we ask him to do which are as impossible as making a square circle, that is, they are contradictory. What makes them impossible is not his lack of power. If we understood his nature better, we should see them to be self-contradictory, and, like the phrase "square circle," meaningless.

A little boy once asked his mother if God made flies. On receiving an affirmative answer, he said, "Oh, Mummy, it must be a ticklish business making flies!" The little boy was guilty of anthropomorphism. But to God that kind of "hardness" is unknown. To put it crudely, God didn't sit back after making elephants and say, "Well, that was a heavy day's work. I think I'm entitled to a rest."

The point of all this is that we simply must not get our human difficulties about size into our thinking about God. Making a star is not a heavier task than making a dewdrop.

Now see how relevant this is to life and to our thought about life. Launching a planet is not, to God, a "bigger" affair, a matter of greater concern, than watching over your baby's illness. God is as much interested in the fact that it is your wash day tomorrow as he is that he is going—for all we know—to create a new world from some flaming sun of which we've never heard. One is not a "little thing" and the other a "big thing." Those are human words.

God is pouring out his omnipotence at every part of his creation, and all that happens, happens to him. "For in him we live, and move, and have our being." He is not looking on, like a big man from above. He is the body of which we are part. Will you misunderstand if I put it like this? He knows it is your wash day tomorrow because it is his. It is his because it is yours. Your life is an extension of his own, and, in a real sense, what happens to you happens to him.

Look at all this in relation to the problem of God's guidance. People will believe that God is guiding "in a general sort of way." They find it hard to believe that he has any sort of interest or concern in the details of that guidance.

But, you see, there are no "details." The significance of one thing may turn out to be greater than the significance of another thing, but as between the things themselves there is no great nor small. Indeed, a screw may be a big thing, and an article in a magazine may hold greater spiritual significance than, say, a whole session of Parliament or the meetings of the Congregational Assembly or even the Methodist Conference in all its glory.

God, you see, is *not* like man in his activities. He is *not* a managing director who steers a business on general lines but can know no details, who does not even know the office boy's name. God is *not* like a general who directs a campaign, but knows nothing of the wounds of Private Smith, or of his ultimate death, or of the sorrow of his widow. When little Margaret Smith, aged ten, learns the terrible news and soaks her pillow with tears, sobbing through the endless night because Daddy is dead, God—if it *can* be put into words—is not in heaven looking on and saying, "Well, of course, war involves casualties." Certainly he is not looking down sternly and saying, "Well, if men will do these things, they must take the consequences." God—if it can, I say, be put into words—is on that bed holding Margaret in his arms, and God is crying too. And Private Smith's wounds are his wounds, and the widow's torn heart is his own. All persons are an extension of his personality. "For in him we live, and move, and have our being."

"Surely he hath *borne* our griefs and *carried* our sorrows." "Are not two sparrows sold for a farthing? and not one of them shall fall to the ground without your Father." Two sparrows! Well, surely that's a detail! What about world unrest and the threat of war that would involve millions? Yes! but the millions are in his hands as well as the sparrows. "Large," "small"—they are man's words. "Infinite" means without end, and greatness *without end* doesn't measure things as we do. It is perfectly adequate to every situation. "Fear ye not therefore; ye are of more value than many sparrows." Not because we are bigger, but because in the realm of creative values we can do more. Sparrows are servants, and men are sons. We are not to be conceited at the thought of sparrows, or frightened at the thought of stars, but happy that through *every* part of his creation, without regard to our labels of important or unimportant, large or small, the unceasing activity of God goes on.

*We* say: "He is such a great man that he cannot be troubled with detail"; "He is such a great general that you can't expect him to be bothered with the rank and file." But of God you must say: "The word 'detail' in regard to him is as foolish as the word 'eating.' He is so different from man and so great that his heart holds them all, and his Spirit can take what we call a tiny detail and fill it with spiritual meaning."

In an English city some months ago a brokenhearted woman sat on a seat in a public park. Why did she go to that park that morning? Why did she sit on that seat? Next to her sat a man who was reading a book. Why did he go to the park that morning? Why did he sit on that seat? Why was he reading that book at that time?

She looked over his book and saw the title at the head of the page. "Sir," she said, "excuse me, but the title of your book makes me wish I could read it. May I write down the name of the author?" "Certainly," said he, "but, better than that, I know the author; and, if you like, I will give you a note, and he will help you, for I see you are in trouble." So a woman was rejoined to her husband, a quarrel was healed, a home was restored, little children found happiness and their birthright—for their birthright is a home where peace reigns and where father and mother love one another —and it was a mere detail, you say, that took those two to that park and that seat and that book? I don't think so. I think it was the loving planning of God, the God of detail.

So mind how you speak of details. On what small hinges big doors swing! Look out for *spiritual significance,* not the things men call important, big, impressive. The Oxford Groupers are as right when they remain sensitive to the thought that God can guide them in "details" as they are wrong if they seek with emphasized enthusiasms to win the "important" people to their way of thinking.

What a lot of surprises there will be for us in heaven! Hudson Taylor says that in his opinion the conversion of a whole village in China depended on the prayers of an unknown woman in an English country village! I know a woman who persuaded another to begin to pray. Suppose the second marries and has a son and teaches him to pray. And supposing he is a Paul! Yet the first woman often says she does nothing for God and lives her life in humdrum details.

Let us not be "anthropomorphic" any more! Let us realize that God is greater than all our thoughts of him based on the nature of man. If we try to think less as man does and more as God does, we shall pour our Christian spirit into every detail and see in detail thrilling adventure, new opportunities, and the signposts of God. We shall watch for his meanings and find a new romance in unsuspected significance.

He who with equal ease can make an ant or an Atlantic, and who pours himself out in all his fullness into every part of his universe, knowing nothing of a scorn for detail, asks from us that we surrender every part of life to him, watching for his message to flash even from the trivial.

"I come in the little things," saith the Lord. Watch, therefore, for in such a detail as ye think not, the Son of Man cometh.

# GOD'S INTOLERABLE COMPLIMENT

SOME TIME AGO I OFFERED IN A SERMON ON "FAITH'S SUPREME Certainty" one little sentence which I should like to develop now. It was to the effect that, throughout the whole Bible, suffering is frequently referred to under the figure of fire. I noted the point that the very use of the word "fire" involves a compliment to human nature; for that which the fire does must be worth doing, and the substance on which the fire acts cannot be destroyed, but must be purified by its action—a compliment indeed to the indestructible nature of that valuable substance on which the fire operates. In a sentence, fire points to gold, not wood. If our nature were thought of as straw or paper or wood, fire would entirely destroy it. The fact that suffering is called "fire" involves by implication that human nature is gold or, at any rate, something that can be purified by the action of the fire. So to grasp the thought of suffering as fire is really to receive a compliment from God.

My interest in our theme was quickened by reading a book recently published called *The Problem of Pain,* by Mr. C. S. Lewis. The phrase "God's intolerable compliment" is one of his. Here is its context: "It is for people whom we care nothing about that we demand happiness on any terms: with our friends, our lovers, our children, we are exacting and would rather see them suffer much than be happy in contemptible and estranging modes. . . . [God] has paid us the intolerable compliment of loving us, in the deepest, most tragic, most inexorable sense."

We see all around us, in these days, widespread suffering both of individuals and of whole nations. It is only misleading to think of that suffering as the will of God. It is within God's will in that he allows it and uses it, but it is not God's will in the sense that he intends it. I believe it is essential to clear thinking to keep those two points separate in our minds, or else we use the phrase "the will of God" in a confusing manner. God *allows* many evil things to happen and uses them, but he does not *intend* them to happen. Similarly a mother *allows* a child to fall on the nursery floor and uses the fall to teach the child to walk better, but she does not *intend* the child to fall or she would push him over. When Jesus met suffering, he tried to heal it. When he healed it, he was not acting in opposition to God's will; he was doing God's will. When Jesus saw a woman who was bowed down by physical infirmity, he referred to her as "this woman . . . whom *Satan* hath bound, lo, these eighteen years." For me that is enough evidence to show that suffering is not the intention of God. We perceive that in a world constituted as this is there must be ignorance, folly, and sin. God is always trying to replace ignorance with knowledge, folly with wisdom, and sin with holiness. Therefore the ills that are consequent on ignorance, folly, and sin cannot be his intention. They are his circumstantial will, his will in the circumstances which man's evil throws up.[1] Further, this is a world in which we are so bound up with one another that the ignorance, folly, and sins of one bring suffering to many, just as the knowledge, wisdom, and holiness of one bring gain to many. In such a world, built up on the family basis, suffering is bound to come to the innocent as well as to the guilty. We both gain and lose by belonging to the human family, and we gain more than we lose, for if life were on an individual basis instead of a family basis, most of us would soon cease to live at all.

But, having distinguished between what God intends and what God allows, we must go on to say that, since he allows suffering, he is ultimately responsible for it, and he takes the responsibility for its possibilities because he can use it toward an end which justifies that possibility. It is fire—fire which he did not kindle, but which he has decreed that certain factors like ignorance, folly, and sin whose *possibility* is necessary to human development can produce, and which, having been ignited, can fulfill a function not utterly destructive but purifying and cleansing.

In other words, suffering has a *possible* disciplinary value. We

[1] I have worked out this idea in a small booklet called *The Will of God*.

must underline there the word "possible," for the disciplinary value of suffering is not inevitable. Many people who suffer become rebellious, resentful, bitter, cynical, hostile, even atheistic. It depends on the reaction we make to suffering whether it spoils or refines our characters.

It is noteworthy, however, that in everybody's mind there is a relationship between character and suffering. Often it is a false relationship, for people imagine that this particular sin brings that particular suffering, whereas suffering usually falls impartially. They put two and two together and make twenty-two instead of four. But let us note for the moment that there is a relationship.

Here are some actual cases which illustrate the point. When bombs were dropping, a woman in an air-raid shelter said of her husband, who, as an air-raid warden, was exposed to great danger: "I wish I had made up with him before he went out into the blitz." Note that she realizes that her life and her husband's are in danger, and that she wants to put right a moral relationship because suffering is imminent and death possible. Here is another illustration which every minister has met. As soon as calamity comes, a person will ask, "What have I done to deserve this?" The answer may quite likely be, "Nothing." But I am using the illustration to point out that people do link in their minds character and suffering. A person will torture his mind for months trying to find out what particular evil he has done to bring calamity upon him, when the calamity is only his share of the whole world's burden of ignorance, folly, and sin. I had a heartbreaking letter recently from a woman who had lost her baby and could not get it out of her mind that her child had been born with a certain deformity because she had given way to a certain sin. The nature of the deformity and the nature of the sin were such that I am quite sure they were not related as effect and cause. But she could not get it out of her mind that they were causally related. She was miserable because her mind was making a false deduction. Here again I am only using the illustration to show the way in which people believe that suffering and character are connected. Everyone will, I think, agree that when we have been ill and are recovering we do take spiritual stock. When pain departs and recovery is in sight, we soon cease to ponder our evil nature and wickedness. Here again we prove to ourselves the tendency to link character and suffering.

We are emancipated, then, from the false idea that God hands out a cancer to this man because he has been a bad man, and tuberculosis to that woman because she has not said her prayers; but let us at the same time realize that there *is* a relation—not necessarily causal—between suffering and character, and that, if our reaction is right, God can use the suffering that comes upon us from the ignorance and folly and sin in the world, our own or other people's, and he can use it as fire upon gold to bring purification and strengthening. And the fact that he does so use it, while often unbearable and intolerable, as we say, is a profound compliment to human nature. The thing that surprises me most in God's ways with men is that he thinks we are beings concerning whom it is worth taking such endless trouble.

Mr. C. S. Lewis makes much of this last point, and I am indebted to him for what I am about to say. There are a great number of people who are fond of dogs. A trained dog who is a household pet lives longer, is far happier, and is more highly cultured—one might say, is nicer to know—than the wild, untrained animal of the prairie or the pariah dog that haunts an Eastern city. A man who loves his dog washes it when it doesn't want to be washed. He housebreaks it, refusing to allow it to befoul his house. He may whip it to stop it from stealing. It is a matter of great importance to the man that the dog should not be repulsive in its habits. He takes infinite pains with it. Why? Because through discipline there is more than a chance that the man can bring the dog into a communion with himself higher and deeper than would otherwise be possible. If the dog could think and talk to other dogs, no doubt the experiences he underwent at the hands of the man would lead him to confide to other dogs that his master could not possibly love him, since he suffered so much. His doggy dignity would often be lowered and his happiness temporarily destroyed. But the sufferings of the dog and the trouble of the man are a compliment. A man does not go to the same trouble with a rat or a frog. Presumably they are incapable of being brought into such a high communion with man.

Look at the relationship between God and man in a similar way, save that God uses a whip already provided by the effects of man's ignorance, folly, and sin, whereas the man in relation to the dog introduces the whip from outside the situation. But God uses the whip of human suffering for the same purpose—namely, to bring man into communion with himself.

We may see the thought of the compliment in a different illustration. A child brings his autograph album to a great composer, who, to please the child, scribbles a few bars in the book, and the child is contented about it. But look at the trouble that composer takes with his great masterpiece, writing, rubbing out, rewriting, introducing this harmony, varying that melody, as Beethoven did with his sonatas. It doesn't require a wild flight to try to imagine that the composition is itself sentient. It might complain and say, "I wish he would not keep rubbing me out and rewriting. I was all right as I was." We know that the truth is that the pains the composer takes are a compliment to the composition. It is just because it is a masterpiece that it merits so much more care than the hastily scribbled bars which please the child.

We could find another illustration in the attitude of the great poet to his poem. Those who have seen the original of Tennyson's *In Memoriam* say that he hardly left a line unaltered. He wrote it, and then scratched it out, and then altered the arrangement of the verses. One might imagine the poem saying, "My lines rhymed before. Why can't he let me alone?" But to be left alone would mean that the poet was content with something less than the best, less than something that the poem might become.

Herein is illustrated in part our attitude to God.[2] When trouble assails us we cry out to God, saying, "I wish you would leave us alone. All we want is to be happy." But the trouble the Artist takes to use every kind of discipline that evil brings into life as a means of purifying our character, though intolerable to us at the time, is a tremendous compliment; and when we cry out to be left alone, we are asking for less care, not more care, for less love, not more love. We are like a dog unwashed, filthy, and with stinking habits, saying,

[2] I say "in part" because in the above illustrations the imperfection is the fault of the composer and poet. In our relationship to God the fault of imperfection lies with us.

"I want only to be left alone." But the God who left us alone as we are now would not be God. Therefore God will use any means, including the suffering he does not will, to shape us and alter us and improve us and win us from our wild, filthy, foul, and unclean habits, so that at last we may be made ready to enter into a communion with him the depths of which have never been plumbed.

Let me lighten our thought by recalling a Sunday-school treat to which with great delight I went as a child. We had a benevolent superintendent who desired only that we should all have a happy day. Those who ran in the races and won got a prize, but those who came in last got a surreptitious sweet. At the end of the day "a good time had been had by all." But the attitude of the superintendent was kindness rather than love. Love has in it a stern note, something stronger than mere benevolence. Kindness makes us happy, but has no power in it to make us improve. Love has.

Here in the City Temple we have what is called an "Adoption Scheme." Poor and underprivileged families are adopted by individuals or groups of individuals, and Miss Jones from the City Temple goes to visit her adopted family and showers pennies and sweets on the children. She doesn't bother much if they are filthy or foul-mouthed or running at the nose. But their *mother* is much more concerned about these things because she loves them with a love that is greater than mere benevolence and kindness. We cannot imagine a true father saying about his son, "I don't care if he is filthy and a liar and a knave and a cheat so long as he is happy." Happiness is not a true end. It is always a by-product. Character is the end, for our character development contributes to the glory of God which is the end of all human existence.

Now look from these illustrations at God's relationship with us. We ask him to be kind. There is a true sense in which God is not kind. His relationship with us is bigger and grander and closer. Kindness is often a love substitute which we offer to people whom we may not love, cannot love, or cannot be bothered to love; and kindness is too poor a thing to express God's relationship to us. We keep on pleading with him to be kind because we want to be happy. His attitude is higher and deeper. He *loves* us because he wants to bring us into communion with himself and he knows that we cannot be really deeply and completely happy until we have been brought into communion with him. If he is merely kind, we shall make happiness our goal and be content with something less than the best, with something less than we may yet become, something less than God can make us. When we ask God to be kind to us that we may be happy, we are asking for less love, not more; we are being content to remain wild dogs; we are being content to be the rapidly scribbled half-dozen bars of music instead of the masterpiece; we are being content to be the rhyme instead of the poem.

When I think about God, I realize that in weak moments of self-indulgence I should like to live in a world where "a good time was had by all," where God was kind, and everybody was happy. But in better moments I realize that it would be asking for a love substitute, kindness. It would be being content with happiness instead of character. If we could see deeper into the nature of reality, including the things that are unseen, we should realize that the things we want which are not his will ultimately bring only more suffering and misery, however innocent they seem, however badly we want them, however passionately we insist on having them, however accompanied they may be by brilliant planning, and however marked they may be by what the world calls success. Our true happiness is a by-product of our quest for blessedness, and blessedness is the complete identity of our will with God's and the fullest realization of our communion with him.

So now at the end of the sermon let me give you the text in II Corinthians 4:17-18: "Our light affliction, which is but for a moment, worketh for us a far more exceeding and eternal weight of glory; while we look not at the things which are seen, but at the things which are not seen: for the things which are seen are temporal; but the things which are not seen are eternal." There is possible to us the glory of sons caught up into the Father's fellowship, honored by the Father's love, brought into communion by his endless patience and the suffering which both he and we endure. This thought can stay us in the hour of our anguish and nerve us in the day of our distress. I have only to look into my own heart to be certain of this, that if God were content with us as we are, it could only mean that he had stopped caring.

# TIME THE DECEIVER

SOMETIMES WHEN YOU HAVE BEEN TRAMPING AMONG THE MOUNTAINS, you have climbed upward through a long, dark valley that led to the open moors and a wide expanse of sky. At one point you looked back into the gloom and darkness below you and then turned and looked forward to the brightening sky ahead, and you had a satisfying feeling that, although the steepness and difficulty of the climb were not yet over, at any rate you were getting away from the imprisoning valley out toward open country.

I think we must all feel a little like that today. We stand on the threshold of this fateful year 1944, which will probably be the most momentous in the history of the world. We look back along the dark valley through which we have come. At one time it looked very, very dark. It seemed as though our beloved land would be invaded. It even seemed as though that invasion might be successful. But strongly believing in our cause, we plodded on under magnificent leadership, and, by the mercy of God, we stand today at a place where we realize that a steep trail is still before us, but the imprisoning darkness of the valley of shadows lies beneath our feet.

I think we must say to ourselves, quite definitely, that probably the steepest part of the trail lies ahead. Sorrow and suffering stand between us and victory. But the hills are falling back on each side of the path. We can see blue sky at the head of the valley. The open country lies before us, and we will go on climbing until we reach peace.

I want to speak especially to those who feel that these war years are stealing something away from them, something that must be written off as permanent loss. For instance, there are the boys whose careers have apparently been broken. Some had started in business; others had gone to the university; many were preparing to do the

163

one or the other; and then war deflected them to paths they never would have chosen, and they wonder where the path will end and what heart they will have for their chosen life when victory is won. There are the men and women who had just begun married life together, with two or three little ones, perhaps, in the home. And now in these important years, when the development of children's minds, and indeed bodies, needs the care and wisdom of parents, the father, perhaps, is away fighting and, it may be, the children evacuated to strange homes. There are the lovers who were proceeding happily to the point when they could marry and who now have been separated, marriage indefinitely postponed. In some cases it must frankly be said that the relationship between them has broken down, and in other cases it has been severely strained. How many people there must be who are tired of waiting and who feel that in various ways something is being filched from them by time, by the mere passing of the years!

I don't know any lines in the whole of literature which express this sentiment better than three from a poem by W. B. Yeats:

> The years like great black oxen tread the world,
> And God the Herdsman goads them on behind,
> And I am broken by their passing feet.[1]

To those who feel thus I want to bring a message which, quite frankly, is hard to understand, for the simple reason that it is so difficult for the mind to escape the prison of time. Even in our imaginative thinking it is hard to escape from the tyranny which the concept of time imposes upon us. Time and space are such strange and deceptive entities and seem to be so much an essential part of the setting of our lives that to ask you to think in terms of spirit where the words "time" and "space" have no real meaning is to make a very heavy demand on your thought. But I make that demand because, for myself, I am convinced that there is a most heartening message for us which comes at the threshold of this year from our timeless God himself.

[1] From "Countess Cathleen," *Poetic Works*. By permission of the publisher, The Macmillan Co.

Note in the first place the immense contrast in regard to the tyranny of time between the Old Testament and the New. In the Old Testament we read of men imploring God for long life. It seemed almost the crowning mercy which they craved. Indeed, I have read that in the Old Testament the impossible longevity of Methuselah and his contemporaries was based on a different way of reckoning years in order to stress their number. But listen to a few passages:

Honor thy father and thy mother: that thy days may be long upon the land which the Lord thy God giveth thee.

A thousand years in thy sight are but as yesterday when it is past, and as a watch in the night. Thou carriest them away as with a flood; they are as a sleep: in the morning they are like grass which groweth up. In the morning it flourisheth, and groweth up; in the evening it is cut down, and withereth. . . . For all our days are passed away in thy wrath: we bring our years to an end as a tale that is told. . . . So teach us to number our days, that we may get us a heart of wisdom. (R.V.)

Man that is born of a woman is of few days, and full of trouble. He cometh forth like a flower, and is cut down: he fleeth also as a shadow, and continueth not.

What man is he that desireth life, and loveth many days, that he may see good? Keep thy tongue from evil and thy lips from speaking guile.

As for man, his days are as grass; as a flower of the field, so he flourisheth. For the wind passeth over it, and it is gone; and the place thereof shall know it no more.

With long life will I satisfy him, and show him my salvation.

These passages are sufficient to show the spirit of the Old Testament in regard to the years. But turn to the New, and we find not only that there is no appeal to God for length of life, but that Paul writes to the Philippians to say that, although he is quite prepared, if God's purposes demand it, to stay and minister to them, he has a greater desire, and that is to end his days on earth and pass into another world: "Having a desire to depart, and to be with Christ;

*which is far better."* And shortly before his death he says: "Now I am ready to be offered [literally, poured out as a drink offering], and the time of my departure is at hand. I have fought a good fight, I have finished my course, I have kept the faith: henceforth there is laid up for me the crown of righteousness."

What an amazing change! We see at once why. The horizon has lifted. There is none of this clinging to the years and fearing their tyranny. There is no dread, such as the Old Testament saints had, that time was so much the tyrant that they might never see the purposes of God worked out. The horizon lifts, and we find that men's feelings could be expressed thus: "We are ready to spend every day fulfilling thy purposes, but *we already live in the eternal world* and know that mere time has no power to destroy anything vital." Now love is vital, and the purposes of God are vital, and the true life of your own spirit is vital, and on these things mere time has no power at all.

It is very hard to find an illustration, for reasons already given. But here is one that may lighten the message a little. You may live in Finchley. You may live in Streatham. You may live in Hampstead. But all the time you live in London. Your work is in London, not in any suburb. You use the suburb only because it is a convenient way of doing the bigger thing and functioning in London. Now can I put it like this? You have to live in time. Last year, this year, next year—these are only suburbs. It is convenient to live in them, and indeed you cannot escape living in them. But your true life is in the central, the vital, the eternal, and all your main purposes are there. A man only puts up with Streatham—I can only think—because it serves the end he fulfills in London. So you may live in today and tomorrow, but really you are living in eternity. Your spirit breathes the atmosphere of heaven already, and eternal life is not something you enter at death. Timeless eternity is all around you now. In Hampstead you can hear the roar of London, and in the life of the body you know that the spirit life is all around you. With Wordsworth you might say:

> Though inland far we be,
> Our souls have sight of that immortal sea

Which brought us hither,
Can in a moment travel thither,

.        .        .        .        .        .

And hear the mighty waters rolling evermore.

You yourself are not a body functioning in time. You are a spirit
functioning in the eternal. You are not a creature of time to whom
time can do anything deadly. You are a spirit making use of time,
imprisoned for a while in time's limitations, but you belong to the
timeless. And if a man moves from a suburb into the real life of the
city, you might be disappointed because you could not have physical
converse with him, but you would not be saddened beyond the
normal sadness of physical separation. And when a man dies, he has
only gone from the suburbs of time to live always in the eternal city.

It is this timelessness of the New Testament, this wide horizon,
that constitutes part of its charm.

There is, however, one passage which appears on the surface to be
an exception in the New Testament, and I must be quite honest
and not only mention it but try to explain it. You will find it in
John 9:1-4. The disciples say to Jesus, "Master, who did sin, this
man, or his parents, that he was born blind?" Now Jesus is reported
to have said: "Neither hath this man sinned, nor his parents: but
that the works of God should be made manifest in him. I must work
the works of him that sent me, while it is day: the night cometh,
when no man can work." Now that emphasis on "the night cometh"
sounds like the horizon of the Old Testament back again. But I
want to do two things in regard to this passage: first to expound its
meaning by a simple device of repunctuating, and second to suggest
that it has no reference to the tyranny of time.

In the old Greek mansucripts there was no punctuation at all. I
accept the suggestion made by some scholars that there should be
a full stop after the word "parents" in the passage I have just
quoted, but no full stop at the end of the third verse, after the word
"him." By this device the passage reads thus. The disciples have
asked, "Who sinned, this man, or his parents, that he should be
born blind?" Jesus says, "Neither did this man sin, nor his parents.

[Put the full stop there.] But that the works of God should be made manifest in him I must work the works of him that sent me while it is day: the night cometh, when no man can work." In other words Jesus is saying, "Don't let us argue why the man is blind. Let us make him better. It wasn't his own fault or that of his parents; but instead of arguing about it, what we must get done before nightfall is the work of God in making him better." In a colloquial phrase, what Jesus says is: "Don't argue; get on with the cure. In the cure the work of God is made manifest."

Certainly we cannot accept the idea that the man had been born blind in order that he might be the occasion of a miracle. Jesus dismisses that in a sentence. He then refuses to be involved in an argument as to why the man was blind. Perhaps part of our Lord's humanity meant a real limitation of his own knowledge of such matters. But perhaps he was unwilling to fritter away time in argument when the man might be made to see before sunset, and thus the works of God be made manifest in him.

This, then, you see, is not an argument about the tyranny of time. It is an exhortation to make time the servant and not the master. In Kipling's lovely phrase, we have "to fill the unforgiving minute with sixty seconds' worth of distance run," but not to suppose that time of itself can steal the vital things of life away.

I wonder if I might put this difficult matter to you like this. As I try to understand the New Testament doctrine of time and its significance, I think it is illustrated by the life of a university student. The university life is only a part of his whole life, but only there can he get his degree and his qualification for the wider life that follows his college course. If he is a wise student, he will remember how important it is to get a good degree. If he allows himself to be satisfied with a third-class honors degree, the whole of his future may be altered, and he cannot go back afterward and exchange it for a first-class honors degree. But, if through circumstances outside his control, the university course is abruptly terminated, he is not to worry, for, to press the figure further than it literally can be pressed, the authority that closes down his course will look after his future. Now while we exist in the university of time, we are to do our very best to qualify as well as we can, for the earth life seems to be a college or school, and the way we graduate from it does mean something significant for the life of eternity that follows. But if the earth life is abruptly closed, the authority that closes it will look after the future.

Part of the trouble we have in receiving this doctrine is that our trust in God is hindered by certain fallacies that we commonly hold about the nature of time. Let me speak of four:

1. Remember that time is like a room in which things happen and has no more influence over the things happening in it than a room has. If your engagement were broken off in a certain room, you would hate the room, perhaps, but could not blame it. Do not blame these difficult years as if *of themselves* they could do something to you, for they simply have not the power to do so. Have you noticed how we misuse words? I cannot undo the bolt of an old shed in the garden, and I say, "It has been corroded by time." But it hasn't. It has been corroded *in* time, but it has been corroded *by* rust. Or again, we speak of "the ravages of time." But there isn't such a thing. Rust can destroy, moths can devour, but time has no such power. We commonly say, "Time will heal." But it won't. If the wound is a wound in the body, the healing forces of nature will do the healing *in* time. But time heals nothing. If the wound be dirty, a limb may be lost by leaving the healing to time. If the wound be a wound in the mind, it is well to remember that there is a *vis medicatrix naturae* of the mind as well as of the body. But time has never healed a repressed complex or a broken heart. Time has never forgiven our sins, though *in* time we may forget them—a dangerous process, for we shall have to remember them again one day, unless they are forgiven. If the wound is a wound in the soul, you will not find that time will accomplish anything. "He will improve with time," we say, forgetting that the mere passing of time only turns a young sinner into an old sinner, a young fool into an old fool. If time were a spiritual healer, all old people would be good, whereas many would say with Hood:

> But now 'tis little joy
> To know I'm farther off from heaven
> Than when I was a boy.

Before you accuse mere time of doing things to you which you resent, be alert and analytical enough to see what are the real enemies of your well-being.

2.  Here is a second fallacy about time. We fall into the fallacy of supposing that time is part of the final structure of reality. In no real sense can this be true, for in no real sense is there such a thing as time. Time does not exist at all in the real world of the spirit. Indeed, many people dream of that which is in the so-called future. But, in reality, the past, present, and future are all the same. The dreamers merely bump into what is *called* the future. Those who find it hard to believe in their freedom of choice, since, as they say, "God knows what I am going to do," would see the difficulty vanish if they remembered two things: (1) What they are going to do, in God's sight, bears the same relationship to him as what they have done. There is no difference between past and future to him. They don't say that, because he knows the past, he made them do what they did. Why do they say that, because he knows their future, his knowledge is coercive? (2) They "know" that if they offer a bone to a starving dog he will move toward it. Yet it is not their knowing, but the dog's hunger, which is the determinant. It is not God's knowledge that determines our doing. Our doing depends on a hundred factors, all of which he knows but we don't. He sees past, present, and future as an eternal present.

Because we mistakenly think of time as part of the final structure of reality, we suppose that all hours are equal. From twelve to one seems just as long a period as from one to two. It is, if you measure time by the clock and the sun. But do you really mean that the hour I spent once in a waiting room while a surgeon operated on the body of one very dear to me was exactly the same length of time as the hour I spent at a Christmas party? And do you mean that from one to four in the middle of the night spent tossing in insomnia is exactly the same length of time as three hours spent at a thrilling film or play? I don't believe it. Indeed, we often say, "I *feel* as if I had known you for years." It is a most revealing sentence. It is your unconscious protest against the tyranny and deception of time. And if a person said that to you, you would not take out your watch and say, "You have known me for one hour and twenty minutes, and so don't you take any liberties." What you "feel" is an indication nearer the truth than the measurement of the watch suggests, for you can "feel" in the real world of spirit, where, thank God, there are no watches at all and no time either.

And I am not just being aggravating and difficult, for the point has an immense significance. A bereaved woman says, "It is twenty years since I lost my dear one, and I'm afraid I shall not know him when we meet again." *But he will know you,*[2] for time has not existed for him. In a sense, time is only a trick. It is only a concession to our limited life on a planet in space. Remember the lovely lines of Laurence Binyon:

> They shall grow not old, as we that are left grow old:
> Age shall not weary them, nor the years condemn.[3]

Not only has this fallacy a relevance to those we have lost in death, but when you meet your dear one after the long separation of the war, you won't find that time has done anything vital. You may have been unfaithful. He may have been. Physical separation may have done something. But *time* will not have done anything, and you will find the amazing amount that can be done in that little anteroom we call a minute, or an instant.

It is wonderful how the poets can always say things that we, whose medium is prose, find it so difficult to express. Listen to Wordsworth:

> One impulse from a vernal wood
> May teach you more of man,
> Of moral evil and of good,
> Than all the sages can.

And those of you who love Browning may remember the passage in *The Ring and the Book* where the Pope is troubled at what seems the inevitable fate which awaits poor Guido, and then, in two lines

[2] Mary did not know Jesus on the resurrection morning, though he had been dead only thirty-six hours, but *he knew her* (John 20:15-16).

[3] From "For the Fallen," *Collected Poems.* By permission of the publisher, The Macmillan Co.

of lovely insight, sees hope for him because it will take only an instant for him to find salvation:

> So may the truth be flashed out by one blow,
> And Guido see, one *instant,* and be saved.

I expect that you have often found that one flash of insight in the tiny dwelling of a second has taken you further than long years of questing. Time, you deceiver, you mocker, you would-be tyrant, I won't be cramped by you! I won't let the black oxen tread me down. I won't be cramped by you, for I belong to the eternal things; and though God has put me in this room which I call time, and though I may have to live most of my life in the slums, I know that I belong to the eternal world. And sometimes when I read grand poetry, or hear wonderful music, or look at the sky, or respond to the love of a dear one, or know the friendship of a little child, I know in that second of insight that I belong to the eternal world. The hills fall back. The valley and its shadows are below me. I escape into the sunshine. "So teach us to number our days," so teach us to deal with this rank impostor, time, that we may get our perspective right, be wise to its devices, awake to the cunning thefts it tries to perpetrate. "So teach us to number our days, that we may get us a heart of wisdom."

3. Look at the third fallacy about time. It would have us believe that long years are an advantage. It would blind us to the horizons of the New Testament and lead us back to the slavery of the Old. Of course we want our dear ones to be with us in the room of time because we live in it ourselves. But never let the idea that long years are necessarily an advantage take hold of you. Would you rather be Shelley or Keats dying in youth, but with the delicious feeling that you had done what you came to do; or would you rather have many, many mere years and be like the old man I knew who died a week or two ago in the nineties, whom everybody supposed it was a duty to keep alive, and who for the last twenty years has been a nuisance to himself and everybody else? There is something beautiful about length of days when they go with a mellowed, ripe, and lovely spirit whose presence is a benediction. But one of the dearest saints I ever knew was very impatient with those who fussed him and who would

not let him do this and would not let him do that. He would say,
"Let me alone. I would rather enjoy myself and die than be miserable and add two more years to my life." Is not that very sound? Is
there *such* a valuable significance, then, in dying at eight-six instead
of eighty-four? Thomas Osbert Mordaunt says:

> One crowded hour of glorious life
> Is worth an age without a name;

and an Italian proverb says: "It is better to be a man for ten minutes
than to be a tortoise for a hundred years." Mark Thrash, a Ten-
nessee Negro, whose estimated longevity was established by Dr. L. P.
Jacks, and whose exact age was proved by "government investiga-
tions," died at 122 years of age, and Siddi Wastad of Bhopal is said
to have been 163; but who would presume to assess the value of
either life in terms of the years? Is not this morbid desire to go on
living for the sake of going on living a way in which we succumb
to the tyranny of time?

4. The last fallacy I want to mention about time could be summarized in a sentence: An obsession with years spoils our perspective. We saw why the Old Testament is so different from the New.
Men pleaded with God for years in which they might see his salvation working itself out, and few of them saw it. There was not time,
and they did not really believe in anything beyond time's prison.
The old doctrine of Sheol, which they held, meant a shadowy life
with uncertain powers and questionable faculties. The old saying
that "whom the gods love die young" was not a cynicism. It simply
meant that it was much better to die young because the mind had
at least the buoyancy of those who die while still looking ahead,
whereas the aged looked at a gray wall called death, toward which
they drew nearer, and beyond which there was nothingness. We have
now no conception of the dread and terror there was in the lives
of the aged before Christ brought life and immortality to light
through the gospel.

What an amazing difference there is in the men of the New Testament! They are certain of immortal life. Time is merely a deceiver.
Life went on, and it was gain to be without a body and away from

earth and uncramped by time. There was no such thing as loss of life. There cannot be loss of life. Life goes on in another room. There is only a passing from one room to another, or perhaps it is more like going out of a stuffy room into the open air of the moors and mountains. "What's time?" says Browning:

Leave Now for dogs and apes!
Man has Forever!

How certain Jesus was of that fact! He didn't even labor to prove it, but took it for granted—an immensely significant thing. "I am the God of Abraham, and the God of Isaac, and the God of Jacob," he quoted, and added, "God is *not the God of the dead, but of the living.*" Abraham, Isaac, and Jacob had not passed out into a darkness, but gone on into a light. And when Jesus on the Mount of Transfiguration stepped out of the room of time, he found Moses and Elijah there, and he did not have to get to know them. Time had had no power with them. They had grown "not old as we that are left grow old." We cannot emphasize to ourselves too often the timeless nature of the life of the spirit.

It dwells not in innumerable years;
    It is the breath of God in timeless things—
The strong, divine persistence that inheres
    In love's red pulses and in faith's white wings.

It is the power whereby low lives aspire
    Unto the doing of a selfless deed,
Unto the slaying of a soft desire,
    In service of the high, unworldly creed.

It is the treasure that is ours to hold
    Secure, while all things else are turned to dust;
That priceless and imperishable gold
    Beyond the scathe of robber and of rust.

It is a clarion when the sun is high,
    The touch of greatness in the toil for bread,
The nameless comfort of the western sky,
    The healing silence where we lay our dead.

And if we feel it not amid our strife,
    In all our toiling and in all our pain,

> This rhythmic pulsing of immortal life,
> Then do we work and suffer here in vain.[4]

I know of a woman whose son in the Air Force was killed, and who, when people commiserated with her, said such a profound thing that, although I have often pondered it, I have never got to the bottom of it: "Why do you commiserate with me?" she said. "He lived for twenty happy, clean years, and then he died for England. What better could he have done than that?" Now if you think that I am the kind of person who could lose my own dear ones and say that kind of thing, I can only say out of sheer honesty that I am not so spiritually advanced as that. I have not got there, but that is where we all must get. And all the heroes of the world, in all the spheres of life in which men have been heroic, would, I think, say to us the same thing.

Our time is going! But think of Edward Wilson, whose life is one of the grandest biographies in literature. Suppose you had put your hand on his arm as he was setting off for that glorious adventure to the Antarctic with Scott and said, "But my dear Dr. Wilson, you are throwing away your medical training. Besides, it is very cold in the Antarctic, and you will get your feet wet." Oh, let him go! He is only going from a limited suburb to where life is more worth living for a heroic spirit, and if he passes beyond all the rooms we call time, he will have found the wisdom which is beyond it. "So teach us to number our days, that we may get us a heart of wisdom."

A friend of mine was once staying in a home in order to preach at a certain church during the week end. When he was shown into his bedroom, all the curtains were drawn for the evening. The black-out had been done for him. The next morning, when the curtains were drawn back, he found that written across the middle of the windowpane, as though with a jewel, were the words, "This is the day." When he went downstairs, he said to his hostess, "I was wondering what those words meant written on the window of the room in which I slept." "Well," she said, "once in that room I was passing through very great trouble. Every morning I wished it were eve-

---

[4] Percy Ainsworth, "And the Life Everlasting." By permission of The Epworth Press.

ning, and every evening I wished the end of life might come with nightfall. One day I opened my Bible at the Psalms and lighted on this text, 'This is the day that the Lord hath made. We will rejoice and be glad in it.' And it came to me that time was no tyrant, that time had no hold on me, that it was just something I could fill with the purposes of God and then pass on gladly to the next room." Yes, that's the idea. Time cannot steal anything vital, cannot hurt or destroy. It is an opportunity to be used, a room to be lived in, a university from which to graduate; but the spirit of man belongs to another category, and his life is in the eternal.

I am no scholar, but I remember in schoolboy days having to translate some odes of Horace. Do you remember the line that contains the famous exhortation *Carpe diem?* I think I am right in saying that the best rendering of the Latin tag is "Grasp the sleeve of the day"—as though a master of olden days should grab the sleeve of a slave and impress him into his service, to use him for a purpose, and then drive him back to the slaves' quarters. So let us seize time by the sleeve. It must be servant, never master, and certainly never thief. The words *carpe diem* seem to have an inner meaning, for conceivably you grab the sleeve of one whose hand is outstretched to steal. Time, you old deceiver, with your bluffing and your pretense, we will *use* you as we step out into life. For that purpose you were created. But you shall not be master. And, what is more, Time, *thou shalt not steal.* No! God is the Master. Time is the slave. And at the end of life's little day, when the last shadows fall apart and the timeless life begins, we shall pass into that dawning loveliness to find that time has taken nothing vital, that nothing of value has been lost.

> We have no hopes if Thou art close beside us,
>     And no profane despairs;
> Since all we need is Thy dear hand to guide us,
>     Thy heart to take our cares;
> For us is no to-day, to-night, to-morrow,
>     No past time nor to be,
> We have no joy but Thee, there is no sorrow,
>     No life to live but Thee.[5]

[5] Edmund Gosse.

# THE DAY OF THE LORD

I WANT TO TRY TO GET OVER TO YOU A MESSAGE WHICH IS NOT EASY for us to receive in these days. It was easier in olden days, for a reason which will appear. But it is a message of comfort and strength, because it fills history, national and international life, and even the personal history of our own lives, with meaning and significance. Its strengthening is still available for us, for it is true, although I think it must be offered and received in a manner different from that of olden times.

In Old Testament days men of God found strength and comfort in the thought that God was enthroned above the life of earth and would act from above in supernatural ways to fulfill his own purposes. Those were days when it was easy to believe in the supernatural. In those days men did not worship science nor shut their minds against anything they could not understand.

Further, those were days when men of God put God in the center of all their thoughts. They did this to an extent which to us is unreal. For instance, if in battle a victory was won, it was because God fought on their side. The victory was due, not to superior armaments or more brilliant tactics, to greater numbers or a clever ruse. Victory was the act of God. If they were fighting uphill and the sunset lingered, they sought no natural explanation. God had made the sun stand still for his own people. If they lost a battle, it was not that they were outflanked by the enemy or that they were poor fighters or that they were outnumbered. It was that God was visiting upon them his displeasure. All was of God.

Again and again their national life seemed to show little sign of the touch upon it of a divine hand, but by stressing the future tense and talking about a "Day of the Lord" these great souls from Abraham to Amos hung on to their faith in God and were strengthened thereby. All the prophets, without exception, spoke of a Day of the Lord in the future, when God would deliver his people, overcome evil, reign in obvious justice, and bring joy to the hearts of his own. "The wilderness and the solitary place shall be glad for them; and the desert shall rejoice, and blossom as the rose." That is only one of an almost countless number of prophecies pointing to a Day of the Lord, when wrong would be righted and the nature and power of God vindicated.

We must not merely dismiss this as "wishful thinking." When we are thinking about God, we cannot, if we think truly, wish better than the truth. The trouble is that we poor mortals have such little power of true thought and true judgment that what we deem would be much better for us would often work out in our undoing. Nothing can be better than the truth about God. Where he is concerned, nothing is "too good to be true," though a lot of things we want and think would be for our good are not good enough to be true. Yet we are plunged into despair when we fail to get them! No, it was not merely wishful thinking, this thought of the Day of the Lord. It was a determined, tenacious hold, by faith, on God and on the proud, unconquerable belief that God would win and that the values man counts precious are indeed invincible. Though that future tense may have strained faith, the Old Testament saints held on by means of it. The Day of the Lord *will* come, they argued. Evil is but for a moment. Rightousness *will* triumph. Evil *will* be swept away. God's reign *will* be established.

Now let us turn to the New Testament days. We find most interestingly that again a hope which is expressed by means of the future tense is the stay of the early Christians. After the ascension of Christ, the whole Christian church believed that in a very short time Christ would return again. The Pauline writings are full of the promise that Christ would come and reign, and that the vindication of his nature and purposes would be seen by his people. "Every knee should bow, and . . . every tongue should confess that Jesus Christ is Lord." "Then cometh the end, when he shall have delivered up the kingdom to God, even the Father; when he shall put down all rule and all authority and power. For he must reign, till he hath put all enemies under his feet." The Day of the Lord was *coming.* Sometimes this return of Christ was thought of as separate from the end of the world, but sometimes it was identified with it. Indeed, the imminence of Christ's return became a dominating idea and one which tended to disintegrate Christian society. Paul seems to have written his first letter to the Thessalonians—the earliest of all the New Testament books, written before any of the Gospels—with the dominant thought in his own mind of Christ's speedy return. In his second epistle he directs them to "patient waiting for Christ," for the simple reason that many early Christians had thrown up their jobs and shown other disturbing signs of unrest and disquietude, because they no doubt argued, "What is the good of going on working, or indeed of engaging in any serious secular activity, when our Lord will return at any moment and catch us up into another life?" No wonder they felt like that when they read:

> For the Lord himself shall descend from heaven with a shout, with the voice of the archangel, and with the trump of God: and the dead in Christ shall rise first: then we which are alive and remain, shall be caught up together with them in the clouds, to meet the Lord in the air: and so shall we ever be with the Lord. Wherefore comfort one another with these words.

Here, then, we see a similar source of comfort and strength, though again the future tense must have strained their patience and courage. They held to the thought that Christ *would* return, everything *would* be put right. Nero would not have the last word. Christ *would* visibly reign, his enemies be vanquished, his own followers vindicated.

What has all this to do with us? Has this message of a future Day of the Lord, so strongly believed by Old Testament saints, so tenaciously held in the early church, no message for us at all? I think it has. I am not now going to discuss the second coming of Christ, save to say that it is very hard for the mind to hold two contradictory ideas together and find comfort in both. I mean that if one is continually thinking of Christ as "coming," one weakens the thought that he is "here"—our ever-present friend, with us and strengthening us day by day. Further, the many promises Christ himself made about his coming, to the effect that his own generation would not pass away before certain things were fulfilled and that those standing around him would see them,[1] were, to my mind, all fulfilled at Pentecost. I feel, therefore, that Pentecost for the disciples did not mean the coming of the third Person of the Trinity—a conception utterly strange to them at that time—so much as the return of their beloved Lord. He had promised not to leave them comfortless, but to come to them, and on Whitsunday they felt just as they used to do when he was visibly in their midst, as indeed he was in the Spirit.

But, reverting to the thought of God's action from above, his intervention in history, which supported the saints of both Old Testament and New Testament days, how can we receive this support, especially if we let go the thought of a visible second coming?

We too may think of a world climax to history. We too must use the future tense concerning it, and it does not much matter whether we regard that climax of history as the Day of the Lord or the second coming of Christ or the end of the world. Faith in God involves *a certainty that God will bring his purposes to their perfect fulfillment.* He will indeed judge the nations. Evil will be certainly overthrown. God will triumph. The eternal values will be vindicated. God will be seen to be King. History will have a worthy climax.

But when this has been said, a difficulty arises for the modern man which did not arise for the early Christians or the Israelites of old. The difficulty really lies in the fact that the modern man cannot look forward to an event which will be a climax of history. It is part of his difficulty in regard to time. Just as it is impossible to imagine time starting, so it is impossible to imagine time stopping, and equally impossible to imagine time going on forever. We cannot imagine an event or climax marking the fulfillment of God's purposes and containing such finality that no other event could follow, or need follow upon it, because no other event could have any relevance, significance, or meaning. To use Professor C. H. Dodd's figure, the end "is such that nothing more could happen in history because the eternal meaning which gave reality to history is now exhausted. To conceive any further event on the plane of his-

[1] See Matt. 10:23; 16:27; 26:64; Mark 8:38; 9:1; 13:26; 14:62; Luke 9:26-27.

tory would be like drawing a cheque on a closed account." [2] We cannot conceive a moment happening in time which could mark at once the end of imperfection and the beginning of perfection.

Shall we moderns, then, throw over the idea of a Day of the Lord because we cannot conceive it? Unable to conceive a time when time ends, or a condition on earth when all God's earth-bound purposes are complete, are we to throw over those great dominating ideas of a Day of the Lord which so strengthened the faith of men and women in both Old Testament and New Testament times?

We need not and must not. Let us, then, try to see how we, as moderns, can appropriate to ourselves the strength of the idea of the Day of the Lord. To do this, I want to take an illustration from the Cross. The Cross happened in the past, but we regard it as a symbol of something that is eternally true. That truth has power for the present and the future. While the Cross means many other things, it stands as a symbol of the victory of love, of the nature of God, and of his reaction against sin. It happened in the *past,* but it has value *now.* It is Christ's pledge, given in time, that he will never leave us.

The idea of the Day of the Lord is an idea which has reference to an unimaginable future. But just as the Cross, though historically *past,* symbolizes a truth which has power for the *present,* so the Day of the Lord, though historically in the *future,* is also symbolic. It symbolizes a truth which has power for the *present;* and just as we speak of "the Cross," meaning a symbol of the love of God for us now, so when we speak of "the Day of the Lord," the very idea of such a day is itself a symbol of the enthroned God, the molder of all history, the triumphant victor over all that happens in the time process, and the omnipotent power who makes all things work out his will, who lives, and would have us live, now partially, but finally fully, in a phase of existence, supernatural and suprahistorical, when all that we call time is caught up into eternity.

This, of course, does not mean any glib thought that "everything will work out all right in the end." From God's point of view, it will, but sin will always temporarily hinder his kingdom and in-

[2] *Apostolic Preaching,* p. 206; cf. J. S. Whale, *Christian Doctrine,* p. 181.

dubitably break the person who continues in it without repentance.

I know that the thought of the Day of the Lord as a symbol is difficult, partly because it is so hard for the human mind to escape the imprisonment of the sense of time. If you have seen any of the plays *Berkeley Square* or *Time and the Conways* or *We Have Been Here Before,* if you have read Mr. Priestley's musings about time in *Midnight on the Desert,* or studied J. W. Dunne's book *An Experiment with Time,* these difficulties will be apparent to you. But when I say that the idea of the Day of the Lord points, not only to a future date, but to a present reality, I mean that when one is talking about eternal things, it is as true to say, "It *is happening,*" or indeed, "It *has happened,*" as to say, "It *will happen.*" Time is a concession to human thought. It has no eternal reality. So we hear Jesus even before his passion saying, "Now shall the prince of this world be cast out." Now! And telling the disciples, "I *have overcome* the world," just *before* that deed of shame when the world thought evil had overcome him. This is what theologians mean when they say that every man must have his teleology—his philosophy of completion—and that eschatology, the doctrine of the fulfillment of God's purposes and the end of the world, *is* that teleology.

The truth is that the whole time-bound world finds its meaning and significance in a timeless world, the eternal heaven that wraps it round. And in Jesus Christ and all he means, that eternal reality has broken into time, and we are assured of the victory of God and the meaningfulness of life. That meaningfulness runs not only through great events of history but through the humblest life of man. It is as though someone picked up all the beads of life that seem scattered, unrelated, and meaningless incidents and threaded them into a necklace. All lives are purposeful because they are part of the eternal world; and the Day of the Lord, though future as far as history is concerned, is an eternal reality, a present experience, as well as a future consummation of the victory of God. Though we must still work for it, pray for it, and indeed fight for it, in the eternal world the victory of God has happened already, and the proof of that happening is the life, words, acts, death, and resurrection of Christ. God's own purpose and grace were given to us in "Christ

Jesus," as Paul said to Timothy, *"before the world began,* but is *now* made manifest by the appearing of our Saviour Jesus Christ, who hath abolished death, and *hath brought* life and immortality to light through the gospel."

Modern as we are, therefore, we must try to receive this thought that lay behind the faith both of the Old and of the New Testament. Life can never pass out of God's controlling hands. The universe cannot run amuck. His purposes can never fail completion. In an eternal world they are complete now. No one can possibly suffer for the truth in vain. All values are vindicated already and will be seen by all to be vindicated. "The Lord God omnipotent reigneth." And he reigns through suffering, said John: "All that dwell upon the earth shall worship him . . . the lamb slain *from the foundation of the world."* Eternal life is here and now. It is future, yes, but present also, and is to be estimated in quality and depth rather than duration and future experience. If we could see all the world's history lying in the eternal, we should find rest for our own minds and support for our own faith. Alas! our vision is clouded. In the days of his flesh men saw in Jesus not the second Person of the Trinity, pre-existent and forever enthroned, reaching from the past through the present to the future. They saw a man going about doing good, but they knew they had seen the nature of the eternal. "We see not yet all things put under him. But we see Jesus, . . . crowned with glory and honor." The Day of the Lord is not to be thought of in time only. Like Christ himself it is also a symbol of the eternal victory of love, the full circle of his eternal purposes, the realization of man's highest dreams, the clue to the meaning of history on this humble planet, the consummation of the plans of a holy, loving God, who has ever reigned, is reigning, and must reign, world without end.

# RESTING IN GOD'S INFINITY

THE AIM OF THIS SERMON IS TO HELP US TO REALIZE A LITTLE MORE truly how great God is and, therefore, how adequate he is for any situation that can arise in our own lives or in the world. As we do this, we can rest our minds and hearts in his infinity.

It has been very hard to choose a text because there are so many. Let me give you some of them:

As the heavens are higher than the earth, so are my ways higher than your ways, and my thought than your thoughts.          —Isa. 55:9

Let all those that seek thee rejoice and be glad in thee: let such as love thy salvation say continually, The Lord be magnified. But I am poor and needy; yet the Lord thinketh upon me.          —Ps. 40:16-17

O magnify the Lord with me, and let us exalt his name together. I sought the Lord, and he heard me, and delivered me from all my fears.
          —Ps. 34:3-4

I should like to add to these passages others from poets who did not live in time to have their words included in the Bible. I hope it will not hurt anybody's feelings if I say that the inspiration of the Bible is not essentially different in kind from the inspiration of religious poets and prophets of later periods. Do you know this passage from Sidney Lanier's great poem "The Marshes of Glynn"?

> As the marsh-hen secretly builds on the watery sod,
> Behold I will build me a nest on the greatness of God:
> I will fly in the greatness of God as the marsh-hen flies
> In the freedom that fills all the space 'twixt the marsh and the skies:
> By so many roots as the marsh-grass sends in the sod
> I will heartily lay me a-hold on the greatness of God:
> Oh, like to the greatness of God is the greatness within
> The range of the marshes, the liberal marshes of Glynn.

And, finally, two lines from Elizabeth Barrett Browning's poem "The Rhyme of the Duchess May":

> And I smiled to think God's greatness flowed around our
>      incompleteness,—
> Round our restlessness, his rest.

So much for texts!

I wonder if you have ever noticed that no biblical poet or prophet sets the thought of God's greatness over against the thought of man's littleness in order to make man feel insignificant and of no consequence. On the contrary, all the great biblical writers set the thought of God's greatness over against the need of man. They magnify God not to make man feel small, but to make man feel that the resources of this mighty Being are at his disposal. We are not to argue, "If he is so great, I must be of no account at all," but rather, "How great he is, and therefore how able to take care of me and look after my interests."

I should be interested if any can find a passage which denies this. Even in that magnificent passage in the fortieth chapter of Isaiah, where the prophet is rejoicing in the might of God, I claim that this point is not denied. We read of God that he "comprehended the dust of the earth in a measure, and weighed the mountains in scales, and the hills in a balance"; that to him the "nations are as a drop of a bucket," and "the small dust of the balance"; and that "he taketh up the isles as a very little thing." But the passage is introduced by the verse: "He shall feed his flock like a shepherd: he shall gather the lambs with his arm, and carry them in his bosom." And the mighty passage ends with the words: "They that wait upon the Lord shall renew their strength; they shall mount up with wings as eagles; they shall run, and not be weary; and they shall walk, and not faint." In other words, this mighty God, whom it is absurd for the maker of idols to try to imprison in a piece of wood or metal, is one whose vast energies are at the disposal of those who trust in him.

Or take that other passage, in Psalm 8, which might seem to dispute my claim. The psalmist says: "When I consider thy heavens, the work of thy fingers, the moon and the stars, which thou hast ordained; what is man, that thou art mindful of him? and the son of man, that thou visitest him?" But don't stop there! For the poet goes on to say: "Thou hast made him a little lower than God"— in the original we have the word God (*elohim*), not angels—"and hast crowned him with glory and honor. . . . Thou hast put all things under his feet." In other words, the poet is rejoicing in the glory of God in order that he may rest the minds of men in God's infinity.

In Psalm 147 we have a similar adjacency of ideas: "He healeth the broken in heart, and bindeth up their wounds. He telleth the number of the stars; he calleth them all by their names."

The psalmists never seem to think of the greatness of God without reveling in the thought of what that means in terms of man's comfort and strengthening.

In Psalm 34—the text already given—the psalmist cries out: "O magnify the Lord with me, and let us exalt his name together," and immediately goes on to say: "*I* sought the Lord, and he heard me. . . . *They* looked unto him, and were lightened." And then, most marvelous of all, "This poor man cried, and the Lord heard *him*, and saved him out of all his troubles." And remember that when the psalmist cries out, as he so often does, "O magnify the Lord," he does not mean, "Let us tell God what a wonderful person he is, and let us in our insignificance crawl at his feet." He means, "Let us realize how big God is and how adequate for all our needs, and let us rest our minds and hearts, our worries, our concern for our loved ones, our whole nation's troubles, on his breast."

> Behold I will build me a nest on the greatness of God.

I am rather jealous for religion in this matter because so often it seems as though the scientist, the poet, the musician, and the dramatist point to a bigger God than ours. I would commend to you the reading of Samuel Foss's great poem "Two Gods." Let me quote two stanzas only:

> As wider skies broke on his view,
>     God greatened in his growing mind;
> Each year he dreamed his God anew,
>     And left his older God behind.

> He saw the boundless scheme dilate,
>   In star and blossom, sky and clod;
> And as the universe grew great,
>   He dreamed for it a greater God.[1]

It is that greater God that so many of us need. And the scientist, whom some may think of as undermining our faith in God, is really a servant of God pointing to the vastness of the Creator.

I am not going to bring to you scientific facts and quote astronomical figures about the vast distance between one star and another or the insignificance of this planet compared with the size and weight of others. (As Pascal said, *"Le silence éternal de ces espaces infinis m'effraie."*) But you remember how Kepler, the astronomer, cried out after much study of the heavens, "O God, I am thinking thy thoughts after thee." If the Milky Way is one of his ideas, what kind of God is this? How, in the light of such a thought, we can hear the intensity of the Master's voice crying, "O men, how little you trust him!" (Matt. 6:30—Moffatt.) Jeans and Eddington and Whitehead have all taught us to have a greater God. Toward the end of Jeans's book *The Mysterious Universe* we find this: "The stream of knowledge is heading towards a non-mechanical reality: the universe begins to look more like a great thought than like a great machine." Popular astronomy is teaching us all to "think God's thoughts after him."

Then think how the poet laments the littleness of religion. Like the scientist, his own God seems bigger than ours. I cannot avoid the feeling that that was in Wordsworth's mind when so passionately he cried:

> We have given our hearts away, a sordid boon!
>
> .    .    .    .    .    .    .    .
>
>                   Great God! I'd rather be
> A Pagan suckled in a creed outworn;
> So might I, standing on this pleasant lea,
> Have glimpses that would make me less forlorn;
> Have sight of Proteus rising from the sea;
> Or hear old Triton blow his wreathèd horn.

[1] *Songs of the Average Man.* By permission of Lothrop, Lee & Shepard Co.

Surely he means that we have whittled down our religion—a religion that should lift us to tuneful harmony with the whole universe —until it has become a triviality.

Or, if you love music and have listened to Bach's "Toccata and Fugue in D minor" or Liszt's "Hungarian Rhapsody"—both of them, you remember, opening in the same way with a series of majestic phrases—I imagine that your heart has been singing, "How great is God, for he is the source of all beauty!"

The dramatist, too, gives one the same feeling. Do you remember near the end of Bernard Shaw's *St. Joan* how Joan lifts up her arms to heaven and cries, "When will the earth be ready to receive thy saints? How long, O Lord, how long?" For myself, I wish Shaw had finished the play at that point. To me everything else is anticlimax. But did you not get in that play the sense of the long, slow processes of life moving out in the hands of a patient God to an end which no man could deny, working through pain and suffering and frustration to some majestic climax beyond all the dreams of man?

And then put over against all that—the revelation of God which the scientist, the poet, the musician, and the dramatist make—put over against that, I say, the conception of religion which you get from so many religious people. It seems trivial, fussy, petty, little-minded, gossipy. Mind! I know the actors quarrel among themselves, and musicians are said to be temperamental, and poets can be odd folk at times, but they keep their pettiness out of their art. Our trouble is that as Christian people we have to practice our art all the time. That is the difficulty. But do let us try to show people a religion that is vast and big. Religion is in the same set of ideas as the boundless sea and mighty mountains and agelong purposes and tremendous courage and adventurous faith and broad tolerance and endless good will. Anyone who is on the verge of the Christian community I would ask to pay no attention to the religion of Mrs. Jones, who has stayed away from church for three Sundays because she was not invited to take an urn at a tea meeting, and who, by her absence, is paying back her fellow Christians and showing God what she thinks of him. Pay no attention to Mr. Smith, who has lost his faith in God because the parson didn't hear of his earache in time to visit him before it was better. No! That has nothing to do with religion at all; and neither, I think, have denominational intolerances or pettifogging committee meetings where, as some wit has said, "minutes are kept, but hours are wasted," or where, as a friend of mine once said, "a group of people, composed of those who individually do not intend to do anything, meet together to decide that nothing shall be done."

Let us *magnify* the Lord together! Let us have a *great* God, not one who appears to be a kind of large-sized, elderly gentleman in a black frock coat, who is almost wholly absorbed in our little denominational chapel. No scientist, no poet, no musician, no dramatist, no artist ought to be able to point to a God greater than the Father of Jesus Christ whom we Christians worship. For all science and all poetry and all music and all drama are but revelations of his nature and his ways with men. Our God, vast and infinite, stands behind them all, greater than man's power to imagine, better than man's loveliest thoughts.

So you can relax your body and hush your mind and quiet your heart and rest in the infinity of God. You have heard of the prayer of the Breton fishermen: "O God, help me. My boat is so small. Thy sea is so large." But on that sea the boat can rest, and a million others too, and on the breast of God can rest every troubled spirit in his world.

Look, if you will, at three things that happen if we have a God who is too small.

1. First of all, he is too small for our lives. We have sung the verse that puts this in a nutshell:

> O Lord, how happy should we be
> If we could cast our care on thee,
>    If we from self could rest,
> And feel at heart that one above,
> In perfect wisdom, perfect love,
>    Is working for the best!

There you have the same idea of resting on his infinity. You see, if you have a little God, you almost get into the mood of one who says to him, "I'm afraid you can't do anything to help me." Whereupon, as my teacher and friend Dr. Maltby would have said, God may turn on you and say, "Oh! I dealt with a much harder case than yours yesterday." If there is a God at all, he is big enough to be trusted, and big enough for all our problems and all our needs and all our troubles. "O magnify the Lord with me . . ."

> Behold I will build me a nest on the greatness of God.

> And I smiled to think God's greatness flowed around our
>    incompleteness,—
> Round our restlessness, his rest.

2. And if we have a little God, the second thing that happens is that he is too small for our prayers. Here I would say a word hoping that you will not misunderstand. It is right for us to imagine God as our Father. Jesus taught us to do this. He built up his parables on this theme. The least erroneous way of thinking of God at all is to think of him as a perfect Father. But I do want very definitely to say this: We are to think of God as a Father as to his character. We are not to think of him as a Father as to his power or the immense scope of his plans or the strange way those plans *appear* to have of going wrong or looking heartless and cruel. God is a Father in that he will never do anything that is unfatherly, whatever appearances may be. But I am sure our conception of God must go beyond the picture of a good human father. Even in terms of character it is often hard to make the word fit, as we shall see.

For example, people have said to me, "I can't understand how God can listen to my prayers if thousands of other people in other places are praying to him at the same moment." But do you see three snags in such a remark? The questioner is imprisoning God in space and in time and in regard to numbers. I know we are all thus imprisoned. We cannot break out of such a prison. We do not know, therefore, what it is like outside the prison of space and time and calculation. But God does not live in that prison. Even though ten thousand prayers come to him at the same time from Greenland or Australia, it makes no difference to God. We can solve the problem only by telling ourselves—what we cannot hope entirely to comprehend—that a numerical system is only a concession to human thinking. If this were not true, God would be like the old woman who lived in a shoe and "had so many children she didn't know what to do." We've overdone the idea of thinking of him as a Father. We've made him only a bit bigger than ourselves. But even we ourselves realize that the greater the human mind the less bewildering are numbers. To an *infinite* mind numbers are not merely less bewildering, but a nonexistent factor in the working out of the purpose. God does not find it "harder" to guide two lives than one. We might express that simply by saying that numbers do not exist to God in the sense in which they exist for us and imprison us. Or, to put it in yet another way, when you pray, God gives himself in loving attention to you *as if you were the only person in the universe*. The difficulty of the questioner whom I have quoted is that his God is too small. He would find rest for his mind in God's infinity.

I hope that does not sound too abstruse, for actually it has a very practical significance. When you pray for Private Jones who is fighting in Germany, don't imagine that God thinks of him as General Montgomery does. The general, however good, is bound to argue, "Well, I must not mind losing several hundred men if I can win this battle and achieve this end." Being human, he cannot possibly give undivided attention to Private Jones. God is not like that. God's love and care and interest surround Private Jones as if he were the only person in the universe, for God is not limited by our prison of time or space or numbers. Said Augustine, "He loves us every one as though there were but one of us to love." If Private Jones is killed, so far from being "lost," as we say, he lives in another and better room in God's house; and when his little daughter, home in England, is sobbing into her pillow because her daddy is killed, the infinite comfort and love of God are round her life as if hers were the only broken heart in God's care. And if Private Jones's wife says she won't believe in God any more because her man is killed, God doesn't desert her or fail to act purposefully in and through her. Indeed, her power to reject him is itself the power of God, and an infinite God is working out purposes which no mere incident like death can do more than divert into another channel. Let us stop thinking of God as though he were only a very great man, even a good man; for, as he says through his inspired prophet, "My ways are higher than your ways, and my thoughts than your thoughts." His power is far greater than anything we associate with the word "father."

3. If we have too small a God, we shall find also that he is too small for our problems. If you think of God only as a Father, you are picking up a key that will not unlock all the doors because it is so hard to stretch the idea of fatherhood to cover all the things which God allows and does. God is good always, to everybody and forever, but the word "fatherly" makes difficulties.

Let me illustrate in three ways:

*a*) God appears to allow vast issues to hang on what we call details. A human father doesn't. He doesn't make a university career depend on whether a boy chooses an egg for breakfast or not. Some vast issues in God's plans appear to depend on details. "Had Cleopatra's nose been shorter," said Pascal, "the whole course of the world would have been altered." Do you not imaginatively tremble when you read the story of Mary and Joseph traveling toward Bethlehem? Here is Mary, expecting her child in an hour or two, and riding on a donkey in the dark. Have you ever thought what would have happened if that donkey had stumbled and thrown that rider off? Have you ever thought about your own life and wondered as you noted what immense things appear to hang on some trivial detail? I could give you illustrations from the lives of men and women in which the greatest happenings have appeared to hang on the most trifling events. Truly, big doors swing on small hinges. Sometimes God seems to take tremendous risks, and chance seems to play such a part.

Here is a paragraph from my friend Isaac Foot's recent booklet on Cromwell and Lincoln:

If Cromwell or Lincoln had been born ten years earlier, or ten years later, the likelihood is we should never have heard of either of them. Some would say it was the mere chance of history that when the Civil War, with all its immense consequences to England and the world, broke out in 1642, Oliver Cromwell was there, aged forty-three, in the plentitude of his capacity, and that when Stephen Douglas, in 1854, proposed the repeal of the Missouri Compromise, Abraham Lincoln was there, at the age of forty-five, at the precise moment when he was best fitted to challenge Douglas and all the implications of his policy. These circumstances, *which we might dismiss as mere chance,* were, in fact, accepted by both men as *the mark of a high vocation,* and, rightly or wrongly, they regarded themsleves as instruments prepared and fitted to meet the challenge which they could only ignore at the peril of their souls.

But, you see, when we are talking like this, we are using words that have no meaning to God. With him *there is no such thing as a detail.* He made a fly's leg as carefully as he made a star. The first wasn't a "detail" and the second "important." With him there is no such thing as chance, for the word, even to us, simply covers those happenings which are the product of laws we do not fully understand. If you knew all the laws that operate when you throw up a penny, you would *know* whether it would come down "heads" or "tails." To an infinite God there is no such thing as chance, for nothing is unknown. Indeed, since there is no such thing as time, there is nothing still to happen which can surprise God, for the future and the past stand in the same relationship to God. Both are eternally present. This is hard for us. It raises immense difficulties including the old bogey that if God knows the future man is not free. Yet when we say God knows the past we don't feel that his knowing determined it. Why do we think his knowing the future determines it? The past and future stand in the same relationship to him. Our only mental rest is in the infinity of God, with whom is no detail, no chance, no unimportant event, no past, no present, no future. All exist in his life, which, being infinite, is beyond our comprehension.

*b)* If you had the power, and you struck a person with lightning, drowned thousands by flood, smote hundreds of thousands by earthquake, you would be locked up in prison, and rightly. As we look at things, we declare that a good father would not allow such a thing to happen if he could prevent it. God, at any rate, *allows* it, and he remains our Father all the time; but I find help by remembering that, while faith must claim for him fatherhood, it must claim for him the infinite purpose acting beyond anything we humans can call fatherly. While we endlessly discuss the problem of pain and suffering, and while there is much light that faith and understanding can throw on such a problem, there is a hard core of impenetrable mystery. I feel it, as you do, when I see a little child suffer. Surely you must see that we need a far bigger conception of God than that he is like a father. We want all that the word "father" can be made to cover, but much more as well.

c) Then, look how unjust life is to many people. A human father tries to be just as he deals with his children. If I took you to Leeds, I could introduce you to two young women. One lived in a happy home, has always had splendid health, went to a very good school, left school and went to Switzerland to "finish," married a nice man, has three lovely children, still lives in a comfortable house, has not suffered through the war, and apparently hasn't a care in the world. But in the same city I could take you to another girl of the same age who lives in a slum. She had an operation, and the surgeon made a mistake. For years she has been in pain and lies in bed in a slum room, from which she can see nothing that God made except a strip of sky. Even that is usually smoke-laden. Further, she isn't a nice pulpit illustration of a person who is always cheerful and bright and into whose room it is a benediction to go. On the contrary, she swears, curses God, and spends hours in bitter, resentful weeping.

But what is God doing to allow such injustice? A human father would put it right if he had the power. And how can that ever be put right? Will the first girl suffer in the next world that the second's troubles may, in some sense, be leveled up? That doesn't make sense, and the second girl doesn't desire it. Can the sufferer have any recompense in another world to make her feel that no injustice has been done? I don't see how. Frankly, I don't know the answer. I don't pretend to know it, and all over the world questions are going up to God from sincere hearts, as well as from bitter, distorted minds—Why? Why? Why? There isn't an answer except that we can rest our minds in the thought of God's infinity. If God is at all, he is infinite. If he is God at all, he is good. For it is incredible that his creatures should be greater than he. Infinite goodness, then, is round about us. We can find peace only in the realization that he must be far greater than our thoughts about him and better than we have the power to conceive. The unquenchable, unsilenceable demand for justice by which we arraign the seeming injustice of God is God's own gift. He planted in our hearts the standards by which we judge him.

I'm not prepared [says a character in a novel by Somerset Maugham] to be made a fool of. If life won't fulfil the demands I make on it, then I have no more use for it. It's a dull and stupid play, and it's only a waste of time to sit it out. I want life to be fair. I want life to be brave and honest. I want men to be decent and things to come right in the end. That's not asking too much, is it? Resignation? That's the refuge of the beaten. Keep your resignation. I don't want it. I'm not willing to accept evil and injustice and ugliness. I'm not willing to stand by while the good are punished and the wicked go scot free. If life means that virtue is trampled on and honesty mocked and beauty fouled, then to hell with life! [2]

Exactly, but what does the last phrase mean? Life has to be *lived,* even though you say, "To hell with it"; and since no explanation is forthcoming which is big enough to fit all the facts, the wise alternative is a faith that rests on God's infinite love and infinite purposefulness.

Let us comfort ourselves by realizing that there are three certainties:

1. We know our values are right—justice, truth, goodness, beauty, kindness, and so on. All who have known God best, assert and exemplify this.

2. We know that our blessedness is his goal; that, in spite of all appearances, he is in charge of the universe, careful of every life; and that we are all within a mighty plan, greater than our conceiving, but the end of which is certainly our highest well-being.

3. We know that our Master, Christ, is a sufficient clue to the nature of God and that in him we can know God as a friend.

Do you realize that when you *know* a person you are content to wait for an explanation of the things he does and allows? "He who hath heard the Word of God," said Ignatius, "can bear his silences."

Some years ago I used an illustration of a little boy whose father

2 From *The Narrow Corner.* Copyright, 1932, by Doubleday, Doran & Co. Reprinted by permission.

was a surgeon. We imagined somebody going to that boy and say-ing: "Do you know that your father gets people on a table and, when they are unconscious and cannot defend themselves, cuts their bodies with a sharp knife and sometimes takes parts of them away? How would you like to have that done to you?" The child could not argue; but if he could, he would rest his mind in the greatness of his father, *and in his knowledge of his father reached by another route*. "I know my Daddy," we could imagine the child saying, "and I have to leave what you say until I can fit the puzzle together."

We cannot comprehend the infinity of God. God will always be beyond the compass of our little, finite minds, and he will both do and allow things that puzzle, bewilder, and affright us; but, al-though we don't know much *about* God, we know God in Jesus and, knowing, can rest our minds in his infinity.

> Yet, in the maddening maze of things,
>   And tossed by storm and flood,
> To one fixed trust my spirit clings;
>   I know that God is good! [3]

> I will build me a nest on the greatness of God.

> And I smiled to think God's greatness flowed around our
>   incompleteness,—
> Round our restlessness, his rest.

"O magnify the Lord with me, and let us exalt his name to-gether," for he is greater than all human thought concerning him and better than all men's dreams.

[3] John Greenleaf Whittier.

# A MESSAGE TO THE SPIRITUALLY DISCOURAGED

I HAVE CHOSEN A NUMBER OF TEXTS BECAUSE I WANT US TO SEE HOW repeatedly Paul offered this message to the Christians to whom he wrote:

If any man be in Christ, there is a new creation.
—II Cor. 5:17 (R.V. margin)

Put ye on the Lord Jesus Christ. —Rom. 13:14

As many of you as have been baptized into Christ, have put on Christ.
—Gal. 3:27

Put on the new man. —Eph. 4:24

Ye have put off the old man with his deeds; and have put on the new man. —Col. 3:9-10

Reckon ye also yourselves to be dead indeed unto sin, but alive unto God through Jesus Christ our Lord. —Rom. 6:11

Ye are dead, and your life is hid with Christ in God. —Col. 3:3

To all these words of Paul I should like to add the words of Christ in the parable of the prodigal son:

Bring forth the best robe, and put it on him. —Luke 15:22

Very few of us really know ourselves, and not one of us knows himself completely. No man has ever seen his own eyes, but only their reflection, since he uses his eyes with which to see. Similarly, no man has seen his own spiritual nature, but only its reflection in his reactions to circumstances. Have you never looked in a mirror and said, "Good heavens! do I look like that?" Have you never looked back on the way you behaved in certain circumstances, on the way you reacted to certain happenings, and said with even deeper dismay, "Good heavens, am I really that kind of person?"

Even that part of our nature at which we *can* look, we see only through colored spectacles. When we try to look at our inner selves, we look at them through spectacles colored by complexes, prejudices, temperamental distortions, influences that affected our childhood, heredity, environment, and so on.

Some people look at themselves through rose-colored spectacles. A man sees himself as "a fairly decent chap," or as a successful businessman, or as a popular speaker. A woman may see herself as a social success, or as a good wife or mother, or perhaps as a beautiful singer. Even those who see themselves in such attractive colors often suspect that deep within the house of their personality are less reputable selves; and sometimes in quiet moments, say of lonely wakefulness, queer forms creep up the cellar steps into the passage, and leer at them in the gloom. But these glimmering ghosts are quickly chased back into the cellar again, and the door is slammed and locked. Such people hate for the phantoms of their unattractive selves to escape from the cellar of the unconscious mind. The cellar is admittedly a better place to keep such ghosts than the living room. But it would be better still to call them all up from the cellar, recognize them, and take steps to throw them out of the house of life forever. The experience called conversion, if genuine, is a good and often a speedy way of driving out devils and giving Christ the key of every room from attic to basement.

I am not going to spend any time talking to those who look at themselves *only* through rose-colored spectacles, because the time would be wasted. Until the spectacles crack and break, such people will probably refuse to be honest with themselves and to see themselves as they are. They can rarely be persuaded that they wear spectacles at all, and no one can help those who say, "There is nothing wrong with me. Nothing is here for treatment or for adjustment. There is no meanness or jealousy, unkindness or resentment, hate or bad temper about me." As Jesus said, with that sad irony of his, "They that be whole need not a physician."

But such people are in the minority. The greater number of people I meet look at themselves through dark lenses. They think the worst of themselves. They think of themselves as those who count for little, who are not much good anyway, who have never been able to make much of a fist of life. The more they know themselves, the more they tend to despise themselves. Some who have been psychoanalyzed feel that they will never be happy again, such depths of depravity and poisoned motive and dark wells of beastliness have they found within themselves.

Indeed, an hour of introspection seems to have made even Paul fall into something like despair about himself, a despair that vanishes only when he turns from himself to Christ. Listen to this:

For in me (that is, in my flesh) no good dwells, I know; the wish is there, but not the power of doing what is right. I cannot be good as I desire to be, and I do wrong against my wishes. . . . I desire to do what is right, but wrong is all I can manage; I cordially agree with God's law, so far as my inner self is concerned, but then I find another law in my members which conflicts with the law of my mind and makes me a prisoner to sin's law that resides in my members. . . . Miserable wretch that I am! Who will rescue me from this body of death? God will! Thanks be to him, through Jesus Christ our Lord.     —Rom. 7:18-25 (Moffatt)

The phrase Paul uses there, "this body of death," is probably a reference to that awful method of punishment by which a corpse was strapped to the back of a criminal so that he had to carry it about with him wherever he went. He could not remove it. He lay down with it at night. He rose up with it in the morning. The stench of its foul corruption was all about him. Even when he sat down to eat, he could not escape it. The burden must have been intolerable. Paul uses it as a figure of speech to describe the inescapable burden of sin which man carries, and which he cannot get rid of by himself. "Who will deliver me," he cries in anguish, "from this body of death—this awful sense of burden and self-loathing, of failure and hopelessness?" And then we almost hear the bonds snapping and the horror falling away from him as he says, "God will! . . . through Jesus Christ our Lord."

Many, I feel, if they were honest and had Paul's gift of self-expression, would go all the way with him in this description of his spiritual despair, and yet, perhaps, could not go on with him to echo his glad, final cry, "God will!" These are the people I should like to help, by getting them to take note of the way in which Paul himself offers encouragement and hope and release to those in the early church who were as heavily burdened as we are.

How can release be obtained? It was to answer this question that I quoted such a rich sample of passages in which Paul says, "Put on Christ." You may possibly feel impatient at those three simple words. The disease is so terrible; the cure sounds so incredibly easy as to be ridiculously ineffective. Here is a man broken by evil, defeated by sin, crushed by its burden; and he goes to this master of the spiritual life, Paul, knowing that he too has passed through these self-same difficulties. He says to Paul, "What *am* I to do?" and Paul simply says, "Put on Christ." It sounds as simple as putting on a robe. Surely it cannot be as easy as that! Surely it means a long, difficult treatment! Surely it demands a tremendous self-discipline over a long period! But no; again and again, to people far worse than ourselves, Paul repeats, "Put on Christ. Put off the old man, put on the new man." Well, this must be looked into! If this is true, it is the most wonderful news in the world.

I heard a little while ago, from a friend who has recently returned from Africa, of an African tribe that used to offer up human sacrifices. In one of their pagan rites the tribesmen demanded that a male member should be selected as the victim who must be put to death. A government official, greatly loved and much admired, did all he knew to stop this practice, but in vain. In desperation, the official finally said, "If you *will* do this, I demand the right to choose the next victim. You will find him tomorrow morning at dawn on the crest of that little hill, robed and veiled. That is the man you must take." The next morning, as the sun came up, the tribesmen looked toward the top of this little knoll, and there stood their victim, robed and veiled. Without any scrutiny, they took him and put him to death. When he was dead, they found that it was their beloved adviser, the government official himself, the man who had pleaded with them to give up their evil ways, and who, finding his words were in vain, had sealed his witness with his life. Is it too imaginative to press that story to our service and suggest that perhaps the robe which that government official wore became for the tribe the symbol of lives that were changed through a noble death?

"Now," says Paul, "put on Christ," as though the nature of Christ were a robe, the robe of one who can still change lives through a noble death, one whose words were beautiful and challenging and healing, but whose words were as nothing compared with the power of a life laid down. "We preach," he said to the Corinthians, "Christ crucified, . . . Christ the power of God, and the wisdom of God."

You may say to me: "Yes, but that's only an illustration, just a figure of speech. To think of the nature of Christ as a robe one can put on may be a beautiful flight of imagination, but it leaves my nature untouched. Underneath the robe I am just the same as I was before."

But wait a minute! Do you believe that Jesus Christ can change a person's life? Ask yourself that question as sincerely as you can. Do you believe that Christianity is a matter of going to church, singing hymns, joining in prayers, listening to sermons, trying to live a good life by the power of your own will; or do you believe that at the heart of Christianity is a tremendous, dynamic, and transforming power, and that Christ can sweep into a man's life and change it utterly? I am going to assume that you believe the latter, for that is the truth of the matter. If it were not, Christianity would not have gone on for so long, would not have achieved the victories which it has achieved on all the shores of the world through two thousand years of time.

If, then, you believe that, let me ask you the next question: When does that change begin? I say *begin* because, admittedly, it may take years to finish completely. But when does it begin? *It begins when you change your mental picture of yourself.* Our great-grandfathers would have said that it begins when you put your faith in Christ. I am expressing the same message rather differently because we live in a different age. But, if you forget everything else in the sermon, try to take hold of this: *It begins when you change your mental picture of yourself.* It begins when you see yourself no longer a man defeated by some secret sin or shuffling along in a state of compromise; as a woman overwhelmed by all her problems, a pitiful, impoverished, weak, defeated person. It begins when you see yourself to be the kind of person that Christ can make you if he has his way with you. When Paul says, "Put off the old man," he means put away the old picture of that broken, defeated prisoner of evil; clean the slate of the mind of that impression of yourself that shows you to be defeated, overwhelmed, incapable of being anything different from what you are now; and see yourself triumphant, victorious, serene, the master or the mistress of your own life.

I am going to ask you to indulge in an imaginative flight that may seem fanciful; but if you are in earnest about Christianity, please do this. Imagine that you are at this moment looking at yourself in a full-length mirror. You are clothed in black, the black of self-despising and failure and defeat. Then, as you continue to look in the mirror, Christ, wearing a red robe—and it would be red, wouldn't it?—comes alongside you, and he puts his red robe right around you. Now, when you look in the mirror, you are a person clothed in red; you are a person very close to· Christ, and that blessed union will make you like him. It may take time admittedly; but already, *already,* you are a changed person, allied with him in a new closeness of relationship. Something has begun—and I don't mind how much you emphasize the time it will take to complete the process—but something has begun which has already made you a person clothed in red instead of a person clothed in black. His radiant personality has done something already. In faith that the old self is dead, its mourning has been covered with resplendent crimson. You have reckoned yourself dead to sin. You dwell in Christ. You are one with him. Your life is hid with Christ. You abide in him. You have put on Christ.

"Bring forth the best robe and put it on him," said the prodigal's father in the famous story, and *that was done in a moment.* Only yesterday the prodigal was in the far country among the swine and the sins; and, if you like to sound a pessimistic note, maybe tomorrow he will have some regrets at what has happened today and think with evil longing of the delights of the far country. But look, he is wearing the robe of the son. He is different already. The relationship is different, and he himself knows in his heart that, although yesterday he was not only with the swine but one of them, today he is a son. He has put on the robe.

So it may be with you, my brother, my sister. You are clothed in the black clothes of the spirit. You are downhearted, frustrated, depressed, frightened, defeated, hopeless—one, if not more than one, of these things. And perhaps in your heart you are saying, "It's no good trying. I'm no good. I hate myself, but I shall never be any different. Life is too hard for me. I give it up."

Now, listen to the gospel! Put on Christ! Here is a new nature like a robe put around you by his loving arm. He is offering himself to you. I beseech you, don't shrink away from him. Let that loving arm come round you. Let that scarlet, blood-dyed robe be put over you. And then, above all, *never again look at your old self, wearing the black robe of self-despising, the dark clothes of inescapable failure and unconquerable sin.* "Reckon ye also yourselves to be dead indeed unto sin." "Ye are dead, and your life is hid with Christ in God." Recall the passages at the beginning of the sermon. Listen while Paul exhausts language, weighing the vessels of his words down to the very waterline to make them carry this precious new cargo of the gospel for which no words that were adequate existed. "You are dead," he says; "don't have anything to do with corpses." That old despairing, timid, defeated person, that victim of sin's power, that plaything of hot lust, is dead. All right! Have done with corpses! You are in Christ, and "if any man be in Christ, there is a new creation."

Now please notice two further points: (1) the importance of seeing yourself thus, and (2) the importance of God's seeing you thus.

1. First of all, then, look at the importance of seeing yourself thus. Try to follow this rather carefully, if you will. You cannot be happy unless you can live with yourself. You cannot live with yourself unless, at least to some extent, you like yourself. You cannot like yourself if you know yourself, and the better you know yourself the more you discover within yourself that is hateful, and the less you like yourself. So, as life proceeds, things get worse and worse, because, as you get older, you get to know yourself better, if you are honest, and thus hate yourself more. That explains why so many

elderly people seem so pathetically hungry for the approval of others. The human mind needs appreciation as much as the body needs food and fresh air. Yet elderly people often find themselves out, and then begin to hate themselves secretly. The reason why they hunger for approval is that the approval of others is an anodyne to deaden the pain of hating themselves. They want others to bolster them up, to tell them they're not such bad folk after all. The approval of others counteracts to some extent their disapproval of themselves. But here, as in every dilemma of the human mind, the Christian gospel comes with its complete answer. Thus the only way to be independent of the approval of others is to approve of yourself; and since he who knows himself can never approve of himself, your peace of mind depends on changing yourself; and your only hope of doing that is found in Christ. In Christ—or, to keep the figure, by putting on the robe, by putting on Christ—you can exchange the self you hate for the new self he is creating; and you are to see yourself *already* as the kind of person you will certainly become, unless you throw off the robe and turn your back on him.

But see the importance of looking upon yourself thus in another way. We all love to be loved, and when things are not going well with us, we all love to get sympathy. But let me indicate one danger to those who, almost morbidly, demand sympathy from others. If you go about asking for sympathy, you are etching deeper into the mind the picture of yourself as a person *needing* sympathy, that is, a weak person. Those who have been deprived of love, and whose nature is emotionally starved, tend quite naturally either to indulge in self-pity or to demand a great deal of sympathy from others, or both; for both are love substitutes, and we want at all costs to be loved. But it would be healthier if, while we admitted our longing for the love of our fellow men and women, we refused to allow ourselves to live with a mental picture of ourselves that showed us to be the kind of people who *depended* on others. The line of the hymn, "Thou, O Christ, art all I want," is literally true, though it may take years for us to realize it; and to "put on Christ" means holding in our own minds a picture of ourselves as already the resplendent, scarlet-cloaked beings, the new men in Christ, which we are becoming in him. Then, instead of needing sympathy, you become the kind of person who offers it to others; instead of showing a pitiful dependence on being loved, you go about among your fellows as one who offers love; and, strangely enough—because this is how God has arranged life—love comes back to the person who gives it in a far greater measure than it comes to the man or woman who demands it. There is a very sound psychology, as well as a deep piety, behind the ancient prayer that says: "Teach us, O Lord, not to seek so much to be consoled as to console, not so much to be understood as to understand, not so much to be loved as to love. Show us that it is in giving that we receive, in self-forgetting that we find, in dying that we waken to eternal life."

Seeking always for sympathy has another bad effect on the soul; it undermines courage. It is easier to put the healing ointment of sympathy on the sore place than to find out why it becomes so sore. The reason is often a fear that must be rooted out or overcome. We tend to accept sympathy instead of facing the fear that makes us want sympathy. The more we can switch attention from the symptom of weakness to the action that will overcome it, the better. The sympathy of others is very lovely, and we are entitled to a measure of it as long as it does not become an anodyne for our own cowardice and for the pain which the recognition of our cowardice would inflict upon us. To "put on Christ" means identifying ourselves with one who will take us, cowards though we are, and change our nature so that we shan't need sympathy, but become the kind of people who can give it. In him we shall assess courage higher than the need of sympathy. Emphasis on the latter makes us permanently weak characters. To see ourselves as courageous "in Christ" makes the beginning of strength, the strength of those who can "stand their corner" and cope with their difficulties and say with Paul, "In him who strengthens me, I am able for anything" (Moffatt). As the new picture of ourselves "in Christ" grows stronger and clearer in our own minds, we tend to become like it and enjoy the power it brings more than we used to enjoy the sympathy of others concerning our weakness. It is better to be "on top of things," as we say, with that exhilarating feeling of conquest, than underneath them, however sympathetic people may be with us in our adversities.

2. Second, turn to the importance of God's seeing us as new men in Christ. You will remember that poem of Tennyson called "The Ancient Sage," where, talking about faith, he says:

> She spies the summer through the winter bud,
> She tastes the fruit before the blossom falls,
> She hears the lark within the songless egg,
> She finds the fountain where they wail'd "Mirage."

That is how God looks at you. Remember that God is not imprisoned in time. You can see yourself only as you are now, and you feel that years and years of hard climbing stretch before you. But I am sure it is true to say that God's assessment of your character is not in terms of present achievement, but of tendency and direction. God, from beyond the time prison, can see you as already perfected, can see you as you are bound to become unless you creep out from under that robe—the robe of Christ's nature—and cut yourself off from its power. And, frankly, God can receive you—since he is utterly righteous and perfectly holy—not as you are in yourself now, for in you is no worth at all, but only as you are in Christ. Man has worth only in what he is capable of becoming, and he is capable of becoming his maximum only through Christ. If I may coin a word, man's "worthness" is established, not in any value he can attain by his own efforts, merit, or abilities, but because of what Christ can make of him. That which he of himself could never become, and that which men would deny as being of any value, is worth a lot to the God who sees him in Christ—a Christ who thought man was worth dying for. As Browning says,

> All I could never be,
> All men ignored in me,
> This I was worth to God.

Thus, in a beautiful Communion hymn, we pray that God will "only look on us as found in him."

I charge you, then, to make this day the day of your conversion. Many of us have never been converted. We have been brought up in Christian homes, but, to be quite honest, we have been content with a conventional sham. The transforming power of Christ has never been released into our lives. We sing the hymns and say the words, but they are forms without the fire. If you doubt this, ask yourself two or three questions of great significance. Could you lead another to Jesus Christ? Have you found something in him that you could pass on? If the early Christians had been like you, do you think Christianity would have spread through the pagan world? We are shy of the very word "conversion." We think it has something to do with emotional excitement, with revivalistic meetings that nice, respectable, cultured, well-educated people despise. But conversion, which of course *may* be a highly emotional experience, has much more to do with a simple act of obedience and with a simple turning toward Christ in some quiet hour of the soul's revelation of its own most desperate need. Don't wait for some great dramatic event or emotional experience. Christ offers himself to you. Take him in faith. Don't bother about your feelings. Indeed, you may *feel* no different right away. But "put on Christ." Make a beginning with him and reaffirm that dear allegiance every morning. Alter your mental picture of yourself, and see yourself, by his grace, as already the changed personality which deep in your heart you desire to be.

But I must give you some warnings:

1. You will often want to slip back and be the "old man" you used to be. That "old man" is an old friend, and it is easier to live with old friends than with new friends. Christ, the new friend, will make new demands, set up new conflicts, bring new challenges. For that reason, many in the early days of Christian discipleship find life much harder and less happy. There was no conflict before, no challenge. They pursued the path of their own will. Now they are pulled up at nearly every step. But if you slip out from under the robe, slip back again; and if you fall and put off Christ, then put on Christ again every evening.

2. The devil will try to tempt you that nothing has happened at all, that all is just imaginative talk. Well, recall that the triumphant history of the Christian church through years of persecution and the history of the church that is being written now—where in India and China and Africa men are finding in these old New Testament

words the very power of God—adequately answer that argument. Why shouldn't it all be true for you?

3. You will hesitate to believe that your personality is being changed, and like a frightened horse you will tremble and shy at the dangers in the road. I would say to you, "Never mind if you do tremble! Put this newly seen, newborn personality to the test. If you believe in yourself, you will find that the new self is stronger than the old, for Christ's personality is now added to yours; and if you feel like trembling, well, tremble!" Do you remember that lovely story of Turenne, the beloved marshal of France, who sacrificed so much that he might maintain his Christian Protestant witness? When he was shaving just before a battle, his hand trembled violently, and he turned on his own body and said, "Tremblest thou, vile carcass? Thou wouldst tremble more if thou knewest where I am going to take thee this day." But though he trembled, he went on. I tremble too, grow sick with feelings of fear, feel my heart turn to lead within my breast. But when I have had the courage to put "the new man" to the test, Christ has never let me down.

4. Remember, lastly, that often when you don't feel any different, and when you feel a failure, neither God nor others see you thus. How well I remember in Leeds a man coming into my vestry and giving me a contribution for the poor because his daughter's life had been changed in a service that I had conducted. He said that the whole atmosphere of the home was different. Yet, five minutes earlier, the girl herself had been talking to me in great depression and almost in tears because she felt such a failure and because, though she sought to follow Christ, she found her home life overwhelmingly hard and thought her witness a failure.

In my study a week or two ago a ministerial friend told me this lovely story. He said that, when he was a little boy, he was out for a walk with his father, and they saw a most vivid rainbow, the end of which lighted up the rocks quite near the path along which they were walking. The little boy said to his father, "Daddy, let me go and stand in the light of the rainbow," and off he went. Of course to the boy the light of the rainbow was always a little bit farther on and never seemed to bathe him in its splendor. But when his father looked at his dear son, the glory of the rainbow light seemed to transfigure him. When we set ourselves to leave the paths of selfishness along which we have been walking and seek to enter into spiritual realities, the light of the glory of God seldom seems to be round about us. It always seems a little farther on. Sometimes we grow disheartened and depressed. Achievement falls so short of desire. But I think when our heavenly Father looks upon us he sees the light of spiritual beauty around us, because the glory of Christ transfigures a man immediately as he steps off the path of selfish desire and longs to be caught up into the light and life of God. You may not discern the light around you, but God sees it, and, more often than we think, other people do too.

Lift up your hearts, then, and take courage, for the man who "puts on Christ" has nothing to fear in this life or the next. Claim your inheritance as a child of God. Realize yourself united with Christ and, remembering that Christ is God and that you are linked with him, remember that there is no power of evil which can defeat God, nor anything that can possibly happen in this world or another that can overwhelm the man who is one with God in Christ. That is what made John Wesley translate the poem of Zinzendorf thus:

> Jesus, thy blood and righteousness
> My beauty are, my glorious dress;
> 'Midst flaming worlds, in these arrayed,
> With joy shall I lift up my head.
>
> Bold shall I stand in thy great day,
> For who aught to my charge shall lay?
> Fully absolved through these I am,
> From sin and fear, from guilt and shame.
>
> .    .    .    .    .    .    .
>
> O let the dead now hear thy voice,
> Now bid thy banished ones rejoice,
> Their beauty this, their glorious dress,
> Jesus, thy blood and righteousness!

Put on Christ! Do it now, as though just you and Christ were alone in a vast solitude. Bow before him in adoration and worship until you feel the robe of his loving nature put around you, and realize that it is you, worthless in yourself, that he thought worth dying for, and will never leave until he has made you all his own. All life can be different for you. Don't let anything put you off this great transaction. "If *any man* be in Christ, there is a new creation." Why not you?

# TO THINE OWN SELF BE TRUE

IS A FAMILIAR PASSAGE IN SHAKESPEARE'S "HAMLET" WHICH
runs thus:

> This above all: to thine own self be true,
> And it must follow, as the night the day,
> Thou canst not then be false to any man.

As we have often reminded ourselves, we are each a number of
selves. Often those selves are in conflict with one another. To har-
ness them all and make them all pull the way of our highest purposes, and thus our truest well-being, is a lifelong task over which
none of us can afford to be dilatory. That task is called by some
psychologists the "integration of personality." Others speak of "adjustment to life," or the "co-ordination of the instincts." Lovers of
Trine speak of being "in tune with the infinite." Whatever we call
it, we know that our truest "self" evolves and emerges to a place of
dominance as this task is successfully achieved. We each become a
unity and attain peace within.

To fail in this task of integration and to allow what we may call
for the moment our "lower selves" to have their way is to lose our
inner peace and, ultimately, to be disgusted with ourselves—in a
literal sense our selves—and land ourselves, either on this side of
the grave or on the other, in remorse. To quote Dante Gabriel
Rossetti's poem about "The Murdered Selves":

> I do not see them here: but after death
> God knows, I know the faces I shall see,
> Each one a murdered self, with low, last breath.
> "I am thyself,—What hast thou done to me?"
> "And I—and I—thyself," (lo, each one saith),
> "And thou thyself to all eternity!"

The true self is in harmony with God's will at each point of its journey. Finding what his will is becomes a demand made on every sincere Christian soul. I have spoken of ways in which we can discern his will,[1] and one of them was a consideration of the advice of others and of the dictates of our own common sense. Yet, for the man who would be true to himself and follow the voice of God within the soul, there may often come the demand that he should discount the advice of friends, and even the dictates of common sense, in order to be true to himself.

There is an incident in the life of the Master which lights this up for us. Jesus had been away in Tyre for nearly a year. We know this because just before he went we read of the green grass on which the five thousand reclined while they were fed, and then the Gospel narrative takes up the thread of our Lord's life again at Passover time, which of course corresponds with our Easter. From early summer the grass in Palestine is brown. No one could describe it as green, so that probably it is right to assume, as Professor Burkitt does, that Jesus was away at Tyre for at least nine months. Hardly anything is known of his movements or his words during that period.

Such study as I have been able to pursue makes me certain that during that period a revolution took place in his own mind. It is no disparagement of our Lord to say that, since his was a human mind, it could receive the revelations of God only slowly. Indeed, as the Epistle to the Hebrews says, he "learned . . . by the things which he suffered." "Learning" involves something done gradually, and I believe that Jesus was led step by step to understand the unfolding purpose of God for his life. At first, I think, he thought his ministry was to the Jews only, and he said so: "I am not sent but unto the lost sheep of the house of Israel"—words which he may have spoken at the beginning of his visit to Tyre. He was to be the *Jewish* Messiah. But away in the solitude of Tyre he learned God's developing plan. He was to be not the Jewish Messiah only but the Saviour of the world. And he was not to win by living; he was to win by dying.

Immediately after he came back from Tyre, he began *for the first*

[1] In a chapter of *The Will of God*.

*time* to speak about his death, and *for the first time* to speak about a message to the whole world. Now Peter loved him dearly. Naturally he could not bear to think of his Master's death. "Be it far from thee, Lord: this shall never be unto thee." But Jesus turned and said unto Peter: "Get thee behind me, Satan: thou art a stumblingblock unto me: for thou mindest not the things of God, but the things of men."

The words sound harsh, but if you have just come to a decision which has cost you immense anguish of mind, and which is far removed from your former plans and natural desires, the advice of a friend to tread the path you have just decided to eschew imposes an almost intolerable strain. It arouses again in the heart the fierce temptation which only with difficulty has just been conquered. I am quite sure, in my own mind, that the measure of the violence of Jesus is the measure of the strength of the temptation which Peter's advice aroused again in his mind. Jesus was completely human, as well as in a unique sense divine. He was a young, fit man who hoped to live. He was a great teacher who desired to be followed. He had the natural shrinking from death which we all have, plus the human fear that his whole ministry would fail if he could not establish it in what we call success. At the very last he prayed, "If it be possible, let this cup pass from me."

It is true that the violence of Jesus to Peter is not as severe as our Western minds suppose. The word "Satan" is not so unkind as it sounds. A friend of mine traveling in Jerusalem a few years before the war heard one cabby call another "Satan." The Arabs still use the word for someone who gets in the way, and Matthew's word "stumblingblock" conveys the sense in which the word is still used.

But in the incident I want us to see that Jesus did not always follow the advice of friends or the dictates of common sense, both of which would have pointed the way to safety. We see him running counter to the wishes of others because he had to be true to that best self—the self that was dedicated to doing the will of God. And from his own experience Jesus whispers to us, "To thine own self be true."

If Jesus had listened to the advice of others at some points in his ministry, perhaps we should never have heard of him. No doubt

Mary, on the advice of the local pastor at Nazareth, had said in earlier days, "But, dear, you have never had a rabbi's training. Why can't you stay quietly at home?" No doubt James his brother, on whom in the absence of Jesus heavy responsibility would fall, since Joseph was by this time dead, said, "Do you expect *me* to run the business?" Peter said, in regard not only to the path of suffering but to the path of duty, "Be it far from thee, Lord"; and there is evidence that the other disciples "walked no more with him," because his interpretation of messiahship was so utterly different from their own. In fact they said to him, "Why don't you use your power and set up your kingdom and reign?" and the Devil had whispered this to him before the disciples thought of it. But Jesus kept on in order that he might be true to himself.

In other spheres of life men have done the same with immense benefit to the world, and I think it would thrust home our message if we glanced down the corridors of history and noted briefly a dozen instances of this:

1. Here is Copernicus, the Polish doctor and priest, stating his astronomical theory in the face of all the learning of his day, and, more right than he ever knew, changing all men's thoughts of the universe. He was true to himself, with immense benefit to science.

2. Here is Galileo, watching a lamp swinging in the cathedral at Pisa, when he ought to have been listening to the sermon, and deducing conclusions which in 1616 led him to assert that the earth goes round the sun. Incredible as it may seem, the church authorities made such a statement a religious heresy. They clung to the current belief that the earth was the fixed center of the universe. Galileo was hauled before the inquisitors, who threatened him with such torture that he recanted in 1632. After recantation, it is said, he rose to his feet and muttered, *"E pur si muove"*—"But it does move." He was true to himself, with immense benefit to astronomy.

3. Here is Luther, the first Protestant, saying bravely in the face of all that authority could do to hurt him: "Here stand I, I can no other, so help me God!" He was true to himself, with immense benefit to religion.

4. Here is Columbus, seeking support for his "mad enterprise," begging for ships, derided at court, disbelieved at last even by his

own men, but determined "to strive, to seek, to find, and not to yield." He was true to himself, with immense benefit to our knowledge of the world.

5. Here is Joan of Arc, a mere slip of a girl, chided and derided, but canonized at last by the church that burned her, and doing more good since her execution than before it. She was true to herself and has ever since been an inspiration to all who read her story.

6. Here is John Wesley, who was harried by the Church of England partly because he would not observe the etiquette of not preaching in another's parish without permission. "The world is my parish" was his challenging response to his critics. He was true to himself, and the historian John Richard Green tells us that John Wesley saved the country from revolution in the eighteenth century. More importantly, he saved men and women from despair, and spiritually set the whole country alight with his evangelism.

7. William Booth inaugurated the Salvation Army, which now is praised by kings, but which, in its early days, was stoned and persecuted, its leader and founder treated with ridicule. Almost all his friends tried to persuade William Booth to settle down in a local chapel as a Methodist minister, but he was true to himself, and every true Christian must thank God for the grand work which the Salvation Army has done on all shores.

8. Here is Robertson Smith, a religious leader at the other end of the intellectual scale from William Booth, perhaps the most brilliant Old Testament scholar England has produced, but equally one of God's pioneers. At twenty-three he was appointed professor of Oriental languages and Old Testament exegesis at the Free Church College, Aberdeen. Practically all biblical scholars now accept his conclusions; but when he announced them, he was tried for heresy, hounded out of his chair, and no longer allowed to be a professor. In the book he afterward published, *The Old Testament and the Jewish Church,* he vindicated his position. He was editor of the ninth edition of the *Encylopaedia Britannica,* and in 1883 was appointed professor of Arabic at Cambridge University. He was true to himself, to the great benefit of honest thinking and the cause of truth.

9. Woodrow Wilson is accounted by many a failure. I think of him as a man who was true to himself. When he arrived in London, people cheered him in the streets, and at one time the hopes of the world seemed centered in him. Crafty politicians proved too much for him, and he died of a broken heart. But his soul goes marching on, and still his principles are the only ones on which we may hope to build a peace that is anything more than an uneasy truce.

10. Frederick Atkins, the journalist, has told the story of his brilliant colleague, H. W. Massingham, a journalist who was three times thrown out of an editorial chair because he and the proprietor of his newspaper lived in different worlds. Massingham lived in the world of right and wrong. The proprietors concerned apparently lived in the world of profit and loss. A writer in the *New Statesmen* said of Massingham: "He cared nothing for money or fame or praise, but he had a furious and impersonal desire for the welfare of the world which literally consumed his energies and destroyed his peace of mind." Massingham was true to himself, to the great benefit of honest journalism.

11. We all know the story of Oates, who accompanied Scott to the South Pole, and who, contrary to all the dictates of common sense and advice of friends, walked out into the blizzard that terrible night, "a very gallant gentleman" who would not let his own sufferings hold up his friends. But not everybody realizes that Edward Wilson, the frail doctor, accompanied the same expedition. Wilson had suffered in earlier days from tuberculosis of the lungs and had the greatest difficulty in persuading medical authorities and, indeed, Captain Scott himself to allow him to go with the expedition. But in one of the tenderest letters ever written Scott wrote as follows to Mrs. Wilson:

If this letter reaches you, Bill [Dr. Wilson] and I will have gone out together. We are very near it now, and I should like you to know how splendid he was at the end—everlastingly cheerful and ready to sacrifice himself for others, never a word of blame to me for leading him into this mess. His eyes have a comfortable, blue look of hope, and his mind is peaceful with the satisfaction of his faith in regarding himself as part of the great scheme of the Almighty. I can do no more to comfort you than to tell you that he died as he lived, a brave, true man; the best of comrades and staunchest of friends.

12. We might conclude our list with Mr. Winston Churchill, who has never once said, "I told you so," even though, if we had heeded that lonely voice in 1918 as to the best way of treating the defeated German nation, I feel quite certain myself that we should not have had to defeat Germany over again at such terrible cost in the lives of brave men.

The voice of the people may sometimes be the voice of God, as the popular Latin tag says—*vox populi, vox Dei.*[2] The wisdom of friends may often guide us. The voice of common sense may, indeed, be a true pointer. But sometimes both will mislead. No one will say to us, "Be it far from thee, Lord!" but they *will* say, "Don't be silly, Tom," or, "I'm only advising you in your own interests, Joan." It is hard to oppose the advice of those we love. Again and again, even when we've taken the difficult step, the way seems so much harder than we dreamed that our own minds fill with misgiving. At such times a man must be alone and be quiet enough to hear the voice of God and not allow the *vox populi* to deafen him. It was the *vox populi* that cried, "Away with this man! Crucify him!" And when I think of Rupert Brooke and Wilfred Owen, and countless others in whose breasts burned the divine fire, I sometimes wonder just how much crucifixion has been done through the voice of the people.

The picture in my own mind at the moment is that of a sensitive compass needle. A mysterious, unseen power swings it to the north and points out the way. But let a bag of steel nails come near the compass, and the needle will turn anywhere but north. You must take it right away from those influences and let it respond only to the mysterious power if you wish to get a true reading. So, deep in every man's nature, a Mysterious Power is at work which no one can quite understand, but which no one can safely explain away. Left to itself, it will point out our true direction. As I brood on the

[2] Accuracy demands the admission that the tag, ascribed to Alcuin, in a letter to Charlemagne, probably meant originally that the voice of the people is irresistible.

incident in our Lord's life, I feel that I must say to you and to my-self that the presence and advice of others must be considered. Indubitably sometimes God guides us through them; but every discerning spirit would do well, having listened, to go away into a solitary place and, putting everything else on one side, listen and wait for that Mysterious Power which cannot always make its presence felt amid the babble of other tongues and the confusion of other voices.

Nor is it only other voices that can disturb the poise of the spirit. Our instincts—which in my own mind I reduce to three in num-ber: self, sex, and social—while they are amoral in themselves, that is, neither moral nor immoral apart from our own handling of them, tend to pull us toward the lower paths of life. With the emo-tions that are attached to them they form the driving power of personality. One might call them the engine of the mind, but he who drives the engine knows how hard it is to direct and control them. The self instinct *tends* to make us selfish. The sex instinct *tends* to make us give rein to sexual impulses. The herd or social instinct *tends* to make us go with the crowd. I think the saints would be unanimous in saying that spiritual achievement involves a battle with the instincts.

The irreligion all around us is another factor which disturbs the poise of the compass needle of which I have spoken. We frequently comment that this is an irreligious age, but we do not always realize that our own communion with God and our sensitiveness to his voice are always threatened by the irreligion which is characteristic of all civilized countries at the present day.

We see this not only in religion but in other ways too. Your taste for Beethoven would tend to disappear if you heard nothing but jazz. Your taste for great literature would tend to disappear if you read nothing but newsstand novelettes. Your taste for great drama would lose its appetite if you saw only those sexy plays which are part of the garbage found in the track of a decadent civilization. Your taste for simple joys and homely pleasures would tend to disappear if continually you tried to speed up the tempo of life by hectic gambling and drinking to excess. When Ruskin said, "If I read this, I cannot read that"—which I think is one of the

most profound things ever said by anybody—he did not mean
if I read this, I shall not have *time* to read that, though such a
statement is true. He meant if I read this, I shall lose my taste
for reading that. I shall satisfy one self, but be false to my true self.

There are cases of physical illness the diagnosis of which is
clearly manifested to the physician partly by the symptom of loss
of appetite. It is not true to say that the patient does not *need*
food, but it is only too true to say that the patient does not *want*
food. We need God, but many are in the state of being unable to
want him. They cannot make themselves want him. They have
lost their taste for him.

You do not need to be a psychoanalyst to interpret this dream of
a patient. "I dream," he said, "that I pay a visit to the zoo and find
a great number of animals all together in one cage. I advance to
the bars of the cage to feed the animals, and I see at the back of the
cage a gentle and graceful gazelle, who looks at me mournfully with
big, brown, velvet eyes. I would like to feed the gazelle, but against
the bars of the cage, rushing up and down, clamoring voraciously
for food, are lions and tigers and wolves. My attempt to feed the
gazelle is defeated by the clamorous demands of wilder animals,
and in my dream the gazelle sinks down and dies." That is a picture
of the selves within the cage of human personality. But so often
the true self is at the back of the cage, gentle, pathetic, pleading,
but not getting its food because of the hungry demands of things
like selfishness or sex desire or ruthless determination to get on
in the world or the wish to be like others and to keep in with the
crowd. So the true self languishes and is near to death, while the
more brutish selves eat and drink their fill.

Let us get right away from famous names and consider a very
human story. I read recently of a girl who was sought by two
lovers. One was a sleek and wealthy youth who took her out in
his car to expensive places of entertainment and refreshment.
Flowers were sent to her nearly every day. She could have had a
house in Mayfair, a cottage in the country, and a month a year in
the south of France. Every whim would have been gratified by
the rich lover. His rival was a poor youth who wore a shabby

tweed coat and gray flannel trousers. He wrote poetry and book reviews, both of which were generally refused by the papers to which he sent them. He entertained her at Lyons' and took her tramping in the country. If he married her, it would mean three rooms at most and, with luck, a week in the summer at Skegness. The parents backed the sleek gentleman. All the girl's friends thought she would be what they called "sensible." If she had mentioned Bob the scribbler, they would have as good as said, "Be it far from thee." She gave no hint of her choice. One night she would go in a Rolls Royce to the Carlton, and then to a box at the theater. The next night she would go in a bus to Tottenham Court Road, dine at a cheap restaurant, and go to the pictures. It was a great drama for all her friends to watch. Would the girl have the grit to defy the purse-proud climber and throw away the furs and pearls and cars and houses waiting to be picked up? "Then," says the narrator of this true story, "I found she was learning shorthand. I asked her why. 'Why?' she demanded, her eyes blazing. 'To help Bob, of course.' So the poor scribbler had won." The girl was true to herself. "Sometimes," says the narrator, "I drop into their rooms. They haven't much money. They seem to live on music, books, plays, ideas, dreams, and arguments. But they are very happy. They laugh a great deal, and when I imagine the money-smothered life she might have lived, I feel glad because of her grit."

Don't misunderstand this illustration. I am not making any cheap sneer about money. If she had *loved* the rich youth, it would have been right to marry him. But sometimes it does your soul good to hear of a person who, after quiet thought, pushes away the advice of friends and the apparent dictates of common sense, and obeys the inward voice, responds to the Mysterious Power that swings the needle of the soul. It does you good to hear of someone who defies common sense and does what the world calls mad, who, in her own little sphere, says with Luther, "Here stand I, I can no other, so help me God."

Yes, there is something to be said for using our own judgment. Only this to be said for it: that it isn't our own at all, but God's. When we are sure of that, we can do without other people's advice, though it's advisable to listen to it. We can even disregard common sense. For where God leads, there the light shines.

Only one last point. Even a magnetized needle gets demagnetized in time. I have seen one that revolved aimlessly round and round the card. A compass needle is remagnetized by bringing it in close contact with a very powerful magnet. You can see the point of the parable. I need not labor an interpretation. But let me say this: If you have drifted, bewildered and confused and wondering which way to go; if you have fallen in with a group of people who are shouting directions in your ear, and maybe what they call "common sense" is clamoring to be noticed; I want to suggest that you become quiet enough to hear what God has to say. Suppose you let him remagnetize the needle. Suppose, then, you kneel quietly and let the needle point which way it will. It will direct your life back to God, and I am certain then that you won't lose your way. "Love God," cried Augustine, "and do what you like." Yes, because loving God determines what you *do* like. Loving God murders the false selves and delivers the true self from the greedy mouths and dripping fangs of those baser selves that strive with it. Here is peace, then, and quiet, and God. "To thine own self be true."

# AS A TALE THAT IS TOLD

L<small>ET US PUT</small> <small>TOGETHER TWO PASSAGES FROM GREAT LITERATURE:</small>

We spend our years as a tale that is told.                    —Ps. 90:9

> Life . . . is a tale
> Told by an idiot, full of sound and fury,
> Signifying nothing.          —*Macbeth,* Act V, Scene 5

The spending of our years, says the psalmist, is like "a tale that is told." But, says Macbeth, it is a "tale told by an idiot, . . . signifying nothing."

It is easy to look at the picture in the mind of the psalmist. Let me sketch it with a few rough strokes as I saw it during my life in the East. The land of Abraham. The vast desert. A community of people eking out the meager existence of the nomad. Life is spent among camels, sheep, and goats. In the center of the camp, set a little apart, is the goat-hair tent of the sheik, divided one third of the way down by a curtain, behind which are the women's quarters. It is evening. The meal is ready. On the ground is a heap of cooked rice with portions of chicken in it. The men partake first, sitting on the floor, and using their right hands only. Following the chicken, dates and figs are served. The servant washes the right hand of each guest between the courses. When you have eaten as much as you want, the dogs and the hens come in and conveniently clear up the fragments. Then you adjourn to the other end of the tent and gather around a brazier, or a fire made on the ground. There are carpets and rugs on which you may recline, with cushions for your elbow. The firelight throws long, flickering shadows as the darkness falls. There are no side curtains to the tent, and you may see the moon lifting her beams above the desert's edge, lighting the world with her supernatural radiance. There is the scent of fragrant coffee, and the men have begun to smoke their hookahs. Entertainment is desired, and it may be that the sheik will entertain his guests by calling in the dancing girls, with graceful forms and a dark beauty of their own. On the other hand, the sheik may call for the official teller of stories, and there, in the quiet of the evening, you may recline and listen to a tale. This, I suppose, is the oldest entertainment in the world.

It must be a good story. There must be at least three things about it:

1. It must have a moral. It is an interesting and rather surprising thing that the great old stories of the world, like Aesop's fables, for instance, all have a moral.

2. The story must have a purpose. I have known the Arabs to hiss a man from the tent whose story ran out into meaninglessness, like a stream that failed in the desert. It may be a tale "full of sound and fury," but if it signifies nothing, the teller will probably be driven out into the darkness.

3. The story must have a satisfying end. If the end is surprising, all the better. I have known the most amazing stories unfolded and brought to such wonderful conclusions that the audience breathes that kind of sigh that expresses both surprise and satisfaction. It is interesting that Dr. Moffatt translates our text: "Our life is over like a sigh."

Let us apply to life this metaphor of the story told. We shall find that, whether we think of life as an individual affair, or the life of the community, or even the life of the nation, the three points we have made about a good story apply.

1. *The story must have a moral.* I think the moral of this strange story that we call human life is that men must co-operate with God, both in their own interest and in order that they may glorify him. Think over the chain of thoughts which I am about to give you, and see if there is a weak link in the chain. I will not use the word "proof," for in religion scientific proof is impossible, but these sentences bring my own mind to certainty as convincingly as science does. Here they are:

*a*) It is incredible that behind all the order we see in the universe there is no mind; and, inasmuch as our minds *recognize* order, that mind must be something like our own.

*b*) It is incredible that such a mind, if it be regarded as the creative force in the universe, is not personal and good; for we manifest both personality and goodness, and it is incredible that that which is created is higher in our own scale of values than that which created it. God—to give this personal Mind a name —may be, and probably is, much more than our word "personality" connotes, aş he is more than our word "good" connotes, but he cannot be less in either case.

*c*) It is incredible that this personal, good, creative Mind has no moral purpose in the lives of men, for even we have such purposes in the lives of children committed to us.

*d*) It is incredible that God cannot make known his purposes to men, since he seems to have ordained that their success depends on man's co-operation. To ordain that man's rightly used free will can serve his purposes, but to withhold from man any notion of what those purposes are, would be foolish and unjust.

*e*) It is incredible that ultimately God can be defeated. He may be temporarily defeated by our lack of co-operation, but it is incredible that a Mind big enough to create this universe, a Mind that is personal and good and purposeful, should be defeated in his ultimate plans by the creatures he made, and be unable to bring the story of human life to a morally satisfying end.

If there is a weak link in this chain of sentences which, in an hour of black doubt, I wrote down for my own comfort, I cannot find it; and the whole chain seems to me to indicate the moral running through the whole story of life. The moral of the story is: "Co-operate with God, for he is working out a purpose that is greater and grander than any human mind can grasp."

2. Further, *this human story is a story with a purpose*. The trouble about it is that men will not stay to ask what the purpose is and whose it is. They suppose that it is man's and that its objective is what he calls progress. It is not. It is God's. The purpose of human life, undoubtedly, is to bring all men and all nations into

harmony with the mind and will of God, living together to promote God's glory and further his purposes. That alone is true progress. Listen to these words from Principal Oman:

The very secret of all profitable use of life is just to abandon the expectation that it ever was designed to forward persons devoted to material and merely worldly purposes, with no higher ends than gain or pleasure or pride of place, and to discern that naturally the only ends it could have been designed to serve are God's.

We might paraphrase this sentence by saying that the only way of making sense of life, of getting the best out of life, of realizing the meaningfulness of life, is to part at once with the idea that it exists to further man's selfish aims and materialistic ambitions. It was created to serve one Person's purposes only, God's. But remember also that part of God's glory is the promotion of man's highest good. Anyone, however, who tries to twist the universe for his own selfish purposes or make it yield its secrets for his own private profit is only asking for the trouble that will certainly follow. The whole trend of the universe, visible and invisible, is toward goodness. It is built to further the purposes of God, not man. If you fight the universe, you only get broken. You may appear to defeat God, but you don't really defeat him; for if he cannot use you as an agent, willingly and co-operatively, he will use you as an instrument though you get broken in the using. But obviously the only ends that the universe is constructed to serve are God's; and that is not a harsh thing to say, for he knows far better than we do that our own highest good is found in harmony with his purpose, and that disaster for ourselves would be inevitable if he left us to our own ways.

Let us go back to the simile of the story. Miss Winifred Holtby was severely criticized by one critic for her novel *South Riding*. The critic said that there was "no completely praiseworthy person in the whole book." Miss Holtby made a very clever reply. "I intended to make them good," she said, "but they would not be." I believe other novelists have found the same thing. A character is created with a certain intention, but the pressure of events has such an effect on the character that the novelist is bound to make him behave in ways unintended at first, for of course the psychological unity of the character must be maintained. If it is not irreverent to put it thus, God could answer Macbeth in a similar way to that in which Miss Holtby replied to her critic. Macbeth says, "Life is a tale, full of sound and fury, signifying nothing." God might have said, "But I made them with the intention that they should be good, and they would not be." The pressure of evil events spoiled the intention of the Creator of the characters. But wait! If Winifred Holtby had not been so modest, she might have claimed that, even in face of all the things that went wrong, she made a fine story that turned out well at last. Will God do less? In spite of the pressure of evil events, in spite of the individual tendency to take the easy way, in spite of the dread entail of human sin, the gold thread of a divine, redeeming purpose runs through your life and mine, through this epoch and that, through good things and bad things, through frustration and defeat, through victory and conquest; and, in the end, God's purpose of bringing all men into unity with himself will be done.

3. This brings us to our third point: *a good story must have a satisfying end*. Have you noticed that when some people read a novel, they have no patience to await its slow development, so they take a little peep at the end? The story seems to get into such an inextricable impasse that it looks as if things will never turn out properly, so some readers turn to the last chapter. Very well! Let us look at the last chapter in this tale of human life. We cannot see it except by faith, but the overwhelming testimony of those who have looked at the last page is very comforting.

The Epistle to the Hebrews says: "We see not yet all things put under him. But we see Jesus . . . crowned with glory and honor." That is a peep at the last page. If you turn up Paul, you will find this: "All things work together for good to them that love God," or this, "He must reign, until he hath put all enemies under his feet." Or turn to John and get his glimpse at the last page. He will show you in the last book of the Bible a picture of the Eternal City, with twelve gates, and all the nations bringing their glory into it.

All the saints have been quite sure, by faith, that the end of the story will satisfy everybody. They do not believe that history, like a stream in the desert, will run out into meaninglessness, "full of sound and fury, signifying nothing." Some speak of the "second coming of Christ," others of the "millennium," others of the "consummation of the ages." We will not inquire now what those phrases mean, but they all reveal the certainty of the saint that the end of the story will satisfy everybody and that no man will be able to look back upon his life and say, "I have been treated unjustly. I have been set a hopeless task. I have had too much pain, or too much sorrow. I was hopelessly frustrated. Life could not be anything but a farce to me. God is cruel. God is unjust. God is unkind."

The hymnbook is indeed a treasury of devotion. Many of the great hymn writers peeped at the last page and then wrote down what they had seen by faith.

> Here I raise mine Ebenezer;
>   Hither by thy help I'm come;
> And I hope, by thy good pleasure,
>   Safely to arrive at home.

Few hymns are good poetry, but consider the optimism of this rhyme:

> His love in times past forbids me to think
> He'll leave me at last in trouble to sink;
> While each Ebenezer I have in review,
> Confirms his good pleasure to help me quite through.

And yet again, in better verse and triumphant faith:

> So long thy power hath blest me, sure it still
>   Will lead me on
> O'er moor and fen, o'er crag and torrent, till
>   *The night is gone.*

They all believe that the night will go. In all Christian literature for two thousand years there is not one exception.

Life's story can contain dark chapters. The earthly life of Jesus contains a chapter full of sorrow and, apparently, full of frustration and defeat. He kneels in a garden, the blood and sweat rolling down his face. Crowned only with thorns, he goes on to the cross, bearing our sins. But this chapter about a lonely man dying in the dark is *the last chapter but one.* The last chapter is Easter morning, with the dawn breaking and birds singing and angels exulting and man rejoicing. The end of the tale that is told satisfies everybody.

Have you sometimes closed a novel and said to a friend who lent it to you, "I wondered how on earth the author was going to work it out. What an amazing story! What an original plot!" I think many of us will be similarly surprised when the tale comes to an end, whether it be the tale of our own life or that of the world. Almost everybody's life contains dark and complicated chapters, full of sorrow and frustration and pain; but in the end we shall sigh with delighted surprise, as I have heard the Arabs sigh in the desert, at the incredible ending of the story. We shall say, in breathless wonder, "This is the Lord's doing; and it is marvelous in our eyes."

So, whether you think of life as the narrative of an individual or the story of a nation or the history of the world, remember that there is a moral to this story, and it is this: Co-operate with God! Remember that there is a purpose in this story. It is the fulfillment of the plans of God. Remember that there is a satisfying ending to this story. It is the glory of God. And go forward with these fine words of Paul ringing in your mind: *"No one who believes in him . . . will ever be disappointed. No one!"* (Moffatt.)

# INEVITABLE MYSTERY

THERE IS A TEXT IN THE BOOK OF JOB—THE TWENTY-SIXTH CHAPTER and fourteenth verse—which I should like you to have in your minds, if you will, as we think quite simply about the matter of mystery: "These are but the fringes of his ways: how small a whisper do we hear of him!"

That lovely poem, the book of Job, with its discussion of the agelong problem of suffering, is full of the most exquisite passages, and here is one of the gems. After Job has described the lovely things in nature, "These," he says, "are but the fringes of his ways: how small a whisper do we hear of him!"

I don't know that I can find any figure which brings that thought of mystery before the mind with the clarity and beauty of that sentence of Job. I can only imagine that a person might land on the shore of a great continent for an hour or two, pick up some lovely shells on the beach, follow a little winding stream into the interior and see growing on the banks lovely flowers, be lured on and on by the thrill of a developing glen and a widening valley, and then perhaps have time only to make his way to one little hillock from whence he could look out over wider and inviting country before it was time to go back, take ship, and leave the remainder unexplored. "These are but the fringes of his ways: how small a whisper do we hear of him!"

Now there are a great number of people who are troubled by the mystery of life, particularly in relation to religion. It is a real problem to them. They say, "Well, of course there may be a God, but life is all so mysterious. You can't really be sure." When you talk to them about our Lord, they say, "Yes, no doubt he was a wonderful man, but I have never been able to make anything of the divinity of Christ. His miracles puzzle me. The Bible is a strange country with a different language and a different atmos-

229

phere from scientific Western civilization. It is all so mysterious."
And when you talk to them about the nature of man, that too is
mystery. We cannot understand ourselves. Man's strange nature,
his combination of God and animal, his queer supernatural sense,
that numinous awe, that queer way he has of reacting to certain
things like beauty—how mysterious a creature is man! So many
people, when they come up against that which is mysterious, turn
back again. It is as though, to go back to the original figure, instead
of wanting to go onward and forward and upward, lured and attracted by the mystery of existence and God and Christ and life,
they are quite satisfied with pitching a little tent on the beach
which encloses a square yard or two of sand. They can understand
that. There is less mystery. They have shut it out, and they settle
down content.

Such an attitude may be partly due to the scientific atmosphere
which our minds now breathe, the scientific age in which we live,
in which, more and more, men are taught to depend on the senses.
Science deals with the things you can measure, the things that you
can weigh and count and see. You do your chemical experiment,
and every time you do it the same thing happens. You put your
little boundary wall around that which seems to be known, and in
that little area you feel at home. There is mystery beyond. All that
is now so familiar was once hidden in the hills of mystery. But
the average scientist is content to leave that. He doesn't have the
instruments with which to deal with that, so he settles down in
the tent of that which can be tested, and the rest he leaves on one
side. And yet some of the scientists who can see furthest are more
and more taking their colleagues by the hand—if I may still cling to
the figure with which I started the sermon—and saying: "Strike
your tent and come up with me a little. Then you won't be happy
in thinking that everything that is real can be weighed and measured and counted and seen and tested."

At the end of his book *The Mysterious Universe* Jeans discounts
that so-called scientific attitude and says that he feels more and
more that the universe is the work of a great mathematician and
runs up into a mystery to which mathematics supplies some kind
of key. And he finishes the book really with a credo, his own

confession of faith that that which is the true reality may be entirely spiritual, and that at any rate you cannot even make sense of the universe if you rule out the spiritual world which has its facts as well authenticated as has the physical world.

I don't know whether those who feel that there is security and safety in science and that in religion the mystery of the unknown undermines even the certainty of the known have realized that as soon as you begin to ask questions in science you are met with evasive replies or an honest confession of ignorance. I am reminded of a tutor of my own college days whom we used to tease because he would sit in the lecture hall at his desk and say to almost every question we asked, "Well, we really don't know."

I don't want you to think that is true only about religion, because if you say to the scientist, "Do you mind telling me what electricity is?" he says, "I don't know. Nobody knows." If you say to the scientist, "Do you mind telling me what caused life on this once red-hot planet?" he says, "We really don't know." If you say to the scientist, "Do you mind explaining to me how, given the animal creation, animals ever evolved into the self-conscious man," the answer is, "We don't know." He may talk to you about the long centuries, as though time could turn the unconscious animal into the self-conscious man. No one knows how that mysterious thing called consciousness began. No one, watching from outside the earth the events happening on it, could have prophesied, from the data before him, the emergence of man. Indeed, I don't know any branch of any science in which it is not true to say that there is a tiny little area of the known and a vast continent of the unknown. You can tie a doctor up in five minutes with questions. What is epilepsy? Nobody knows. What causes it? Nobody knows. What cures it? Nobody knows. And so with a dozen diseases. I hear that the question on which the Brains Trust privately spent the most time was one sent up by a little girl of eleven who said, "Will you please tell us why sugar is sweet?" I am only saying these things to suggest that we should not be put off from resting in religious reality and from making religious quest by that vast hinterland of the mysterious which lies all around every tiny area of the known.

The known is a tiny, tiny island in an immense sea of the mysterious and the unknown.

When you turn from science and talk to explorers who have been where no human foot has trodden before their own, do you not catch, as you read their books, that same strange sense of inevitable mystery? Read *South,* by Shackleton, or read that wonderful book of Cherry Garrard, *The Worst Journey in the World.* Read how these men, as they tramped through the icy wastes, had a most amazing, and sometimes terrifying, sense of the mystery of those silent, uninhabited wastes of untrodden snow. "We dared not stop talking," they tell us; "we had to talk to one another. The veriest gossip would do, but if we kept silent we could not bear the mystery that bore down upon us in those unbearable silences." Do you see what they are doing? They are putting up that little tent of conversation, putting a little wall, as it were, around the known and familiar and homely. "Let's talk about your aunt at Finchley. Let's talk about keeping rabbits or poultry. Have you heard the yarn about the man who . . . ?" and so on. The mind clinging to the little area of the familiar and the known and the homely, because all around is the mysterious unknown.

When you turn to the artists, the musicians, and the poets, who in a sense are the high priests of life, then the point becomes more and more obvious. Do you know this little poem of Ralph Hodgson?

> He came and took me by the hand
>   Up to a red rose tree,
> He kept his meaning to himself
>   But gave a rose to me:
>
> I did not pray him to lay bare
>   The mystery to me,
> Enough the rose was heaven to smell,
>   And his own face to see.[1]

Indeed, I think part of the explanation—if it is an explanation—of great poetry is that, because of the particular artistry in the use of words, the poet is taking us by the hand, saying to us, "Now come

[1] "The Mystery," *Poems.* By permission of the publisher, The Macmillan Co.

away from that comfortable little patch you have made for your-self on the beach of life and follow this winding stream, and let us go up into the foothills," until he gets us as far as words can take us; and then he leaves go of our hand, and we come back again, down to the old, familiar, homely things. But it is with an inex-pressible awe in our hearts, because we have been shown that beyond the familiar and known is the mysterious and the terribly beautiful which cannot be put into words. It is as much as you can do sometimes to bear the meaning of great poetry.

It seems to me as though, when the poet leaves go of your hand, the musician takes it and leads you farther because he can say more. What is violin music but the crying out of humanity in the wilderness of the infinite with no language but a cry? What is it but an attempt to express the inexpressible? I remember hearing Kreisler do a wonderful thing. After a program of classical music, in response to encore upon encore, he took his violin and, without any music at all, played what I still believe was music never written by anybody. I am not a musical person, but it seemed to me that he was doing the very thing I have tried to describe—as though he said, "If you do want more, you shall have it. Come away from the beach. You have landed there. You are content with your little tent, and I have tried to interpret a few things to you; but if you want more, come along." First you could hear the sounds of nature that are in a sense familiar—the wind in the trees and the songs of the birds and the running of a mountain brook down the hillside. You could hear the murmur of the wind growing in strength until it became a tremendous storm, sweeping through the forests, and you could hear the swish of the rain and the roar of the thunder. The lightning was flashing. The terrible forces of nature were unleashed. Then the storm died away again; the birds began to sing; the rain stopped. But when his listeners had been taken through that particular country that we can all bear because its music is familiar, he went on and on and on, until you almost rose up in your place in the concert hall and begged him to stop because you felt you were *overhearing* something which it is not lawful for man in the flesh to hear, as though you were listening to the angels around the throne of God, as though you were being carried up to worship before the throne of God, sharing the agony of a God brokenhearted over a world gone wrong. And that violin of Kreisler's sobbed and moaned and agonized and wailed, until you nearly said, "For God's sake, stop! I can't bear any more!" At last he stopped. He could not play any more. Even he could not take us farther out into the waste of the universe where no device of man, no word or music, could imprison for us mystery overwhelming.

Now if the scientist, longing to know, if the explorer, longing to see, and if the artist, longing to feel, all take you to the edge of utter mystery, is it surprising that religion, which longs to know and to see and to feel all in one, should have its frontiers in the realm of inevitable mystery?

The nature of God will be, of course, forever beyond us. That ought not to need saying, except that man gets so conceited on his little wayside planet. How well Cecil Day Lewis protests against such conceit in one of his poems:

> God is a proposition
> And we that prove him are his priests, his chosen.
> From base hypothesis
> Of strata and wind, of stars and tides, watch me
> Construct his universe
> A working model of my majestic notions,
> A sum done in the head.
> Last week I measured the light, his little finger,
> The rest is a matter of time.[2]

When you think of the things I have spoken about, like music and poetry and the solitary wastes and the questions the scientist never attempts to answer, what about the nature of the Creator of all these things? Is it strange we do not understand his being and his ways with us? Yet men are heard saying such little things. "I don't understand him, and so I shan't love him, and I shan't worship him, and I shan't think about him any more." Isn't it childish, utterly silly? Why, the totality of all that is known, compared with the unknown, represents one pebble compared with all the beaches in the world. "These are but the fringes of his ways: how small a whisper do we hear of him!"

[2] From *Collected Poems*, Hogarth Press.

Then think of the nature of Christ and the nature of man. All we know about color is what we call the spectrum. The red and the orange and the yellow and the green and the blue and the indigo and the violet—just the spectrum of color. But we know from other devices that there are waves below the violet, the ultra-violet, and waves above the red, the infrared—ranges of waves coming to us that we cannot receive as color because our little apparatus of sight is incompetent. Now Jesus is the spectrum of God. Jesus is as much of the nature of God as our tiny little natures can register and take in, but the nature of God goes on beyond either end of the spectrum into infinitely mysterious realms where man has no power to penetrate. Or you could take your illustration from sound. The birds can hear sounds that we cannot hear at all. There can be sound waves in the air so fast that they are beyond the top note that the human ear can pick up, and so slow that they are below the bottom note that the ear can detect; all music lies within a few octaves. That is all. Beyond that is utter mystery. Jesus is the octave of God. Just a few notes—true, beautiful, lovely notes—but beyond it all the utter mystery of God, as far beyond us as Beethoven's music would be beyond a man who could hear only six notes. "These are but the fringes of his ways."

I want to get over to you this one message: Don't be put off religion because of its mystery. Don't say, "Well, I don't understand the strange ways of God to man, and I don't know why this and that should happen." Of course you don't. Nor does anybody. That old professor I made fun of was quite right; "We really don't know." We know hardly anything. Let it suffice that we know enough to live by, and what we do know is not illusion. We apprehend though we cannot comprehend.

There are two things about mystery that are of value, and the first is this: when we are at our best, mystery lures us on. Who could worship where all was understood? If God were so small that the mind of man could understand him, he would be unworthy of our worship and incapable of achieving his purposes. And isn't it one of the sweetest things about being in love that the personality of the loved one is mysterious to the end? We know enough to make us happy, but a delightful mystery lies all around the area of the known, and we are lured on to make delicious discoveries. We know enough about God to love him, but "these are but the fringes of his ways." A holy and lovely mystery lures us on.

Then I think mystery has this second value: it purifies motive. It is mystery that calls out faith and hope and patience, and the counsel of God becomes more truly counsel when we follow it in faith and hope and patience, and not in sight. If mystery were banished from religion, motives would be less religious, because if mystery were stripped away, religion would be seen to pay. If you could see the whole nature of God's plans with man laid bare, and if by a miracle you could be given such a vast mind that you could see the whole scheme of God's purposes and understand them as something that has been completely explained, then you would no longer walk step by step in patience and hope and faith and trust. You would say, "Well, I never dreamed that *that* was what he was after or else . . ." What? You would have followed anything that paid such a dividend as that. It seems to me that it is necessary that God should conceal his ways with us, or else he would lower in value our very motive for following his way. It is more valuable to the soul to walk a road the end of which is indiscernible, which to walk at all is hard and apparently valueless, than to see the end and appraise the value so clearly that all the time the motive could not be other than self-interest.

So I hope that, so far from being put off by the mystery of religion and life, we shall be glad about it.

I love that story about Mrs. Einstein, wife of the scientist who discovered relativity, and who was banished from Germany because he is a Jew, even though he is one of the greatest minds in the world, perhaps the greatest mind since Newton. Somebody said to Mrs. Einstein, "Do you know all about relativity?" And it is said that, with a smile, she replied, "No, but I know my husband." I like to imagine that they are very happy, that she rests her mind in her love for him, that the mystery of his immense knowledge endears him to her even more than would be the case if she understood his theories, that his greatness gives her pride and the delicious sense of being loved by one so great.

Do you understand the ways of God to men? Ways that bewilder and confuse us and make us almost certain that religion not only does not pay, but is untrue, unreal, and irrelevant. Good people suffer agonies of body and mind. Crooks and rogues flourish. Behind many a façade of happiness is heartbreak and disillusionment. We cannot make sense of life. Violence and greed and cruel rapacity turn the whole world into a shambles. Young men of sound body and healthy mind, with high ideals of unselfish service, are killed in thousands. Imbeciles and incurables survive. Sleek, complacent, well-fed, selfish women flop from one bridge party to another, parasites of society, scum of a false civilization. The poor are bombed in their homes. The rich evacuate themselves to safety. An industrial system makes a few folk wealthy and a thousand a means to the end of the few. Yet the thousand are deep in sin. Many have no mind for a new world. They gamble and drink and lust and sweat in their slums. They don't even rise up and demand their own rights. Some rarely ask for anything more than the "pictures" and the pubs, a holiday at Hampstead and a "binge" at Christmas. Their days of outstanding happiness are blurred in their own fuddled memories by the fumes of beer. And God seems to sit in heaven and wait and watch. Oh! I know another side can be put, but what a world of evil this one sometimes looks, and how remote and futile religion often seems! How mysterious are life and destiny and man and God!

I do not understand God's ways, but I know God. For in Jesus is to be seen all of God that a human life can carry and reveal. Mystery enfolds everything beyond that little area on the beach of history where he pitched his tent. The Word became flesh and *pitched his tent* among us. That is what "tabernacled" or "dwelt" means. Yes, all else is mystery and most of that too. "I don't know much about relativity," says Mrs. Einstein, "but I know my husband." I don't know much about God, but I know God is Jesus. I'm proud to be loved by one like this mysterious God, proud to share his life and to be of some little use as he works out his plans. In Jesus I can guess what those plans for a new world must be.

> I do not ask what joys or woes time holds for me,
> I simply seek a love that goes out unto thee,
> As surely as the river flows to meet the sea.

Or, if I may misquote another poet:

> I do not ask *thy* way to understand,
>     *My* way to see,
> Better in darkness just to feel thy hand
>     And follow thee.

Yes, men and women, I think that is true. Many of us during the past several years have learned a lot about that darkness. Better the darkness and the mystery, so long as there is the feel of that pierced hand and the obedience of our loyal hearts. "I said to the man who stood at the gate of the year: 'Give me a light that I may tread safely into the unknown.' And he replied: 'Go out *into the darkness* and put thine hand into the hand of God. That shall be to thee better than light and safer than a known way.'"